A
MAN
CALLED
LION

A
MAN
CALLED
LION

by
Peter Hathaway Capstick

Artwork by
Joseph Vance

SAFARI PRESS, INC.
P.O. Box 3095, Long Beach, CA 90803 USA

Capstick, Peter H.

Second Edition

ISBN 1-57157-011-X

1994, Long Beach, California, USA

10 9 8 7 6 5 4 3 2

Library of Congress 94-067702

Readers wishing to receive the Safari Press catalog, featuring many fine books on big-game hunting, wingshooting, and firearms, should write the publisher at the address given above.

This is the 54th title published by Safari Press.

TABLE OF CONTENTS

ILLUSTRATIONS

AUTHOR'S NOTE

The author has elected to use the singular convention with reference to animal species, such as elephant, lion, etc., even if a group is discussed.

The use of the name "Aly" rather than the more correct and common "Ali" for John Taylor's adopted son reflected Taylor's own spelling of Ndemanga's first name and is retained in this manuscript although certain documents show clearly that "Ali" is likely the correct form.

There was an inconsistency that was faced by the author inasmuch as the three main characters all spoke different forms of English. John Taylor was an Irishman; Brian Marsh is a Zimbabwean, and I am an American. Each branch of the English language has its own preferences of spelling and usage and it was felt that to conduct the entire story line in one form would be at the expense of the others. Thus, when quoting John Taylor, British conventions and spelling are used and when I am speaking American English, I have written it in the American style. Brian Marsh's contributions are a combination of British and American, with spellings and conventions of both. In short, all three forms are used for authenticity.

ACKNOWLEDGMENTS

Brian Marsh and Peter Capstick would like to express their gratitude and appreciation to the following people for their many favors and courtesies: Alexander Maitland, for his photos, Tayloriana, and anecdotes.** Bill Feldstein, for his encouragement and friendship.** Karin Brettauer for her incomparable service in locating Charles Taylor, John's brother.** Norman, Mavis, Fletcher Jr., and Jan Jamieson for their help in researching C. Fletcher Jamieson and the days that are no more.** John Dawkins for many photos, letters, and diary recollections.** The late Charles Taylor, M.D., for his long tapes and valuable correspondence.** Ivor Jones, for his recollections and the use of his historic photo with John Taylor.** Dan Landrey, Ian Nyschens, and Gus du Toit for their many recollections of Taylor and details of those days of yore.** Mike LaGrange, for his kind permission to use many of his observations and entries in his excellent book, *Ballistics in Perspective*.** Harry Manners, the late Wally Johnson, and Ken Warner for their many recollections and anecdotes about John Taylor.** Samson Nyamhoka, John Taylor's old gunbearer, for his help to Brian years ago in the bush and for his many stories of "Jack."** Bob Blair for his invaluable assistance with the acquisition of Taylor books in New Zealand.** Isa Vatiwa, Brian's old friend, employee, and associate, whose advice and interpreting skills were invaluable in Malawi among the Yao.** All of the late Aly Ndemanga's clan and immediate family at Nombo and Mwambwajila villages in Malawi for their cooperation and help in matters of the memorial plaque.** Professor Argyle, Department of African Studies at the University of Natal, for his perception and professional advice.** Steve Mack, Psychologist, for his insights and predictions into the life and behavior of John Taylor.** To Petersen's Publishing Company for the use of the article "Buffalo!" from Petersen's *True* magazine files.** Last, a very special note of thanks to Jillie Marsh and Fifi Capstick for their help, patience, and advice as well as their technical assistance in matters of editing, spelling, and generally how *NOT* to do this manuscript. We love you both!

Dedication
For Jillie and Fifi
with all our love

FOREWORD

Among the most famous African hunters of the past, a few have shown particular interest in their chosen weapons, as well as in the subject of sporting rifles as a whole. I am thinking specially of Karamojo Bell, Denis D. Lyell, and, of course, John "Pondoro" Taylor. Bell and Lyell wrote extensively about rifles in their books, mainly in the context of their own experiences and the hunting adventures of others. In Bell's *The Wanderings of an Elephant Hunter* (1923), he listed a variety of calibres that he had used with greater or lesser satisfaction. Bell's experiments confirmed his lifelong preference for light magazine rifles, such as the .275, .303, and .318. Lyell did much the same. In *The African Elephant and Its Hunters* (1924), he admitted that he had "a craze for buying rifles." In *The Hunting and Spoor of Central African Game* (1929), Lyell wrote, "I have owned and used quite forty rifles of all kinds," adding, "I unhesitatingly say that for African sport the magazine action is the best."

I have no idea how many rifles Bell used or tested during and after his hunting career, but I imagine that he handled a great many. According to his own testimony, John Taylor asserts that he was familiar with more rifles than either Bell or Lyell. In Mozambique, Taylor hunted in thick cover and what in Africa is termed open forest, as well as the less-restricted surroundings described by Bell, Lyell, and their contemporaries. After the First World War, when Taylor's elephant-hunting career began, hunting conditions in many areas had changed and big game had grown accustomed to being pursued with firearms. Taylor soon found that the light repeaters favoured by Bell could not be relied upon to stop a charging elephant, a criticism that applied equally to other dangerous game. Taylor's experience proved that much more powerful rifles were necessary for this purpose. In dense bush, interlaced with tangles of thorn where the hunter's vision and movement are severely limited, double-barrelled rifles again and again showed themselves to be quicker and more reliable than single-barrelled magazines. While to some extent keeping

FOREWORD

his options open, Taylor would mainly become associated with large-bore double rifles—notably Holland & Holland's .500/.465—and an eloquent opponent of the smallbore magazine rifles advocated by Bell and Lyell for use against potentially dangerous animals, such as elephant or buffalo.

In whatever way Taylor's actual hunting experience may be compared with that of other celebrated hunters, regardless of their period, circumstances, or surroundings (or indeed with the rifles available to them), the main thing that sets Taylor apart from the rest is the fact that he would one day write about African sporting rifles and cartridges and discuss them at greater length, in far greater detail, than anyone before him. Taylor's classics, *Big Game and Big Game Rifles* and *African Rifles & Cartridges*, both first published in 1948, broke new ground and raised standards of criticism for every subsequent writer on these topics.

Both books became very popular. During and after Taylor's lifetime, they both ran to several editions. Of the two, *African Rifles & Cartridges* remains the finer, an outstanding work that has been read by enthusiasts the world over. This book and Taylor's autobiography, *Pondoro: Last of the Ivory Hunters* (1955), established his literary reputation. Taylor wrote two more books: *Maneaters and Marauders* (1959) and a novel, *Shadows of Shame* (1956). *Maneaters and Marauders* contains much exciting, authoritative material drawn from Taylor's experiences of hunting man-eating lion and herds of crop-raiding elephant and buffalo. Fiction, however, was never his métier and *Shadows of Shame*, in contrast to his other books, consequently seems artless and unconvincing.

I was given a copy of *Big Game and Big Game Rifles* by my mother for my fifteenth birthday. The book enthralled me and, in due course, like D.D. Lyell, "I could have passed an examination . . . on the type of weapons used by the various hunters of big game." Although I had no head for figures, I was eventually able to recite, parrot-fashion, the bullet-weights, muzzle-velocities, and muzzle-energy of all the rifles listed by Taylor. The ballistic tables in *Big Game and Big Game Rifles* became a sort of litany, and the subject of sporting rifles, for me, like a religion. Not surprisingly, this delighted Taylor when we met some years afterwards. It gave our friendship a firm foothold and created a bond that lasted for the remainder of his life.

FOREWORD

Even more than *Big Game and Big Game Rifles*, Taylor's auto-biography fired my youthful imagination, which had already been primed by Baldwin, Selous, and the then more recent works by J.A. Hunter. Soon after reading *Pondoro*, I wrote to Taylor at his publisher's address and a few months later received Taylor's reply. His sympathetic letter aroused mixed feelings of pleasure and dismay. It was thrilling for me, an impressionable seventeen-year-old schoolboy, to receive a letter from someone whose books I so much admired. Taylor, however, made it perfectly clear that he saw little or no hope of anyone being able to hunt in Africa or live off his rifles, as he had done in the past. This news dealt a crushing blow to my dreams. To my surprise, however, Taylor's letter had been sent from London and not, as I had expected, from Mozambique. This now meant that I should be able to visit him. With all the simplicity of youth, inspired by imperishable visions of adventure, I brushed aside my first disappointment, confronted my anxious, though remarkably tolerant parents with Taylor's letter, and a few days later travelled to London from Scotland by the overnight train. This was early February 1958, about six weeks after Taylor's arrival in England from Zimbabwe.

I have written several times before about my first meeting with John Taylor. Since his arrival, Taylor had been staying with friends in a large, well-furnished flat in Kensington with two Irish sisters, Grace and Dorothy Dow. As far as I recall, Taylor at age fifty-four looked older than I had pictured him to be. He stood above middle height, a few inches shorter than myself, and he had a clipped gray moustache and hair that was graying at the temples, thinning slightly, and brushed straight back from a con-ventional parting. His eyes were set well apart, and I noticed that they made an instant reflection of his mood. When he grinned, Taylor's whole face lit up, an effect like turning up the wick of an old-fashioned oil lamp.

In a brief note correcting the Dows' address, he had stated, "I've no use for formality" and had signed himself, "John T." Forgetting this, in my excitement, I called him "sir," and he immediately replied, "Ah, none of that! It's John. That's how I like it, d'ye see?" [The phrase, "d'ye see?" was one of Taylor's favourites, and it was always part of his speech. I can remember him standing there, grinning and giving a slight, interrogative lift of an eyebrow, and saying "d'ye see?"] Hearing this phrase never fails to bring him clearly and vividly to mind, or to trigger memories of that winter meeting: the cold gray slush in the London streets, the sudden warmth of the Dows' spacious ground-floor flat with its all-pervading smell of furniture polish, its thickly carpeted floors, and its dark corridors.

Grace and Dorothy Dow came out to greet me from a morning room at the rear of the flat, where they had prepared a delicious breakfast of cold smoked ham, cracker biscuits, and freshly ground coffee. Taylor and the sisters had breakfasted already, but joined me over coffee. The Dows chatted for a while before leaving us by ourselves. In the Dows' company, Taylor was quiet and reserved, almost too courteous, and yet strangely guarded. The younger sister, Dorothy, was tall, slim, and dark-haired; Grace was gray-haired and elegantly dressed. Of the two, Grace seemed the more assertive and, towards Taylor, I thought noticeably protective.

Like Taylor, both women spoke with cultured Anglo-Irish voices; both had the same charming tendency to drag the last consonant of any word. When referring to Taylor, they would not say "Jack" but "Jackhh." The use of Jack, instead of John, added to the sense of intimacy among them, but it also appeared to grate, however mildly, on Taylor's nerves, like some reminder of a past he would have preferred to forget.

This sense of intimacy was very obvious at the time, and is, incidentally, no mere invention of hindsight, for later that same day Grace Dow told me how she and "Jackhh" had once been engaged to be married. "It was all a very long time ago," she said. "I was 'great' on him, as we say in Ireland, but he really loved Africa more than me, I'm afraid." Of course, she offered this revelation when Taylor was out of earshot, having left the room—as he often remarked before visiting the lavatory—"to crack a whip." Grace Dow was evidently deeply concerned about Taylor's future plans, which, even then, she had connected with my visit. "Jack talks about nothing but getting back to Africa," she said. "Are you intending to go there with him? I do hope not. Please don't encourage the idea. All that's in his past." And she added prophetically, "It's all over and done with now."

When Grace and Dorothy had left us, Taylor settled back in his armchair and lit a cigarette. Without any sort of introduction, he began at once to discuss various thoughts he had been "mulling over" about large-medium-bore magazine rifles. He said,

FOREWORD

"I'm really a doubles man, as you know from my writings, but I could never afford to buy one nowadays." Taylor spoke about these rifles as you or I might refer to close friends or members of the family. He spoke slowly, very precisely, but with infectious enthusiasm about Jeffery's "four-nought-four," Rigby's "four-sixteen," and the Westley Richards's "four-twenty-five." His words gave character and real substance to these calibres that, until then, for me had meant little more than evocative numbers on the printed page. By doing so, Taylor vividly created in my mind portraits of the rifles, and their strengths and failings took on an almost human quality.

I could hardly fail to observe that he spoke just as he wrote, especially the freer writing I remembered in *Pondoro*. I would find this again, mixed with a phonetic Midwestern slang of his own invention, in *African Rifles & Cartridges*. Taylor smiled ruefully: "When you read *African Rifles & Cartridges*, you'll see that I've written it differently from the books published over here. Tom Samworth, my American publisher, insisted that I should do this. It was all a question of appealing to the American market, d'ye see? Normally I would never write like that, but it was what Samworth wanted and who was I, a poor devil of an elephant-hunter, to refuse him?"

Despite the flat's comfortable central-heating, now and then Taylor shivered and rubbed his big sunburned hands together. Then he clasped them in what I would learn was a typical attitude—the third and fourth fingers of his left hand filling a gap left by the missing middle finger on his right. It was then Taylor mentioned how he had lost this finger when the jaws of a lioness closed over his hand—"she, thankfully, at her last gasp"—and sliced it off at the knuckle. This version was one of his little romances, for he had already written that the missing finger was due to a war wound. But I did not realize this at the time.

Shivering again, Taylor chuckled: "Two things I dislike intensely. The cold, and walking uphill." He grinned at me, "Of course, you must be used to cold weather. Isn't it true that you Scots are born with antifreeze in your veins?"

After a long morning's talk, during which Taylor scarcely drew breath, he proposed that we should lunch at a pub around the corner and afterwards visit some of the gunmakers' showrooms in London's West End. Lunch consisted of sandwiches, which Taylor washed down with strong lager, while I drank a glass of bottled cider. I remember that he paid for lunch from a thick roll of bank notes bound with an elastic band, which he pulled from a trouser pocket. It looked like a great deal of money to be carrying about, but it did not occur to me that it was probably all the money he possessed. Over lunch, when I asked him why he had come back from Africa, Taylor was evasive at the beginning, but then he came right out and said that he had been ordered to leave. His passport had been canceled "with two strokes of red ink." He added, "Now I'm strictly *persona non grata* in any of the British territories. But, dammit, Africa is a big place. I will miss Aly and Nyasaland, to be sure, but from what I hear French Equatorial might still be worth considering. I've been looking into the prospects for hunting in that region."

Mentioning Aly Ndemanga cast a temporary gloom over our conversation, but Taylor soon dispelled this dark mood. We made our way to three gunmakers in succession. Tramping in wet streets under a gray sky, Taylor looked utterly miserable. He wore a thin mackintosh over his lightweight jacket and flannels, but this and his thick woolen jersey gave him little protection against the damp, bitter air. He strolled along at an unhurried pace, carrying a stick. His whole demeanor seemed better suited to the wide spaces of Africa, or even the English countryside, than the London pavements that echoed with the heavy clop of his hobnailed brown *veldschoen*. I was better clad for the winter cold in a warm overcoat, one of my grandfather's castoffs, the Edwardian cut of which Taylor much admired.

As we turned into New Bond Street, on our way to Holland & Holland's showrooms, Taylor enquired: "Tell me, my friend, do you own this part of town or have you merely rented it?" This was a typical example of his quaint humor, I discovered. Though he deplored deceit, Taylor loved to exaggerate for effect. Years later he would often say, "I've but three topics of conversation: African hunting, Rolls Royce cars, and seagoing yachts!" While this was far from the case, there was an element of truth in it. A whole range of subjects remained beyond his ken or liking. For instance, unlike other hunters I have met, Taylor took absolutely no interest in music, general literature, or the arts. Nor was he particularly concerned with the details of people's lives—except when these in some way involved or came into collision with his own. Yet in those early days, I never found him tedious, over-bearing, or dismissive. Instead, he was fascinating to listen to, frequently very amusing, and always his distinctive Irish drawl, his wheezy gasping laughter, enhanced the most trivial observation to make it somehow memorable.

As an illustration of this, when I was with Taylor one evening in his room near Clapham Common, he happened to glance at the small electric fire, which he had turned down to half its power in order to save a few coppers and still provide a glimmer of comfort. Shaking his head affectionately, he muttered "Man oh man! What a warmth this little squirt gives out, and the one bar only. . . ." Another of Taylor's bed-sitting-rooms was located on the upper floor of a house owned by an Irish builder and his family. The builder was a decent, though slightly vulgar man, rough at the edges and certainly a stranger to tact or discretion. Coming there once from Scotland, I brought Taylor a bottle of malt whiskey, which he immediately opened and sampled with enormous relish. The bottle now stood on a table beside Taylor's chair. As we sat talking, without warning, the door burst open and Taylor's landlord strode into the room. The man exclaimed heatedly, "You owe a week's rent, Mr. Taylor, and there you are drinking expensive whiskey. . . ." Whereupon Taylor exploded in a fury, "Heaven and Hell, man! If you had a Rolls Royce, would you drive it on cheap petrol?"

Over matters such as rent, Taylor was usually very meticulous, but perhaps not invariably so. By the end of the week, he was, as he put it, usually "skint" (broke). His small wage as a park keeper barely covered the most basic expenses: tinned bully beef and rice, which constituted his evening meal, a packet of Rothman filter cigarettes a day, his rent money, and every now and then, a bottle of cheap whisky or gin. Life at this meager level must have been truly awful for him. Robbed of hope, by the mid-1960s Taylor's life had become little more than a drab existence, an instinctive clutching at survival. Like his single-bar electric fire, in 1958 still some vestige of hope gave a touch of warmth to Taylor's days. But even then it was a small, frail thing with scarcely more substance than a dream. Perhaps this, too, helped to forge a bond between us. I dreamt of one day going to Africa for the first time and Taylor dreamt of returning there.

That February afternoon, at Holland's, then Westley Richards's and Rigby's, Taylor was once more in his element. The gunmakers gave him a warm welcome and showed him the respect which, after all, had been his due. He derived immense pleasure from

FOREWORD

showing me their beautiful rifles, discussing details of design and construction, and poring over samples of ammunition. He drank mugs of the gunmakers' sweet tea and smoked the cigarettes they offered him, as he talked longingly of his plans for another elephant-hunting safari, this time by canoe, following Karamojo Bell's route to Lake Chad. For a while this seemed feasible, but only for as long as it remained a dream. The letters of enquiry I wrote, and the bleak replies I received from Paris, Fort Archambault, and Fort Lamy soon confirmed the harsh reality.

I now suspect that Taylor had been fully prepared for the inevitable disappointment that seemed to confirm that elephant hunting, as he knew it, was finished. The letters he wrote to me were consoling, but it was impossible not to recognize in them Taylor's growing sense of resignation and despair. For him, at least, there was always the recollected past. He had his own precious memories of experiences, some enshrined in his books, others that, with the passing years, his imagination sometimes embellished. A buffer against his depressing circumstances and the inescapable poverty and loneliness that dogged him, Taylor's fantasy world magnified as time went by. He later adopted an arcane style of dress that included breeches, leather gaiters, and goggles, taking as much care with his dress as he did with all his personal effects. He also grew a white beard, which markedly aged him. His African sunburn faded to a sickly pallor, much like old vellum. He even went so far as to assume his father's knighthood, a harmless ruse that apparently bolstered his self-esteem and kept his drowning spirits afloat.

When he died of bronchitis in March 1969 (or it may have been a broken heart), ironically the Irish builder's wife was at his bedside. Like her husband she never understood Taylor, but she was a good woman and held his hand until he finally slipped away. She told me afterwards, "There was just a flicker of the eye, then he was gone. He never struggled. . . ."

A Man Called Lion contains much interesting information about Taylor, which has never been published before. This includes a wider background of his early years in Ireland and South Africa. Taylor's adventurous life, carefully researched over several years by Brian Marsh, has been written by Peter Capstick. The biography is vivid, and it captures and reflects the energy and sparkle that anyone who met Taylor will instantly associate with him. After reading the manuscript, I found this foreword easy to write. I think this is because Capstick has presented the diverse, occasionally complicated material in an informal way that makes it very readable. He has made Taylor accessible, tangible, and completely real. There is much skill in this, and it shows in the obvious and touching commitment by the author to his work.

Fascinating though it was, John Taylor's life could not possibly justify a lengthier biography than this. Instead, it actually benefits from the author's more modest treatment and his matter-of-fact approach, an approach that Taylor himself would have been among the first to appreciate and commend. It was very much his own way of thinking, giving his material sufficient weight, choosing words with reasonable care, and, above all, "getting it said" in plain, unambiguous language without too much artifice or premeditated design. The best-remembered melodies are often the simplest. The same is true of writing.

A Man Called Lion makes a fitting tribute to Taylor the hunter, amateur ballistics expert, enthusiast of sporting rifles, and lover of Africans and African bush life. It is an uncompromising book. This may be one of its most noteworthy features, since it so accurately mirrors Taylor's unflinching dedication to his career, his devotion to unsophisticated tribesmen, and his sometimes unconventional relationships with certain individuals. Taylor paid dearly for his entrenched views and emotional attachments, ending his days in lonely exile in what was then a rundown backwater of South London.

To his English contemporaries, he was a renegade, an outlaw, a sworn enemy of the British colonial establishment, a fantasist, a drunkard, and, according to hearsay, an alleged homosexual. Admittedly this was more of an expatriate view, since few people in London knew of Taylor's existence. It seems, however, that the few who did know him also shunned him. Taylor's alleged bad character and his uncertain temperament, which to some was like an unexploded bomb, made it impossible for firms such as Holland & Holland to employ him, however great an asset his experience might have been.*

A Man Called Lion deals very frankly with Taylor's sexuality and this, to me, is absolutely as it should be. In Taylor's case, for a biography to be complete, a candid treatment of his many-faceted character is necessary. His homosexual relations with young Africans in Malawi allegedly led to his deportation from

FOREWORD

Africa in December 1957. This was a cross he bore silently. Brian Marsh, who by then knew Taylor well, had no inkling of these tendencies. Nor had I as a boy of seventeen—nor indeed at any time before his death. Like Brian Marsh, had I heard such rumours, I should not have believed them. I think that this says much for Taylor's fundamental integrity.

In a sense, it is probably true that Taylor never quite grew up. He took an impish delight in remaining a rebel, a thorn in the flesh of colonial administrations. Yet he could never escape from his social background, or turn his back on the establishment values that were the foundation of his youthful upbringing in Ireland. Privilege, good breeding, and the ingrained, established traditions of his past remained with him always. Had he lived more conventionally, saved his money, kept his sexual life discreet, and remained on closer terms with his family, his last years might have been comfortable and secure. This he could never bring himself to do. His obstinate yet admirable pride, his attachment to freedom, and his untamed nature forbade it. In this sense, I suppose, the very freedom he cherished and strove to preserve in the end served only to imprison him. It was Taylor himself who threw away the keys to his self-imposed prison, and to an extent he accepted this. Besides, when all is said and done, had he played safe or else, like many another far more flawed than himself, chosen to live as a hypocrite, he would quite simply not have been the man he was. We might have known John Taylor, but never "Pondoro," nor would we have had the pleasure of reading *A Man Called Lion*.

Alexander Maitland
London, England
9 July, 1994

(Editor's note: Mr. Roger Mitchell, Managing Director of Holland and Holland, kindly had the archives of that firm searched and found no record of John Taylor ever having formally applied for a job at that firm, after he returned from Africa.)

INTRODUCTION

It was 1939, the chill of war already settling like a cold, damp fog over Europe when John Taylor wrote the first lines to his first book:

> It is an astonishing thing how little the average sportsman in Africa knows about the rifles he uses. It is only a trifling exaggeration to say that all he really does know about them is: that a bullet comes out of the end that has a hole in it!

Today, more than fifty years later, a half-century of controversy has proved him quite astute, and that same five decades has established him as one of, if not the, foremost characters of African hunting legend and literature. Yes, Hemingway was more artful with his prose and Ruark more politically facile with his best-selling concepts of such things as *Uhuru* and modern safari. Yet, when the deadwood campfire burns low and the hyenas begin to whoop, it is Taylor's turn to take center stage, and they are *his* ideas that fly across the gleaming, croc-eyed coals; ideas so basic to the magic of safari that they are as much a part of modern big-game hunting as the professional hunter, the gunbearers, and the distant, night-muffled yap of a lonely jackal—or the grunt of hunting lion, the symbol of Africa that is his namesake.

By the grace—and perhaps the foresight—of Allah, John Howard Taylor is dead. But, he left his mark deeply scored on Africa and in the imaginations of those who accumulate dream books that are found with arrowheads, migratory duck bands, strange nuts, slingshots, possible fossils, and other detritus dear to the heart of any small boy in a man's body. To many, even though twenty-five years have passed since he died, alone, cold, and beaten in an alien London, he is still *Pondoro,* the Lion, and his great works such as *African Rifles & Cartridges* are not only classics—they are also the stuff of which adventure is manufactured . . . the ore of imagination, the alloy of individualism, the element of energy.

To refer to John *Pondoro* Taylor as an individualist would be to make the same relative observation by saying that Babe Ruth didn't hit a baseball too badly, that Paderewski knew something about the piano, and that Raquel Welch is definitely female. Given the Greek theatrical choice, the story of *Pondoro* Taylor is definitely a tragedy. In fact, I suppose it could be called a super- or mega-tragedy. The leprechaun that should have been on his Irish shoulder all his life turned out to be a gargoyle, and he spent his sixty-five years in various degrees of disharmony with his generally more conventional-thinking contemporaries.

John Taylor was a brilliant elephant hunter, a gifted theoretical ballistician, and a devoted homosexual. There is no other way to put the truth. We may pussyfoot behind the lace curtain until the cows come home, but the facts don't change, nor are they about to. But, and I suppose, tragically enough, herein lies the fascination of his story, his portrait if you will. One doesn't run across that many gay professional elephant hunters; certainly none with the savagery and talent that Taylor's restless soul exuded and sometimes wept.

Most certainly, neither Brian Marsh nor I, who have collaborated on the tale of Taylor, presume to make any sort of judgment of the man, not that a judgment is remotely called for. What he did was his own business, conducted between consenting adults, and we neither condemn nor applaud his actions. We do applaud his skill with and his knowledge of firearms, especially fine English double rifles, and one only has to read a few passages from one of his hunting books to realize why one of his works is a world-renowned classic today

This biography is really Brian Marsh's. Brian personally knew Taylor, gladly received the advice that the Old Master gave to a neophyte, and researched Taylor's career to the extent that he made many investigatory trips that resulted in this manuscript. Brian was the first professional hunter to conduct hunting safaris in the old Rhodesia, an ex-professional crocodile hunter, a grand gentleman, and an old and treasured friend. So is his wife, Jillie, a lady who understands and appreciates the bush and its hunters in all their connotations and convolutions.

Brian and I have known each other for fifteen years or more, and I had known of his reputation as a great hunter and pioneer of the safari trade for much longer. He is the author of the highly acclaimed novel, *The Last Trophy* (St. Martin's Press, New York, 1982) as well as contributing editor of *MAGNUM* magazine in South Africa. We decided to do this book more or less together,

INTRODUCTION

based on not only his excellent research on *Pondoro* Taylor but the fact that what we knew in aggregate dovetailed exactly and that we would only have half a book if we were to do two books alone, each by ourselves.

So, we give you *Pondoro*, literally "A Man Called Lion." You may like him or dislike him, approve or not of his way of doing things, be astonished at his logic, and either hate or admire him. But, he was as he was and never left any doubt about that!

Peter Hathaway Capstick
Waterkloof, RSA
17 January, 1994

JOHN *PONDORO* TAYLOR'S AFRICA

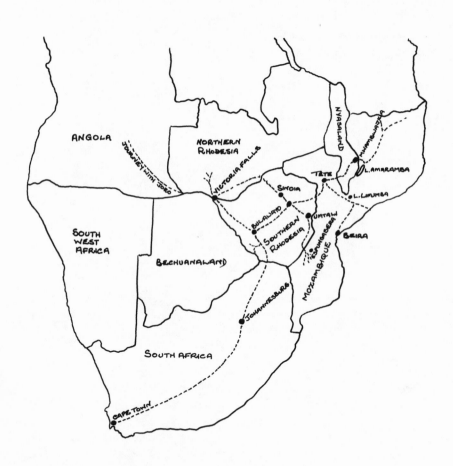

CHAPTER ONE

It was Sunday morning in the early months of 1957. Brian Marsh, a twenty-nine-year-old professional crocodile hunter in Nyasaland, and Ricky Philip, a fifty-three-year-old retired policeman from West Africa, were evicting a pair of slight hangovers with cold beers on the veranda of Ricky's beach cottage at Namasso Bay on Lake Nyasa. The aroma of frying bacon drifted along with the offshore breeze that was blowing through the kitchen where Rene, Ricky's wife, was fixing breakfast. The wide expanse of the lake stretched to the purple hills of Mozambique in the far distance and glinted flashes of dazzling silver off the slow-rolling surface. Ricky struck a match and touched the flame to the tip of his Gold Leaf Plain, as a shaft of amber, early morning Nyasaland sunshine lanced the blue cloud of tobacco smoke and sulphur fumes.

"I say, old boy," he said suddenly. "You couldn't use an assistant for a while, could you? On some sort of share basis? I've got an extremely good friend who rather needs to make a bit of money. He's down on his luck at the moment. If you could let him use your other boat and lend him a rifle, you'd be giving him a hand up and I think he'd do quite well for you."

Marsh took a pull of beer. He wasn't too enthusiastic. In fact, he wasn't enthusiastic at all. He had similar requests before from fellows wanting a bit of adventure as professional croc hunters, which had not worked out too well, to say the least. "God, spare me egos," he mused.

"I'd really like to help him, Ricky, particularly as he's a friend of yours. But you know I'm having a rather slim time of things myself at the moment, and until they blow that bloody bund (embankment) at Liwonde and the lake begins to drop again, I don't see things improving."

"Pity," said Ricky, taking a swipe at his own beer. "But I see your point. You should meet him anyway; he would interest you. He's an extremely experienced hunter, hunted elephant in Mozambique for years, and he has written a number of very good books.

Packed in the hunting now and wants to settle in Nyasaland to become a full-time writer but needs a bit of lolly to get him going. He's in a bloody bad way financially, poor chap."

The young crocodile hunter perked up. "Sounds interesting! Who is he?" With dreams of taking up professional hunting as a lifetime career, he was always anxious to meet the old pros.

"Fellow by the name of Taylor—John *Pondoro* Taylor. Ever hear of him?"

Marsh's chair swayed as he nearly fell off it. John *Pondoro* Taylor! Good God! He had read both his *Big Game and Big Game Rifles* and *African Rifles & Cartridges,* Taylor's classics on rifles and ammo, almost to ragged tatters. Without any doubt, it was the impact made by reading these two books shortly after he left school that had sparked Marsh into pursuing his present profession. John Taylor, he was ready to admit, had already influenced his life substantially. He did not know then that John Taylor was about to influence it again.

"How do I find him?" he asked eagerly when he had steadied himself.

"Can't miss it, old boy. Right on the side of the Namwera road, just after you get up onto the plateau." Ricky gave him detailed directions to Aly Ndemanga Village.

Marsh had planned to go to Blantyre that Monday to deliver his skins and buy his supplies. His usual *modus operandi* was to hunt for three weeks nonstop and then give his crew a full week off. But this called for an immediate change of plan. The next morning he would drive to the Mangochi Plateau to visit the legendary John Taylor.

He had no trouble finding Aly Ndemanga Village. It looked like any other in that part of Africa, except a white man was sitting at a square unpainted deal table under the shade of a small grove of *brachystegia* trees with a typewriter in front of him. The man was smoking a cigarette, holding it between the fingers of one hand, with his elbows on the table and both hands cupped before his face, as though lost in deep concentration. He struck his visitor as looking very much out of place, especially as he was wearing a turban. The man raised his head, watching quizzically when he observed the Land Rover pull off the road and stop. Then he rose easily to his feet.

Marsh's first impression of *Pondoro,* the man called Lion, lives with him still. He had never met a real, live professional elephant hunter before. He had, in fact, only once even seen a genuine elephant hunter. He and Keith Curle, a pal of his from school, were treating themselves to a Nickabocka Glory at Pocket's Tea Room in the great Southern Rhodesian metropolis of Salisbury. It had been during the Great War to-keep-the-world-safe-for-democracy and, at the time, it had looked like Hitler and Tojo were winning it.

"Hey! See that man over there?" Keith had asked Brian excitedly. "That's Fletcher Jamieson, the famous elephant hunter. My dad *knows* him! My dad's in the building business with his brother."

Had the young Marsh not been so intimidated by greatness at the time, he would have demanded an introduction. All bush-minded young Rhodesians knew who Fletcher Jamieson was; he had a sea of mystique lapping his reputation that would have floated an ark. How Brian was to regret that he had never actually shaken Jamieson's hand. He was, much later, to become firm friends of the whole Jamieson family, but by that time Fletcher had since departed for other hunting grounds, as even young professional ivory hunters had a decided tendency to do with depressing regularity. Even then, Fletcher was only a few steps from the grave.

Fletcher was to feature very prominently in the John Taylor saga, the two of them becoming the best of friends and even doing an ivory safari to the Elephant Marsh on the lower Shire River in Nyasaland together. And as all Taylor fans will know, it was Fletcher's magnificent photographs that were used to illustrate Taylor's first two books.

Taylor, Marsh recalled, was a big, powerful man as he rose from that table, yet he moved with the ease and grace of a hunting cat. His movements were brisk and smooth, almost studied in their decisiveness, and his eyes were quick and alert, as if they could never get enough to see. He had grin lines to the sides of his graying mustache and a friendly smile; in every way he looked like a man completely confident in himself and his surroundings. To Marsh he oozed vitality and physical fitness.

Taylor was dressed in a freshly laundered khaki shirt and a pair of those cheaply-cut shorts one finds in the rural Indian *dukas*. His sleeves were neatly rolled to the elbow revealing tanned, heavily-boned and muscled forearms, and the hems of his shorts turned up above a pair of legs like those of an alpine guide. There were sockless, newly-bleached tennis shoes at the base of his tall figure, but actually, Marsh later realized, Taylor was not overly tall. Years later, Taylor's British South African Police records revealed him to be just five feet, ten inches tall. (When going through Taylor's effects after his death, Alexander Maitland found Taylor's passport and made a photocopy of it. Taylor's passport lists his height as five feet, eight and a half inches tall.) Perhaps he appeared very tall because he was among his Yao followers, who were generally short and stocky.

Marsh, feeling somewhat self-conscious, stepped forward to introduce himself. "I'm a good friend of Ricky and Rene Philip," he said. "They said it would be okay if I just dropped in on you. They send their regards."

Taylor grasped his hand in a firm grip, and Marsh remembers thinking how big the brown hand felt. Later, once they had become friends, Taylor would shake Marsh's hand using a "bush handshake," linking the thumbs.

"Ahhh! Sure, it's the crocodile hunter. Ricky's spoken about you often."

He led his visitor back to the table under the trees where he had been writing. Marsh glanced around the village while they were talking. It showed all the signs of being newly built. It was small with only five or six identical huts, so it was more of a kraal, a village really in name only.

The huts were of pole and thatch, with clean and yellow new grass, and were of rectangular Arab design, instead of the usual African Bantu round beehives. On each was a roughly hewn native timber door—to dull the enthusiasm of nocturnal unpleasantries—fastened to their bush-pole frames with squares of tire rubber acting as hinges. The huts were spaced some thirty paces apart in a rough circle, with a small thatched shelter around a low pole wall that was the communal kitchen. There was no stove inside, only a ring of stones upon which the cooking pots were placed over the open fire.

The yard had been swept clean and there was no litter. There were the usual African village accouterments to be seen: water buckets made from five-gallon oil tins and blocks of tree trunk that served as stools, and Marsh saw some boxes, which were obviously packing cases stacked neatly under the eaves of one of the huts. This, he guessed, was Taylor's.

A MAN CALLED LION

In the trees beyond, he saw a small open-topped grass enclosure around a pole frame from which was suspended a shower bucket. This was the single non-African trapping in a habitation that was wholly African. Yet, there was the obvious evidence, by its white mark, that a large campfire in the center of the yard was much used at night, the fire itself being African enough, but not in this setting. Africans will sit around their small cooking fires at night. But apparently, Taylor persisted in his link to the old life by having a large campfire built, next to which he sat in the evenings and smoked.

There was an abundance of wood to collect on the Mangochi plateau, and the ashes of the fire were gathered each morning and deposited down the *chimbuzi*, the village long-drop. Taylor was very clearly satisfied to live a primitive life, but his life was orderly. He had never let himself go "bush" as was popularly believed by those who sought to discredit him.

"I'm pleased you came up," he said. "Have a seat." Marsh noticed that he might well have been in Kilcullen for the Irish lilt of Taylor's speech. His speech was not a case of *begorrah*, but of that small class of Anglo-Irish aristocrats. There was another chair across the table from where Taylor had been sitting and Marsh wondered who might habitually use it. He sat down as Taylor moved the typewriter to one side and sat down himself.

"I can only type on days when the wind's not blowing," the old elephant hunter remarked conversationally, giving a wheezy laugh. "Otherwise, my papers blow all ohhver the place, d'ye see?"

"I hope I'm not disturbing you," Marsh said, conscious that there were probably not too many days on the high plateau when the wind *didn't* blow.

"No, not a bit, not a bit. Any friend of Ricky and Rene's is a friend of mine. Grand pair, aren't they? Two of the best. Can't imagine though why a fellow like that got himself mixed up with government." Marsh was to learn of Taylor's seething hatred of absolutely anything to do with any form of colonial government. It was a wonder he and Ricky were friends at all.

Marsh had brought Taylor a bottle of Johnnie Walker Red. Ricky had told him Taylor was down on his luck and he guessed he wouldn't be buying too many luxuries like whiskey, but what Marsh did not know was that the Irishman was a practicing Muslim and may not have welcomed the present. Theoretically, those of the Islamic faith do not touch alcohol, but the Holy Koran puts it interestingly, so it is not outright condemned. It decrees there is some profit for man from wine, but that the sin exceeds the profit.

Marsh, however, immediately noticed that Taylor's native Irish practicality seemed to be uppermost in the matter of his religion. It was apparent at once that Taylor concerned himself more with the profit than with the Prophet, for when Marsh took the bottle from his briefcase and handed it to Taylor, Marsh noticed the approving gleam in Taylor's eyes.

"I've brought something for you," he said.

Taylor took the bottle and gazed at it like the face of an old love, lost but miraculously found. "How very noble of you, me dear fellah, and my favourite label, too! I have always greatly admired Johnnie Walker. (Actually Taylor's favorite was Jameson's or Power's Irish whiskey, but Taylor would have felt that a gift like Marsh's deserved a bit of elaboration.) Yes, indeed, I have always admired the way his square bottle won't roll off the table when it's er, ah, . . . accidentally bumped."

Marsh naively thought that Taylor would put the bottle away at least until evening, but the Irishman broke the seal and held the bottle to his nose.

"Ahhhh, I knew it! Brewed in heaven by a cellar full of angels!" He turned round in his chair. "Aly!"

Another turbaned head appeared like a displaced *djinni* from around the back of one of the huts.

"*Bweresani makomichi mawiri.*"

The turbaned head disappeared as if it had been decapitated.

Marsh glanced at the typewriter and the ream of paper next to it. The Mangochi winds were not blowing. The machine was a well-used Remington portable. "Writing another book?" he asked somewhat inanely, as it seemed fairly obvious. There was an awful lot of paper for a couple of letters home to Eire, but the overawed young crocodile hunter was at a loss for spontaneous conversation and was having to search his mind for something—anything—to say.

"Planning another at the moment and may it have better luck than its predecessor," Taylor grumbled, an edge of bitterness sharpening the lilt of his Irish brogue, "which I sent off an age ago and now my publisher writes that it's gone astray."

A MAN CALLED LION

The missing manuscript was of *Maneaters and Marauders,* Taylor's fifth book. The manuscript must have either reappeared or Taylor retyped it, because the book came out in 1959. But at this time, Taylor was very upset at the loss of the manuscript and subsequently complained to Marsh on several occasions about his publisher's carelessness, even suggesting it was a ruse to cheat him. From the way he grouched, it appeared to Marsh that he did not have a copy.

Thirty years were to elapse before Marsh came upon a copy of Maneaters and Marauders. *It may have appeared on the shelves of the book shops in the major centers, but being away in the bush with game ranching and sport safaris, Marsh was not to see it. The finding of this book was to become the pivotal factor on which the writing of this Taylor story depended.*

The turban came back into view. There was a young black man under it, dressed in a sleeveless knee-length white cotton shift of the sort known as a *kanzu* farther to the north in East Africa. He was carrying the ordered two glasses on a tray.

"And this," said Taylor, smiling benignly, while gesturing with a sweep to the young man, "is Aly Ndemanga."

Marsh greeted the young African cordially and the young African smiled widely but without replying. He was stockily built and only of average height, but Marsh saw that the bare arms and the calves, protruding below the hem of the shift, were muscular. He looked a very bright young fellow with a cheery face, very cleanly turned-out, and the young white man took it that Aly was simply Taylor's cook. He did consider it a little "different" that he should have been introduced formally, though. They were still very much in Africa's colonial era and it was not usual to introduce another white man to one's domestic servant. However, Marsh had already deduced that Taylor's lifestyle was considerably different from that of any other white man he had met.

He noticed that Aly also had a quick way of moving, like John Taylor, and that he too seemed very much at ease and completely sure of himself. Aly took the canvas water jaw-sack from where it was hanging on a twig above, handed it to Taylor, and quietly went away again. Marsh thought Taylor lucky to have found such a pleasant and agreeable-looking young fellow to run his kitchen for him.

Taylor poured out two gargantuan shots of whiskey, following each with a dribble of water from the bag, hung the jaw-sack on the back of his camp chair, and handed Marsh a glass. He held his own up to a shaft of sunlight and peered through its amberness.

"May the glint in it blind the eye of the Prophet!" he murmured solemnly. He took a huge gulp and sat back with a long rattling sigh.

Marsh followed suit and felt the liquid lava flow down his gullet. Taylor hadn't put much water with it at all. Marsh only drank beer and wine in those days and felt completely ambushed by J. Walker, Esq. almost straight. But at least it untied the young crocodile hunter's tongue—when he found he could talk again.

Taylor's third and fourth books, *Pondoro, Last of the Ivory Hunters*, and his novel, *Shadows of Shame*, had both very recently been published. For some reason Taylor did not have a copy of *Pondoro* with him, or probably more likely, he did have one but did not want to lend it. He later, however, offered Marsh the loan of his novel after Ricky and Rene were finished with it, but Marsh didn't take him up on it. Rene had actually shown him the book on a subsequent visit to the beach cottage at Namasso Bay, which he had glanced through quickly, but it was not about hunting, and other subjects in novel form didn't much interest him at that point. In fact, Marsh was not to read it until quite recently when he was sent a copy by Alexander Maitland. When it arrived, Marsh recognized it as the same "author's copy" that he had held in his hands at Namasso Bay all those long years ago.

Marsh was, however, very conversant with Taylor's first two books. He talked at length about them and asked Taylor to enlarge on a number of well-remembered incidents, which probably flattered the older man and made him aware that he had gained a disciple. They talked a great deal about crocodile hunting. Taylor had shot slathers of crocs in his time, but these were mostly man-eaters harassing the villagers and fishermen, and he had never hunted them at night. He had sold a few skins when it was convenient and knew that a living could be made from the trade if only he could get a foot in the door. Marsh then told him of the current problems caused by the high water level of the lake.

In order to strangle its flow to conduct a hydroelectric survey at Livingstone Falls, a part of the series of tumbling rapids and foaming gorges that separate the lower Shire (pronounced Shi-re) from the upper, an earth bund had been thrown across the river at Liwonde, just below the ferry on the road between Blantyre and the lake. But the bund, naturally, had a twofold effect. The Shire drained the overflow from Lake Nyasa to the Zambezi. While the bund had radically *decreased* the river's flow below, it did not stop it completely. Secondly, it had *increased* the level of the lake above, so that the crocodile's habitat had been changed and rendered hunting it extremely difficult, if not well-nigh impossible. Marsh was then no longer able to ply his trade profitably.

The fishermen below the bund had screamed official bloody murder, saying quite rightly, that the government had taken their river away. Anxious to please in the face of the winds-of-change, the colonial government had promised to blow the bund as soon as the survey was completed, but so far there had been no action. Marsh told Taylor, however, that as soon as conditions came right again, he would be delighted to have him join him. At that time things had tightened up and it was a practical certainty that Taylor would not have been granted a license to operate on his own.

Marsh did, however, make the suggestion that they should go out together one night so he could show Taylor what commercial croc hunting was all about. As the level of conversation expanded in direct proportion to the dwindling level in the Johnnie Walker bottle, so the younger man's enthusiasm mounted. He declared that he would move his own camp to the base of the lake at first light the very next day, and he would drive up to collect John Taylor to go crocodile hunting the very next evening, come high water or no!

When he hunted in remote places, which by the definition of croc hunting meant most of the time, Marsh was obliged to live fairly roughly. These places where the big crocs congregated could only be reached by a small boat and there was not much room for luxuries aboard. Marsh had two identical flat-bottomed skiffs, wide-beamed fourteen-footers, and hunted from one while carrying his skins, supplies, and some of his crew in the other. As he had seven men, space was always at a premium, especially when he moved camp.

But in the more accessible areas he was able to move with his Land Rover and trailer while his crew followed with the boats, which allowed him space to carry the more refined aspects of his camping equipment. Rene Philip, who had experience of bush life from her West African days, was very insistent that he "keep up standards."

"I will not have you pitching up here like an unwashed and unshaved beach bum," she would scold. So the casual crocodile hunter, through her motherly insistence, had been embarrassed into acquiring such exotica as folding chairs and table, and a box of cutlery and crockery, replete, as Rene saw to it, with tablecloth and napkins. Of course, she was absolutely right. She well knew that standards and comfort, when spending time alone in the bush, were essential to a person's well-being, both mental and physical. And she had also seen to it that the young hunter was also equipped with, well, a *reasonable* cook.

Later in the afternoon of that first visit to Aly Ndemanga Village, Marsh took his somewhat tipsy leave of Taylor and returned to his base at Nkhudzi Bay. Early the following morning he sent the two boats off with Tawali and Masamba, his two regular boatmen, in control. They went to a campsite he had previously used on the eastern shore close to the toe of the lake. He then set off with the rest of his crew in the Land Rover, the faster mode of travel, to set up the camp.

On his way there he stopped briefly at Palm Beach Hotel, a very popular holiday resort and his regular watering hole in these parts, to beg a bottle of Cape Pinotage from Pixie Sweetman's hotel stock. Pixie was the hotel proprietor, and she guarded her wine stock like her young, but no doubt aware, as women generally are about such things, that the young croc hunter was madly in love with her, she agreed to let him have a bottle.

As soon as he reached his new campsite, Marsh hung the bottle in a wet sack in the leafy branches of a mango tree in an endeavor to maintain "room temperature." When the camp was up and ready, he drove to the top of the escarpment to pick up John Taylor, who had no transport of his own.

"You won't mind if Aly comes along with us?" Taylor asked when Marsh arrived.

"He's actually a very experienced hunter in his own right and he'd like to come along to see the fun."

"Not a bit," Marsh replied. "But you'd better tell him to bring a jacket or something. It gets pretty chilly on the lake in the early hours. But I didn't know that Aly was a hunter. I thought he was your cook."

A MAN CALLED LION

Taylor gave another of his wheezy laughs. "Aly is just about someting of everyting. (In his charming Anglo-Irish speech, Taylor habitually dropped the "h" in thing.) He cooks for both of us, but he's my headman really. He's in charge here and that's why we call this place Aly Ndemanga Village. But in the old days when we were out in the bush, he also hunted. I taught him and he's very good. He's shot a great deal of everyting entirely on his own."

Aly wasn't waiting for a second invitation. He jumped into the back of the Land Rover and they headed back down to the lake with Taylor sitting in the left-hand passenger seat. Marsh began to chatter, pleased to be in the Great Man's company again, but soon discovered that Taylor could not hear what he was saying above the noise of the motor. Taylor had a bad case of "cordite ears," nerve deafness, every professional hunter's eventual hearing problem if he lives long enough. After Taylor had asked, "What d'ye say?" a half-dozen times, Marsh lapsed into silence and concentrated on his driving.

It was just becoming dark when they got back to camp. Carmine bee-eaters and African skimmers riffled the glowing water and winged termites were already starting to gang the pressure lanterns. The table had been set up under the trees and William, the cook, had hung another Coleman in the branches, flooding the area with a warm gloss that seemed almost to stick to the dark green of the leaves.

While Taylor and his host had a sundowner, Aly took over from William, Marsh's cook, at the cooking fire. Marsh was to discover that Aly was a very good cook. He turned William's chicken casserole into something surprisingly different and the rice didn't stick in a lump at the bottom of the pot. For a side dish Aly made pumpkin fritters and he also made *pao*, Portuguese bread, unleavened and cooked in a frying pan. It came out like pancakes and buttered hot it was delicious. Both Aly and William waited at the table and served an excellent meal, not depreciated in the least by having to serve the wine in whiskey glasses.

The moon was full as only a central African moon can be—a great, golden coin that radiated light strong enough to throw hard shadows of men and gargoyles. Croc hunting wasn't feasible then. The crocodiles could see the boat with the hunter in it approaching behind the spotlight, ready to give them a 300-grain dose of terminal meditation, and they would swirl away into the black depths before a shot could be fired. Marsh always took a brain shot on the saurians, at a range of two paces. This would anchor them, more or less, with their tails thrashing like paddle wheels. The governor would be stuck open until the croc slowed with the lull of death, and the hunter could grab and hold it while it was roped to stop it from sinking.

Normally when there was too much moon for successful croc hunting, Marsh would have waited till it waned, which on this particular night would have meant waiting till the early hours of the following morning. His guest was anxious to see what went on, however, so they went out shortly after dinner. They went under outboard power to a long sandy beach lined by a wide bed of reeds, their eyes, ears, and hair full of the water insects that blew into their faces. Here they cut the motor, lifting it out of the water, while Tawali and Masamba took up their punting poles.

The hunting boat slipped silently through the shallows as the two boatmen, standing in the stern, evenly dipped their long poles, sending it slicing through the mist-swirls like a gliding wraith. Scores of fireflies pulsated rhythmically in the reeds, winking on and off like the window lights of a busy city. Now and then a Senegal coucal would wake and give its bubbling hooting call as the passing boat disturbed its roost, setting up a chain reaction as other coucals along the lake shore answered. Others further along answered in turn, until the sound faded at the outer limits of their hearing.

From a hunting point of view, the night was a flop. They saw crocs, quite a scad of them, but because of the artificially high water they were all lying up on the wrong side of the reed beds where they could not be reached. Each time the spotlight picked up the keyhole-shaped red reflection of an eye, Taylor kept up a low-toned running commentary on what he thought of crocodiles in general and these in particular, but after a couple of hours they realized that it was hopeless and decided to head back.

It was shortly after midnight when they reached the camp. They immediately reestablished their friendship with Mr. Walker of Scotland (only to relieve the chill, of course) and Marsh brought out his treasured box of Duc Georg cigars. He smoked a pipe in those days but carried cigars for special occasions. Then started a most entertaining night, one the young croc hunter would well remember thirty years further on. Taylor revealed himself as an unsurpassed raconteur and kept the younger man enthralled with hunting stories until the roosters in the nearby village pleaded for mercy at the first light of dawn. And that night, Taylor also told Marsh about Aly, how he had adopted him as his son.

Perhaps it may seem surprising that even then Marsh did not suspect that there might be something else between the two beyond the inevitable bond that grows between a hunter and the men who share daily hardships and dangers. A more worldly person no doubt would have guessed. But Marsh did not, possibly because of his own experience of Africa, falling between that of his white friends in Blantyre, who only experienced the African as a messenger or domestic servant or a petrol-pump attendant, and that of Taylor, who would not have treated his bank-loan officer any differently from the bank janitor.

A bond of friendship had grown between Marsh and his two boatmen, Tawali and Masamba, who had shared many a dangerous situation together. They had had their boat sunk by rogue hippo at night, three times in fact, and had been swamped by the sudden wind squalls, which blew up out of the night, and been lost on the lake at night when storm clouds closed over the heavens and shut out the guiding stars. He just supposed that Taylor thought about Aly in the same way that he thought about his two boatmen—good comrades who need not be kept at arm's length for fear of what other whites might think or say.

While Marsh sat enthralled by the stories he heard, Aly rolled out the sleeping mat he had borrowed and stretched out by the fire, which they had kept burning throughout the night of yarning. Aly neither smoked nor drank and did not speak English, so he had not been tempted to relive the old days with Taylor and Marsh. At sunup he awakened and rose quickly, rolling up the sleeping mat and, putting it on one side, he hurried to the lake shore to wash his feet, face, and hands and then, in the manner of the true Muslim, he went into the nearby seclusion of some mango and pawpaw trees to bow down and say his morning prayers. Returning, he stirred up the embers and placed the kettle on them and soon had coffee boiling. Taylor told him to bring three cups and Aly did so; then he pulled up a box to sit on, and from that time on, he joined the two white men at table whenever they had a meal together.

Marsh was to come to know Aly very well. He did not know exactly how old he was, at the time thinking that Aly was a few years older than he really was, placing him in his middle thirties.

The bush African keeps no record of the date of his birth. In his culture, the important thing in life is dying. A newborn child is of little importance. It is only after a lifetime of friendship, enmity, struggle, accomplishment, and failure that a person in that culture is important. The funeral is the event by which a life is marked, not a birthday. Makes a lot of sense. He was to learn much later from Aly's brother, Kandulu, that Aly had been a boy of probably thirteen when he and Taylor had first met at Lake Amaramba just before the war, so Aly was probably born in 1925. This would have made him a man of thirty-two when Marsh first met him.

Marsh knew that Aly was married to a Sena woman from the Tete region of Mozambique. She lived with her children at Aly's home, which he concluded, as Aly and Taylor had been so long in Mozambique, must be somewhere in that country. It was of little importance at the time and he did not inquire. If only he had! If he had known that Aly's "home" was in Nyasaland and only twenty-five miles down the road, the course of this book would have taken a markedly different turn.

CHAPTER TWO

John Howard Taylor was born on January 6, 1904, at 32 Harcourt Street, Dublin, Ireland, the son of Dr. William Taylor, F.R.C.S.I., Fellow of the Royal Academy of Medicine, then a surgeon at Meath Hospital, and Catherine Maria (née Walker), an American heiress from Louisiana. Dr. Taylor was thirty-two at the time of John's birth and his wife three years older. The family was staunchly Presbyterian, which was to lead John and his elder brother, Bill, into serious trouble after the First World War, all, of course, in the name of Jesus. Both were expelled for political and religious reasons from their own country, which was why John ended up in Africa at the age of eighteen. It was also partly why, many years later, having witnessed what went on between the two groups of Irish "Christians," Catholics and Protestants, he abandoned his Presbyterian religion to become a Muslim.

John, known as "Jack" to friends and family, was the third of four children born to the Taylors. William Hepburn Hamilton Taylor, the eldest and called Bill, was born May 25, 1900. He was in Moser's House at Shrewsbury (pronounced Shrowsbury, for reasons best known to the English) school from 1913 to 1917, when he served as second lieutenant in the Royal Fortress Artillery during the last years of World War I. John's sister, Eleanor Mary, was born April 30, 1902, and became the wife of Erwin C. Ridlington. He is the brother-in-law mentioned in Taylor's first book who was shot in the arm by his own service revolver when it fell from his Sam Browne belt while he was cranking a car. The youngest of the children was Charles Morrison Taylor, born January 17, 1907. Charles followed his father's path into medicine and died in 1989 in Los Angeles, California.

Taylor's father was knighted in 1920 after serving as a military surgeon in the war. Colonel Sir William Taylor is listed as follows in the 1921 edition of *The Dublin Directory*:

Taylor: Colonel Sir William, K.B.E. (Knight of the British Empire) (1920)., C.B. (1919)., B.A., M.B. (Dublin University), F.R.C.S.I., Presbyterian. Royal College of Surgeons, Ireland, 1916., Colonel, Army Medical Services.,

PETER HATHAWAY CAPSTICK

Consulting Surgeon to Forces of Ireland., is a D.L. for the county Dublin., served in the European War, 1914-1918 (Dispatches, C.B.). Son of John Taylor, of Callifen, County Donegal. Born 1871. Married 1898. Catherine, daughter of the late Dr. William Hamilton Walker. Residence: 47 FitzWilliam Square, West Dublin, St. Annes, Killiny, County Dublin. Dublin University and Royal Yacht Clubs.

From all accounts the Taylors were wealthy and the four children were brought up grandly, mixing in the best sets. Dr. Taylor drove a Rolls Royce on his rounds and owned a country home at Kilcullen, in the foothills of the Wicklow Mountains some twenty-five miles from Dublin. The 1901 Census of Ireland records that the family had two servants, Mary Matterson and Mary Haughney, while the 1911 Census records that they had four, Maggie and Lizzie Donegan, Maggie Croake, and Rosanna Kelly. Besides inherited money, Dr. Taylor's medical practice must have been very good before the war.

John Taylor started his education at Monkstown Park preparatory school in Eire, a weekly boarding school about six miles out of Dublin, following his elder brother to Shrewsbury in England to be a boarder at Moser's House, a residence that was and still is considered to be as much of a character-molding force as the school itself. It was rather like an American fraternity and the bonds arising from the experience lasted throughout one's life.

But Taylor was only to remain one year at Shrewsbury, despite his later implication that he had graduated. In his autobiography, he doesn't say that he left early, referring instead to the "years" he spent there. Later, he would write in a letter to a friend that one of the poachers in the "Great Tana Raid" with him had also been at Shrewsbury. After leaving Shrewsbury at the end of his first year there, he returned to Ireland to attend an agricultural college on the outskirts of Dublin, a fact that he also omits.

Knowing in retrospect that Taylor was a homosexual, one is tempted to assume that this was why he was asked to leave Shrewsbury, but his brother Charles told Marsh a different story. Charles alleged that Jack fell out with one of the senior students on the very first day of his inauguration at his new school over the traditional system called "fagging." It has always been considered in British schools the duty of juniors to attend to the menial needs of seniors: cleaning out lockers, fetching and carrying, and generally being on hand to make life easier for their elders. Taylor absolutely rejected this system.

A MAN CALLED LION

This resulted in his being placed under the direct supervision of the senior house prefect, who demanded that Taylor clean and polish his shoes. Taylor responded by throwing the said shoes out of the window. This was in 1917, and at thirteen Taylor was already rather powerfully developed, and the story goes that when the senior prefect approached the first stages of apoplexy, John offered to give him an impromptu face-lift and general redesign. There is no way to confirm this story, but it is most likely true. All his life Taylor fought against authority in any form, and a traditional school like Shrewsbury simply would not brook a nonconformist. Taylor's father was sent for and John was withdrawn.

However, what he later wrote of Shrewsbury clearly shows that he wanted to be associated with the school. He mentions that he was on the school rowing team, which must be a grand invention. He would simply not have been accepted for senior athletics at the age of thirteen. But, for all this, he appears to have been popular with his contemporaries, as nonconformists at school always seem to be. An Old Salopian Club (Shrewsbury's alumni association) official told Marsh in a letter of reply to an inquiry, "John Taylor was clearly an engaging character. I have read the extracts you sent to the present house master of Moser's and we both at once recognized him as a typical Moserite."

Charles continues the saga of his brother's schooling in a letter he wrote to Marsh:

> After Shrewsbury Jack enrolled in an agricultural college in Dublin—how much he attended however is questionable because shortly afterwards a Sinn Feiner was shot and on him was found the Black [death] List— Jack and Bill's names were on it! As a result Jack was taken into the Black and Tans, and Bill into the Auxiliaries. But when the Irish Free State was formed (in 1921), Jack and Bill were out in the cold. They came to stay at home but we were raided, and they were arrested. They were tried and kicked out of the country and shipped to England. They were told that if they returned they would probably be shot. Bill went to Canada and Jack to Africa.

The Auxiliaries and Black and Tans were paramilitary groups assisting the British after the First World War (shades of *Ryan's Daughter*) to keep the peace in Ireland. The Auxiliaries were made up of British ex-officers and the Black and Tans of other ranks. Bill, as mentioned earlier, had been an officer in the Royal Fortress Artillery. John was accepted into the Black and Tans despite his tender age, but what he and Bill had done to earn themselves a place on the Black List is not on record. None-theless, they both must have been fairly active in extracurricular affairs to have been singled out!

Bill at the time was enrolled in Trinity Medical School, intent on following his father's surgical footsteps. (Charles graduated from Trinity later and did become a doctor.) The two brothers, Jack and Bill, were actually staying with their mother at Kilcullen when they were arrested by four Sinn Feiners with silk stockings pulled over their heads. One was a family "friend," who was recognized despite the disguise and later apologized to Lady Taylor for his part. They spent a week in jail before their trial and Charles, who was still a boy, was allowed to accompany their mother to visit them. Charles records that Jack's belligerent attitude to his jailers resulted in them firing a revolver into the wall above his head in an effort to get him to retaliate; had he retaliated, they could have shot him. Bill wisely held his brother down. Jack at the time was just eighteen years old.

Actually, both brothers went to Canada when they were kicked out of Ireland. Bill, abandoning his ambition to become a doctor, took a job with an electrical firm in Montreal, while John went to Ontario to work on a ranch, which was situated close to the United States border. Taylor discovered that bootleg-gers were taking advantage of the winter freeze to drive a truck illegally across the narrows of a border lake and he immediately joined them, finding this a lot more fun than cattle punching and hog slopping.

Brother Bill got bored with short circuits, ohms, and amps in Montreal, and took a job as a bodyguard to the Mexican presi-dent, but things went wrong again politically. He moved again, this time to Venezuela to work in oil. At the start of the Second World War, then in Borneo with Shell Oil Company, Bill joined Montgomery's Eighth Army as a private and ended this long, bloody adventure as a lieutenant colonel! Although Bill made a great success of his life, it seemed that he always regretted that events in Ireland had prevented him from becoming a medical doctor. The three boys greatly admired their famous father and Bill and Charles wanted to emulate him, but John had no ambi-tion in that direction. John writes of his early hankering for Africa:

A MAN CALLED LION

It was at my preparatory school in Eire that I discovered Rider Haggard's *Nada the Lily* (a name he used for his heroine in *Shadows of Shame*), an extremely well-illustrated edition. From that I knew there was only one country for me—Africa. Later I came across *Golden Glory* by Horace Rose, which only deepened my determination to live among the Africans. The years spent at Shrewsbury—one of the Big Five of English public schools—in no way lessened my determination. Neither did a winter spent in Canada. In fact, it was when I returned from Canada that I first mentioned to my mother and father my determination to go to Africa. They were the kindest of parents, as their customary remark to me clearly shows: "All right, son. So long as you are happy, we are."

Marsh gathered from Charles that the last few lines were written with tongue-in-cheek. More likely they would agree to anything to see the back of him. John had caused his parents practically all the gray hairs they had accumulated over the past five years.

Taylor continues his narrative:

When I first set foot on African soil with twenty gold sovereigns and a Harley-Davidson motorcycle, I was not discouraged by the settled and peaceful atmosphere of the Cape. I mounted my Harley and rode north. I guessed that all Africa could not be so civilized like this, so I just continued riding until I had no more money left with which to buy petrol. I thereupon sold my motorcycle and proceeded to jump freight trains—always heading north—as I wanted my money for the rifle I hoped soon to be buying. On my arrival in Bulawayo, Southern Rhodesia, I passed a sports-goods store with rifles in the window and went in. The fellow behind the counter did not seem to know much more about them than I did, and, as I did not know the difference between the various Mausers and their calibres, I plumped for a brand new B.S.A. .303 Sporter and a hundred shells. With this and my old (.455 calibre) Webley revolver, which I was carrying in my knapsack, I jumped more freight trains until I reached the famous Victoria Falls in the Zambezi River. Here I parted from the railway with the intention of wandering away up the Zambezi.

Taylor goes on to describe his first meeting with Joro, who was to become his first gunbearer, and their journey together up the Zambezi. This did happen but was to come later. When he arrived at the Victoria Falls, Taylor was broke again. First he needed to get some money together before he could go wandering off into the blue.

There is a written "reference of work" in the Archives of Zimbabwe that shows that Taylor was employed during 1922 as an overseer on a mission farm near Umtali, on the other side of the country close to the Mozambique border. The reference indicates that the mission fathers were well pleased with his efforts and the fact that the mission farm was right next door to "elephant country" may well have been significant. There is a snippet in his writings that must refer to the time when he was on the mission farm. It concerns an African who was blinded by a spitting cobra: "I once had a native working for me in the Transvaal who got blinded in this manner. . . ." Taylor never did work in the Transvaal, which is a province of South Africa. Clearly, he substituted Transvaal for Southern Rhodesia to bury any reference to his first year there.

On the twenty-second of December of that same year Taylor wrote a letter on Victoria Falls Hotel letterhead paper applying to join the Southern Rhodesian British South Africa Police. The B.S.A.P. has one of the sterling records in southern Africa and when the British South Africa Company was disbanded, this unit voted to keep the name for the sake of its glory. Taylor took great pains to keep his police experience a dark secret, never writing a word about it, making it seem as if he and Joro had left immediately for upriver after his arrival in Africa. Marsh learned about this short but, shall we say, distinguished period of his career only by a chance remark to his wife's uncle, George Style, one of Rhodesia's early hunters and a pioneer game rancher. Marsh was visiting George one day and noticed a copy of *African Rifles & Cartridges* on his bookshelf. Marsh took it out.

"Did I ever tell you that I knew John Taylor?" he said, expecting a warm response from the older man. He knew George was a lover of classic rifles and knew more than a bit about them.

"Taylor!" responded George with an amused glint in his eye. "He was an absolute bounder. Don't tell me he was a friend of yours!" Smiling quietly to himself, he rose to pour himself another whiskey. "Shocking conduct. A disgrace to the force." He glanced up at his nephew-in-law inquiringly as he passed him the bottle. "You do know, I suppose, that he was given a dishonourable discharge from the B.S.A.P.?"

"A dishonourable discharge! I didn't know he was ever in the police." Marsh was shocked. His mind turned back to the nagging rumors he had heard before he left Nyasaland. "What did he do?"

"Never met him personally," continued George, adding a squirt of soda to his glass. "Joined the force just after he left, but of course, they couldn't stop a thing like that being talked about."

A MAN CALLED LION

At this time, Marsh still did not believe the rumors he had heard. He put them down to a character assassination attempt by the British administration in Nyasaland who wanted an excuse to refuse Taylor resident status. Now he began to feel uneasy. Was he about to learn of the fire behind the smoke?

"I did hear some rumours," Marsh ventured, "when I was in Nyasaland. . . ."

"Oh those! I know there were all sorts of rumours about his later life, but never knew if there was any truth in 'em, but this had nothing to do with it. Fact is, Taylor's first station was Sinoia. Sent there as a mounted trooper. Arrested a poacher one day, a local black, and had him locked in the cells for the night. But then he started to feel sorry for him, so he took a crowbar and broke the lock on the cell door to make it look like an outside job and told the prisoner to skip, but the wretched fellow wouldn't budge. His home was nearby and he knew he'd be picked up again. Of course, there was a hell's own row. Unlawfully releasing a prisoner and all that, and Taylor was court-marshalled and convicted. He had a lot of pals though and they were sorry to see him go. He was well liked by the other troopers, but it was generally conceded he would never make a policeman's bootstrap."

A full account of the matter is contained in the Archives of Zimbabwe, reference number S1202: British South Africa Police Record of Service Number 2528: John Howard Taylor. Attested May 1923. Born Dublin 6 January, 1903. Next of Kin: Sir William Taylor.

What? Born 1903? No sir! Taylor was born in 1904. His discharge came through on January 5, 1924, the day before his twentieth birthday. So, he had lied about his age, as the minimum age for acceptance by the B.S.A.P. was twenty, and Taylor was only nineteen when he joined.

The file also contains the previously mentioned letter from the mission farm and some other interesting glimpses of Trooper Taylor. Above-average rifle and pistol shot. Above-average horseman. A report from his member-in-charge to say that Taylor lacked the discipline to ever make a good policeman, together with the comment that Trooper Taylor possessed the remarkable ability to appear completely sober when he was actually motherless drunk! There are also numerous records of five shilling fines for various misdemeanors and bad behavior, and there is the complete, word-for-word transcript of his court-martial.

Proven guilty—Taylor did not deny the charge—he opted for a jail sentence rather than a fine because this would have meant compulsory dismissal by the rather complicated regulations of the force. He had been in the police for only eight months, and like everything else in his life so far, it had proved a disaster. It looked like John Taylor was not fated for success. . . .

Taylor makes much in his novel, *Shadows of Shame*, of the fact that he came from a country where racism was completely unknown and it is likely that his already liberal views rightly made it abhorrent to him that tribespeople were sent to jail for petty offenses because they lacked the money to pay the option of a fine. Certainly, too, in the case of poaching, Taylor's sympathies would have lain foursquare with the accused, even though he had arrested the man in the case that got him court-martialed. But, after leaving the force, he made no effort to conceal his liberalism, and made his feelings clear in his writings.

In passing, it is worth mentioning that George Style's amusement at Trooper Taylor's demise was entirely due to the fact that he all but suffered the same fate. He confessed to his nephew-in-law after telling him what an absolute bounder John Taylor had been that when he was member-in-charge at Binga, a remote dot in an all but blank segment of the old maps of Rhodesia, he pressganged the services of a cook from one of the European-owned cattle ranches in the area to do his cooking for him, a man whom George himself had a short time before arrested for slaughtering his wife's lover.

George ate like a duke for the months it took for the circuit judge to get around to visiting Binga to try the case, and as George grew fat he grew lax, no longer even insisting that an armed warder be on guard at the mess when the murderer was on duty there. On the day of the trial, the cook was let out of the cells early so he could give George a last breakfast before the judge arrived, but instead of reporting to the court house after washing up and cleaning the house, he vanished. . . . The circuit judge, after risking flooded rivers and fixing punctured tires on the bad road to get there on time to try the case, was not at all amused.

It was almost certainly at this crossroad of Taylor's life, at the time of his dishonorable discharge from the force in the early months of 1924, that Taylor acquired the aforementioned .303 Sporter and went on his fifteen-month walkabout along the Zambezi and into

Angola with Joro, his first mentor and guide in Africa. He lived by hunting antelope and trading meat with the natives for pumpkins, maize meal, and the small, brown local eggs.

If this guess at timing is right, it would have been the middle of 1925 when he returned to Southern Rhodesia and took a job as vermin controller on a West Nicholson cattle ranch. The "vermin" consisted mostly of cattle-killing lions, and this was when he presumably parted with the .303, since he never mentions it again. Perhaps he thought it a trifle light for lions.

Taylor had meanwhile fallen for "that grand little gold-inlaid Martini-Henry and invested in it." This was a .577/.450 caliber under-lever single-action, firing a 480-grain lead bullet in front of a nasty load of black powder, by then antiquated in both caliber and pattern, but a piece that had a proven ability against lions. The piece had originally been made for an Indian prince, but it could not be imported into the Raj because .450 caliber bullets had been outlawed. There had been too many uprisings and rebellions over the years and the insurrectionists had captured many Martini rifles, which were making nice new blue-edged holes in British khaki. The idea to outlaw the service caliber of .450 (even though the British had long since gone to the .303) was because there were still too many rifles of that caliber floating around in brown, bloody hands. Where the rifles could not be recovered, at least they could be denied ammunition.

After gaining some experience, Taylor was offered a similar position with a big—even by African standards—cattle-ranching company in Northern Rhodesia (now Zambia), which was when he added a .400/.350 Greener Farquharson single-action to his battery. This also proved effective on lions, but Taylor preferred his Martini for night shooting because it had a flip-up night sight with a large ivory bead that folded down into a recess at the muzzle when not required.

The spotlight that Taylor used was quite different from what is available today, to say the least. It was a carbide lamp, generating acetylene gas led by a rubber tube from a double container affixed on the shooter's belt to the headpiece strapped to his forehead, a regulated flow of water dripping from the top compartment of the container onto the carbide underneath. The gas was ejected from a jet in the headpiece to burn with a small white flame in front of a shiny metal reflector. The light it gave was more of a yellow glow than a white beam, and it was not exactly the sort of thing most would choose today to venture out in the dark to tackle a pride of feeding lions.

Taylor tells of meeting another professional vermin hunter who was operating at the time, the famous "Yank" Allen, whose lion-hunting exploits on the one-million acre Nuanetsi Ranch earned him a place in Rhodesian history, as well as some fairly hairy memories of his own. Taylor describes him as a "tall, steady, unhurried Texan." In the days when "Yank" operated, his name seems to have been synonymous on the Dark Continent for every American, but one wonders how he must have felt about this appellation, being from a Confederate state. Allen disposed of over 200 cattle-killing lions on Nuanetsi, but armed with a double-barreled .577 Nitro Express, then considered the cat-gun *sine qua non.*

Considering all he had done since he first arrived in Africa, it was probably not until 1927 when Taylor was twenty-three years old, that he actually shot his first elephant. From clues given in his writing it can be deduced that his first elephant was taken within rifle shot at the coordinates 20'38"S and 32'49"E, a spot hidden in the green-gray bush of central Mozambique, about midway between the small Xinica and Mossurize Rivers.

He set off on his first elephant poaching expedition into Portuguese territory from Southern Rhodesia, now Zimbabwe, with Joro, his gunbearer, a short string of "Irish lions"—his name for pack donkeys—and his gold-inlaid, black powder and lead-bullet .577/.450 Martini-Henry rifle. He had another rifle he could have taken, the .400/.350 Greener Nitro, which fired a 310-grain metal-jacketed bullet with a muzzle velocity of 2000 feet per second, giving a muzzle energy of 2760 foot-pounds, which most elephant hunters today might feel was the superior weapon for elephant. But it appears that even then Taylor had already acquired his high regard for "obsolete" black powder, which was not as much affected as cordite by the high ambient temperatures of tropical Africa. Taylor also liked the heavier, slower bullets compared with light, fast ones and right to the end he regarded Friar Bacon's invention as the best propellant for the tropics, with only one drawback—smoke!

Taylor's first elephant hunt was not that much of an adventure. This part of Africa is still wild and the elephant then would have been plentiful and not much hunted. He tells that he conducted a stalk up on a big, lone bull that had been raiding the maize granaries belonging to a nearby village and placed a 480-grain lead bullet into its lungs. "All I really knew about shooting elephant," he wrote, "was that you must never shoot aft of an imaginary perpendicular dropped from the hindermost edge of his ear when that ear is back against the shoulder. This fellow's huge ear was back against his shoulder, so I took most deliberate aim exactly halfway up his body and right on the imaginary line, hoping my bullet would slip in close up behind the shoulder."

After the smoke from his black powder charge had cleared, there was nothing but Africa. The bull had vanished, but shortly afterward there came a breaking of branches and a crash, followed by a long deep groan as the bull fell in the dense undergrowth where it had stopped. With loud shouts that it was down, Taylor and his team ran to where they had heard it fall. Having admired his first elephant, he told how he felt after shooting it, admitting that "I suddenly found that I was trembling from head to foot." He cut the tail off in the approved manner as proof of ownership and set about moving his camp up closer to his prize.

Returning, he found "a seething, shouting, yelling black mass of humanity all over the carcass . . . hacking and jabbing and sawing and slashing at great chunks of meat." He then chopped out the tusks, which Taylor records as being "good," probably forty to fifty pounds as anything better would surely have produced some further comment, and then set about finding another.

Two days later, having been called out by one of the local villagers who had run across them, Taylor stalked up on his second elephant. The bull was with a herd of cows and calves and was not so easy to approach. This one he also shot in the shoulder but not with the same result. This bull was still on its feet when Taylor again caught up with it and required two more Martini-Henry rounds in the lungs before it finally went down. Taylor records that "all the gold inlay in the world would not have helped my little Martini stop him had he come then," realizing that he needed steel-jacketed bullets to shoot elephant safely. Having again chopped out the ivory and given away the meat, he tied the four tusks from his first elephant poaching expedition onto the donkeys and hastily departed the way he had come.

Taylor made his second elephant poaching trip within a few days of returning from the first. He went to the same area but now explored further afield and the hunt was of a longer duration. He had sold the "Irish lions" to the first person who would take them. (He was more than glad to get rid of them, having found them more a hindrance than a help). He sold his first ivory, most likely to an Indian storekeeper or *dhukawallah* at Chipinga, which was the nearest settlement on the Southern Rhodesian side.

This brought in enough illicit loot to enable him to invest in his first double-barreled rifle, a .600 Nitro Express, which the seller, an Afrikaans farmer in the district, sportingly warned was a double-discharger. This meant that both barrels would fire when only one trigger was pulled and the farmer warned Taylor that he should use it as a single loader by only loading one barrel at a time. Taylor, however, with the brashness of youth and after having now shot two elephants successfully, did not see the necessity of heeding this sage advice. He loaded up both barrels— 1800 grains of jacketed lead—when he set out to tackle his third elephant. His reward was just:

> There came a thunderous, crashing roar like the last crack of doom: The rifle leaped out of my hands, and I was knocked flying backwards into Joro and the thornbushes. It was as though I had strayed into the railroad track and been hit by ninety-mile-an-hour express. . . .

He did, however, hit the elephant, with both barrels, so he probably wasn't in a fit state to appreciate the humor of it all, but thereafter he loaded the .600 in just one barrel. Taylor tells of shooting a number of good bulls on his second trip before escaping back over the Rhodesian border with a string of porters carrying his poached ivory. He learned that the *chefe de posto* at Espungabeira, the nearest *boma*, had gotten wind of him and was out to arrest him. His activities had been given away by the huge amounts of elephant meat the chief's spies had found drying in all the nearby kraals. One elephant here and there, he may have been prepared to overlook, but the chief no doubt realized that someone was in there blasting away at them in earnest.

Taylor sold the ivory and also the .600, which he reports gave him enough to invest in a new battery of rifles of undisclosed types and calibers before returning with Joro to Victoria Falls and embarking on a poaching trip to Angola. The Angolan opportunities appeared to be not as promising as he had supposed, however, and he now decided to set himself up in Portuguese East Africa (Mozambique) as a legally licensed professional hunter.

A MAN CALLED LION

It was a neat concept. Using illegally gained money to become a legal elephant hunter.

CHAPTER THREE

Taylor went to Tete, which lies on the south side of the lower Zambezi River. Tete has the distinction of being the oldest inland town in Africa south of the equator. It was founded by the Portuguese in 1632, precisely 1000 years after the death of the Prophet Mohammed, on the site of the old Arab slave center of Inyungwe (later Nyungwe). The north bank of the Zambezi that is opposite the town is still known by this name today.

Taylor moved onto the north bank of the river, which in his day was only sparsely populated with families of Sena fisher folk who lived by trading their catches of Zambezi bream, bottlenose, tiger, and catfish to the residents of Tete. These people were not agriculturalists and the riverine fringe with its giant trees was not cleared as it is today to make way for fields of maize.

With the aid of some African helpers, Taylor built himself a pole-and-thatch camp under the umbrella of shade close to the river. This was to be his home for the next ten years. The year was either late 1927 or early 1928. He now joined the ranks of licensed professional ivory hunters. He took a dugout across to Tete and presented himself at the offices of the Portuguese *chefe de posto* to buy an elephant hunting license.

Taylor had parted from Joro at the same place he had found him, on the Zambezi near Victoria Falls. He went alone to Tete, but this parting had greatly affected Taylor. One doesn't have to read literally between the "lions" to see that his affection for his gunbearer was probably his first mention of his sexual affinity for black Africans and males in general:

> Joro came with me until we were in sight of the canoe, then he halted, we faced each other, and he said his farewells. He said them without words. He raised his hands, placed them on my shoulders, and looked deep into my eyes. My hands were on his shoulders and I looked back at him. For long and long we stood like that; and then without a backwards glance he was gone. I never saw him again. I remember I blew my nose loudly and stumbled a bit as I made my way to the canoe. There seemed to be a slight mist in front of my eyes and I couldn't see too well.

Later, when Taylor couldn't forget Joro, he wrote:

> But things began to go wrong. I became restless and irritable. I could
> not settle down and stay put, even when there were plenty of elephant around.
> I had to keep going, I had to see what was on the further side of those hills, I
> would leave the elephant here and go and look for others. My men must have
> thought I was crazy, and I guess they were not far from wrong. The fact of the
> matter is I was lonesome. I missed Joro. Several times I was tempted to go and
> get him—maybe I was foolish not to, but I didn't. I started to drink too much,
> something I'd never done. But then I'd never been lonesome before. I had
> not realized just how fond I'd grown of that constant companion of mine. And
> then one day I was nearly killed by an elephant I wounded when I was half-
> tight—that shook me badly.

Joro, by the way, came out of the arrangement much sunnier
than he went into it. Taylor had gifted the man with half of all his
profits on the basis that they had been partners through thick and
thin. By bush standards, Taylor had probably set Joro up as a
local cattle and goat baron! But Taylor was not so lucky. Lone-
some and miserable, Taylor decided that a change of scene was
indicated:

> If I did not pull myself together, I would never make an elephant hunter—
> even if I survived. The best thing I could do was get away for a spell. So I sold
> nearly everything and sailed for Australia, where I stayed for some months.

An account of the elephant he wounded while tipsy appears
under the heading "How NOT to Shoot an Elephant" in "After-
thoughts" at the end of *African Rifles & Cartridges*. This, however,
as with many of Taylor's anecdotes, was only half the story. Tete
and its surrounds has an extremely hot and unhealthy climate.
The young, unacclimatized Irishman very shortly went down
almost for the count with mosquito-borne malaria that developed
into blackwater fever. Blackwater was all but always fatal in
those days and still has an awesome reputation as a man-killer.

As the story unfolds, it can be seen that it was not that he was
pining for Joro that prompted his move to Australia. He went
there because he had just escaped the grave, with his constitution
all but destroyed. He may have decided that it would seem more
romantic if he left the malaria out of his story, who knows!

Happily for him, there was another elephant hunter who had
made his base at Nyungwe. He was a German named Muller (the
German hunter Taylor often refers to by the initial "M"), an ex-

officer in the First World War and an old African hand. Muller treated Taylor with calabashes of locally brewed millet beer, a nutritious, low-alcohol opaque brew found in every native kraal, which kept Taylor in the right frame of mind while flushing out his affected kidneys. Taylor pulled through the crisis, but the fever stayed with him, keeping him in a chronic state of weakness and ill-health.

Meanwhile, Muller, fearing the worst, had sent for Taylor's mother. She sailed immediately for Cape Town, taking Grace Dow, a young family friend as a traveling companion. From Cape Town, she took the train to Salisbury, Southern Rhodesia, and from there went by car—which she presumably hired despite the fact it was well before the Hertz or Avis era—to Tete. It was a phenomenal feat for the two women to get there on their own over such roads as existed then, which shows the mettle of which they were made.

Arriving in Tete, Lady Taylor grabbed her still very ill son by the ear and carted him back with her to Ireland. No sooner was he back home than the fever broke out again. John's brother Charles told Brian Marsh that John demanded aspirin, quinine, and a bottle of the best Irish whiskey. He then got into a bed piled high with blankets. He became delirious, shouting in an African dialect they couldn't understand—which was probably just as well—while he sweated right through the mattress. Forty-eight hours later, the malaria had abated, defeated but not conquered. It now lay in some dark corner of his body while sharpening its talons for its next attack, which would be anytime he was tired or run down.

Lady Taylor now implored her son to give up the hazards of Africa and elephant hunting in favor of a steady job on a New Zealand sheep station that his father had arranged for him. The owners of the station were old friends of the family and John complied. He was broke, as usual, and did not have the resources to take himself back to Africa, and the family no doubt put on the squeeze. But the job didn't work out, and he was canned. Possibly it was the lack of lions. It was after New Zealand that he went to Australia, not immediately after having lost Joro, as he had implied.

John wrote to his family that he had found a nice quiet job on an Australian sheep ranch that didn't involve anything more dangerous than riding around on a horse counting sheep all day, and his family was relieved. What he did not tell them was that he had, in fact, joined a roughneck adventurer who was looking for a partner to go on a bird-of-paradise poaching expedition to New Guinea. As it turned out, this was almost his last trip anywhere. Japanese poachers who were there ahead of them objected to their presence somewhat strenuously. They murdered Taylor's partner by sneaking up and shooting him, and John came within an ace of being shot, too. The young Irishman had almost been trampled by an elephant and had barely pulled through Death's bony fingers with blackwater fever, but to his dying day he was to reckon that the New Guinea episode gave him his closest call.

Poaching is poaching, we suppose, but the bird-of-paradise project was really the bottom of the barrel. In Africa, ivory poaching was merely against the law of that time because the various governments didn't get their financial tax rake-off by licenses and fees. It wasn't a matter of endangering a species. It was rather more like rum-running or selling tax-free cigarettes. Tens of thousands of elephants were killed by crop controllers. The relatively few tuskers the ivory poachers took didn't really endanger elephant as a species in the least.

But, the bird-of-paradise had been completely protected since 1921 when it was noted by an expert ornithologist that "there were more specimens to be seen in the millinery shops around the world than in their native forests." These gorgeous, exotic creatures, of the family *Paradisaeidae*, of which there are some forty species, were all but out of business. Occurring only in New Guinea, Australia, and the surrounding islands, they were first seen in Europe when Magellan's crew returned in 1522 with a pair of the Greater birds-of-paradise. Apparently native hunters had cut the legs off this particular pair (presumably alive as no mention is made of their being just skins), for reasons unknown. The European title for them was "legless wonders from heaven."

These birds, with capes, plumes, and trains of such startling metallic colors, were all but exterminated, sacrificed on the altars of European fashion, some fifty thousand skins being sent to Paris and Amsterdam alone each year before the trade was banned. Of course, there was big money, a fast buck, to be made from the business, but Taylor didn't get any of it. He was more than happy to get out of it with just his life.

A MAN CALLED LION

Taylor wrote that he had sold "pretty near everything" before he left Tete, so it is unlikely that he had any ideas of returning. Perhaps his nerve had failed when that elephant had nearly killed him. Taylor was still very much an untutored novice at that time and there are few things on this earth more terrifying than the world's largest land animal when it has decided it doesn't like you. After the debacle in New Guinea, Taylor decided to return to Portuguese East Africa, and once there he found himself keener than ever on hunting. Taylor actually returned to his camp on the Zambezi with virtually nothing to his name. He had no rifles or equipment, and this was 1930, just after Wall Street entered the Black Hole of Depression, "the reverberations of which were felt even in Central Africa." Taylor glosses over his predicament by saying it was because a consignment of ammunition had gone astray from London. He always insisted in buying "fresh" ammo, soldered up in sealed tins to keep tropical conditions at bay, obliging him to borrow a "10-bore muzzle-loading *bundook*." But this was probably the only firing-piece of any sort he could lay his hands on.

The muzzleloader, which Taylor estimated to have been made about 1830, but must have been a bit younger since a cap-percussion gun first appeared only in 1836, apparently worked well enough after he got some hardened spherical ten-to-the-pound lead balls, Curtis & Harvey black powder, and a supply of percussion caps from South Africa. Shooting by moonlight from a pit blind at a water hole, he claims to have bagged an elephant bull and two rhino his first night out with it. He was undoubtedly correct when he wrote:

> Men with their modern breechloaders and repeaters are all too much inclined to sneer at the muzzleloader. But a good muzzleloader, properly handled, is a deadly and efficient weapon—provided its limitations are fully realized.

Generations of great African hunters had proved this for many decades before smokeless powder appeared. The 10-bore, muzzle-loading *bundook* would have to be deadly and efficient if Taylor was set to make his fortune with it. With the depression, the price of ivory fell like a shot bird, until about 1933 when apparently supplies were so low that there was something of a recovery, even with the relatively low demand. The value of ivory settled about that time to a price of 80 escudos to the pound, which equates to one pound sterling to one pound weight, and held that price till well after the war.

Taylor averred, in a letter to a friend, that he considered he was doing well if he averaged £30 per tusk throughout the twelve-month hunting period, and in his autobiography he hazards a guess at how many elephants he thinks he had shot:

> As near as I can figure it, I've killed about three hundred elephant on license and I am quite sure I am on the conservative side when I say I have poached four for every one shot legally. That must sound a great many but when you spread it out over thirty-three years you will find that it works out to barely one elephant a week. Even that would be a lot to the occasional hunter, but you must remember that I lived all year round in the bush.

Thirty-three years had indeed gone by from the time Taylor landed in Africa in 1922 to the time he wrote his autobiography in 1955. He was not, in fact, hunting elephant for much of this time, only seriously from 1930 to 1940, and perhaps for two years after the war. If Taylor shot the 1500 elephants in his claim of the ratio between poached and legal animals, he would have had to take ten a month, one every three days with no days off for twelve years. At an average of thirty pounds weight per tusk and an average of one pound sterling per pound of ivory, he would have realized £90,000 over this period, equal to an income of £7,500 per year for the time he was actively hunting.

The prewar United States dollar was five to the British pound, so this would have been the equivalent of $37,500 annually. In those days before gut-gobbling inflation, that was a huge income. He also shot a few leopard for their skins and some rhino for their horns, and he shot buffalo, which he sold on site to the native meat-vendors for £2 apiece. He should have been making big money if his claims were true. After all, a luxury car in the 1930s cost only $2,000 in American funds, even though $2,000 was a lot a money in those days. Yet, we know of his almost constant poverty, so something was very wrong somewhere. . . .

The price that Harry Manners, a prewar Mozambican ivory hunter known for his record-holding tusks, quotes applies to legal ivory. Poached ivory had to be sold for what the purchaser would give, the classic buyer's market. Taylor sold all his tusks to a Chinese in Tete, who ran a general store and traded in wildcat skins of all types as well as ivory. He also supplied gin-traps to the natives who set them at night around their kraals.

A MAN CALLED LION

Taylor told Marsh that he had once been inside the store-room of the store when it was filled to the ceiling with every type of wildcat skin: genet, serval, leopard and such. Harry Manners maintains that the Chinese would most certainly have demanded an all-or-nothing deal on Taylor's ivory, taking both Taylor's legal and illegal tusks. Harry quotes the price for illegal ivory at that time as only seven shillings and six pence a pound, one third the legal price. That would probably have been the price that Taylor was getting. But even this would still have added up to a fair amount of money.

Taylor must have made *some* money from ivory during the '30s, but he was a reckless adventurer who lived for the moment, never putting anything aside for his old age or even tomorrow. If he had enough in his pocket for his immediate needs, that was enough. The excitement of a professional hunter's life was meat and soul food enough for the day.

Although Taylor was actively hunting elephant right through the 1930s, his real heydays of elephant hunting were only from about 1933 until he joined the army in 1940. This was a period of some seven years. "The Great Tana Raid" was supposed to have occurred during this time. He wrote of it: "I'm not going to be too specific about the date of this adventure—it's all too recent. And I doubt that there has ever been a bigger, or more highly organized, or more successful poaching raid anywhere."

Taylor told Marsh that it had come off in 1936. If it happened at all, we doubt that it could have been on the scale claimed. The logistics alone would have been prohibitive, almost impossible, and a number of things about the "Raid" do not ring true. Taylor makes no mention of leaving Africa for good. He says that he was on his way home to Ireland for a vacation when the raid came up. If he was only going on holiday to Eire, why did he have his elephant guns and ammunition with him as well as numerous other items of camping gear? There haven't been any elephants in Dublin for quite a while, since the *Dinotherium* in fact.

Taylor ended the chapter about the raid in *Pondoro*:

> Not so very long afterwards, when I happened to be in Kenya and was talking to a certain official of the game department, the question of poaching was mentioned. The official's florid face turned an expensive purple as he spluttered and fumed into his gin and water over the recollection of that particular raid. I clucked and tut-tutted in sympathy and condemned the audacity

of the rascals. Blackguardly! Outrageous! Dastardly! I gave them every adjective I could lay my tongue to.

In response to an inquiry about the raid, Taylor wrote in a letter dated April 22, 1958, that the "certain official of the game department" was the famed Captain Archie Ritchie, Chief Warden in Kenya at the time of the supposed raid. We don't think that Archie Ritchie ever even heard of the "Great Tana Raid," which of course he would have, had the incident happened other than in Taylor's nimble mind.

During the time Taylor was based at Nyungwe, he hunted mostly up and downstream along the Zambezi, using dugout canoes for portage. He did not own a motor vehicle, preferring to hunt remote places that could only be reached by water or on foot. Taylor would make a camp at a convenient place along the river and strike off inland, hiring porters locally as he went. He writes that the minimum number of men he kept permanently was eight: Saduku, his head tracker before the war; his cook-cum-personal servant; and six camp hands who also acted as porters.

Living off the land, his needs were meager. Since he went around clad only in a *moochi* or *kikoy*, a piece of cloth around his waist (if that), he did not have a wardrobe to cart around. Taylor had much to say about the virtues of nudism in his writings. He claimed that his nakedness while hunting kept him cool by day and, as his body absorbed the heat of the sun, warm by night. Sometimes these hunts would take Taylor as far as fifty miles from the river, sleeping on tracks or at the nearest water hole. He traded meat in the kraals for native staples, carrying only salt, tea, coffee, and condensed milk by way of luxuries.

At certain times of the year Taylor would concentrate on hunting buffalo. This was during the late winter and early summer when the buffalo herds came down onto the plains at Lake Lifumba, the "Lake of the Woman's Anklet." Lifumba is a small L-shaped lagoon on the north bank of the Zambezi, connected to the river by a narrow channel overgrown with reeds, kept open by the movement of hippo. Taylor built a permanent camp there on the small island that lies in the angle of the "L."

Taylor shot Cape buffalo on the plains, where even in recent times they still occurred in hundreds, jostling, bellowing, black, swirling pools of wild cattle. He sold them where they fell, to meat-vendors from Nyasaland for the sum of £2 apiece. The vendors walked in over the border to butcher and smoke-dry the meat before tying it into manageable bundles with strips of rawhide cut from the skin. Taylor sometimes shot as many as ten in a day by running after the herds and shooting every time they stopped. Taylor describes how the herds would sometimes perform:

> A large herd will sometimes come towards you when you encounter them out in the open with all the grass burnt off, so that there is no cover. They will start at a walk but those in the rear are so anxious to see what it's all about that they will jostle and push until the whole mob breaks into a lumbering gallop. The dust and the black pall of burnt ashes of the grass thrown up and the clashing and rattling of mighty horns are certainly awe-inspiring if you aren't accustomed to them, and the beginner might well be excused for believing that it's a mass attack. But it's nothing of the sort; it's merely curiosity. And the bigger the herd the more curious they are. If there are several hundreds of them, as there well might be, don't let them scare you. Just wait until they are forty yards or so, and then let loose a yell: "Hi-ya, there!" Anything will do. They'll stop. A couple of mighty bulls, the leaders of the herd, will come perhaps their own length out from the dense black mass of the remainder of the herd, and paw the ground and snort and toss their great heads. But that's sheer bluff. Don't take any notice of it. Throw up your rifle and drop the better of the two, and then slam your left barrel into the other as it wheels around to go. It's quite on the cards that if you should lose your head and run, the herd will come on and run you down without having any evil intent.

Running after a big herd when you have fired under those conditions will almost certainly ensure you will get another crack at the animals, because a big herd will indeed shortly stop to see what's going on. The ones that were at the back are now the leaders and they don't know what it is all about. When they stop, the ones behind will also stop. But you will only get another shot if you have been able to keep up with them, which isn't easy. When the herd thunders off, the dust and ash from the burnt plains is as thick as raw molasses. You cannot see and you cannot breathe, and you stand the excellent chance of running onto the horns of one you may have wounded. Brian Marsh and I have tried it!

On one occasion when Taylor walked in from the south bank of the Zambezi after elephant he ended up in Changara, a small village about midway between the border and the Zambezi on the main road from Southern Rhodesia to Nyasaland. There he met up with Crawford Fletcher Jamieson, the Rhodesian professional who had established a base there. Although the two men shared a similar age and love of their profession, they really had little else in common. Yet they were to remain the best of friends until "Fletch"'s death in 1947.

In 1938, Taylor and Jamieson spent several months on an elephant hunting safari together in the Elephant Marsh on the lower Shire River in Nyasaland. Both were looking for new hunting grounds. Toward the end of the 1930s some changes in the hunting scene had occurred in Portuguese East Africa. Bush tracks had been opened into the more accessible places with mopane-pole (a resinous, indigenous, and termite-proof hardwood) bridges constructed across water courses and dongas. These all led into the best hunting areas that had previously been remote country but were now available to every visiting, casual sportsman. Portuguese, Rhodesian, and South African hunters arrived in Tete in their Ford and Chevrolet trucks to buy licenses to hunt, carrying fuel and supplies for a few weeks in the wilds, greatly interfering with the professionals.

When Jamieson and Taylor split up after their Nyasaland safari, Taylor left the Zambezi altogether and headed north. There was a mine labor-recruiting organization running buses from the gold mines in Johannesburg, South Africa, through Nyasaland to Mandimba in P.E.A. Taylor got a lift on one of these buses in order to explore new territory. He got off at Mandimba, the small Portuguese administration and border post, and walked the twenty-odd miles to the top of the waters of Lake Amaramba. This is a comparatively small lake lying some fifty miles to the east of the southern tip of Lake Nyasa and is the source of the Lugenda (pronounced Ruzhenda) River, which drains the lake into the Ruvuma River—the border with Tanzania—and then to the sea. He found exactly what he was looking for: good elephant country that was still unmolested and a small town with a *boma* that was an easy distance away where he could buy his supplies and hunting licenses.

In those days, licenses to hunt elephant were issued on a renewable basis, five elephant per ticket, the licensee being entitled to another as soon as the first one was filled. Delighted, Taylor hired some staff and set about constructing a permanent base camp where the Mandimba River runs into the Lugenda, only a short distance from the lake. Once the camp was up and running, he began hunting elephant again in earnest.

Taylor did not have to go far to hunt. He found plenty of good bulls around the lake shoreline where they came to drink and to feed on the green shoots growing in the sudd, matted masses of papyrus. Although shallow, Lake Amaramba was swarming with fish, and the fishermen on the lake smoked or sun dried their catches to sell to their agrarian cousins from Nyasaland. This was the country of the Yao, a staunchly Islamic tribe that had been split in two by the European-aligned border between Mozambique and Nyasaland, which ignored the existing cultures. The mode of transport for the fish merchants from Nyasaland was the bicycle. On the back two long bamboo poles protruded and the bales of dried fish were tied on, a custom that is still prevalent today in that part of the world.

One bright morning, two travel-worn young African boys arrived at Taylor's camp. The elder was about seventeen years old while the other was probably three or four years younger. Taylor noticed that in spite of their age difference they were so alike they could have been identical twins. They were dusty and covered with grime and sweat, and on their heads they wore the badge of their religion, the string-crochet *kofia*, as it is called in the local language, Chichewa. It is the skullcap worn by the adherents of Islam.

They looked half-starved. They had obviously been on the road for some time, and Taylor, always sensitive to the wants of the needy, cut them some lengths of dried buffalo meat from the strips his men had hung in the trees. The two boys would not have questioned its fitness to eat. It was a local convention in that area that the buffalo would have been *halalled*, their throats cut in accordance with Islamic dietary law. The two boys thanked him profusely and sank their teeth into the meat.

Then the older one said, "We have heard about you. You are *Chimpondoro*, the elephant hunter from the Zambezi."

Taylor nodded. "Yes. I am he. And who are you and what is your business here?"

"I am Kandulu, and this is my younger brother Aly. We are from Nyasaland, the sons of a farmer, but last year's rains failed, so we have been sent to buy fish to sell to make money."

"Fish vendors! You are younger than most who come here. And where are your bicycles upon which to carry your purchases?"

"We are poor, bwana. We have no bicycles. What we buy we must carry on our heads."

Taylor wondered just how much two such fellows could really carry. To make the venture worthwhile, they would need to buy a fair weight. Well, nothing he could do about it. They both looked fit and strong, so he wished them luck and they departed. But he did wonder how successful they would be.

Because of the drought, the fish vendors, generally farmers whose crops had failed, were arriving at Lake Amaramba in large numbers, and the fishermen had a seller's market. He wondered just how easy it would be for two such young fellows to compete. He was not long in finding out. A couple of days later the same two boys were back in his camp, looking woebegone. "We have failed," said Kandulu, rubbing his big toe in the dirt. "All the fish have been spoken for. We have come too late and there is nothing for new buyers like ourselves."

Taylor was not surprised. "You may sleep here tonight and my men will give you food," he told them, "and I will see that you do not return empty-handed. You may come out with me tomorrow. I will shoot you a buffalo. I am sure if you have no fish to sell that you will find a ready market for dried buffalo meat."

The two boys' look of sorrow changed quickly to one of elation. "But we do not know how much you will charge us," said Kandulu cautiously. "Perhaps we do not have money enough to pay you."

"Keep your money," said *Pondoro*. "Times are hard and you may need it later." He was going out next morning to shoot a buffalo for camp meat anyway, and with any luck he would be able to shoot two. Large herds drank nightly near his camp and it would only cost him one extra round of ammunition.

The next morning Taylor shot them a buffalo and left them to butcher it and cut it into long strips to dry in the sun, ready to carry back to Nyasaland. On their way back a few days later, they called to thank him.

The young boy then made two spooky predictions: "You are my father," he said, using a polite idiom to express his overwhelming gratitude. "I am Aly Ndemanga, and when I grow up I will work for you."

A MAN CALLED LION

Eerily both these predictions were to come true. A few years later Aly entered Taylor's employ, and Taylor figuratively became Aly's father when he adopted him as a son.

CHAPTER FOUR

Taylor had been established at his base camp in northern Portuguese East Africa at Lake Amaramba—he calls it Lake Namaramba in his writings—no doubt he got this phonetically rather than from a map—when war was declared. Having no radio, Taylor did not even hear about the war until it had already been on for some months. He had sent one of his men to Mandimba, the small Portuguese town on the border with Nyasaland, to buy supplies, which were delivered wrapped in sheets of the Beira newspaper. Taylor, being fluent in Portuguese, sat down to catch up on what had been going on.

He stopped hunting immediately and hurried off to England's defense, which was quite commendable considering his animosity toward British colonialism. He dismantled his camp and went to Zomba, then capital of Nyasaland and the H.Q. of that famous African regiment, the Kings African Rifles, to join up. As it happened, the very well-known safari outfitter and professional hunter, Norman Carr of Zambia, had joined the regiment shortly before John Taylor arrived. Carr in a letter to Marsh tells of Taylor's arrival and enlistment:

> When war was declared, I thought I was one of the last to hear about it. I was hunting in the Luangwa Valley and it was two weeks later that I received a note from the D.C. [District Commissioner] Lundazi. It was several months later that I was called up for service (I was on the Kings African Rifles Reserve of Officers). Whilst in Zomba with the 2/2nd KAR training recruits, a man walked in from the bush to say he had just heard there was a war on and he wanted to join up. When his beard was shaved off, we saw it was . . . (John *Pondoro* Taylor).
>
> Our battalion (2/2 KAR) was transferred to Namwera (S.E. of Lake Nyasa on the Mozambique border) to a new training depot for completion of field training some weeks before embarking north. *Pondoro* was posted to our battalion as a sergeant. Within a short space of time, some of the troops with family commitments were allowed to apply for embarkation leave. *Pondoro* applied but the C.O. was reluctant as it meant his going back to Tete and leaving Nyasaland into neutral P.E.A. However leave was granted for seven days.

Taylor went to Tete to leave his personal belongings for safekeeping, which included all his hunting equipment and his valuable battery of rifles, with a Portuguese friend until he returned from the war. The story of what happened when he got there was told to Brian Marsh by Harry Manners.

Harry is one of the very last survivors of the prewar Mozambican ivory hunters, and he is best remembered as being the record holder for the second largest pair of elephant tusks ever taken by a white man—standing at number four in Rowland Ward's *Records of Big Game*. Harry Manners and John Taylor had a mutual friend, McKenna, the Irish-Australian telephone linesman mentioned in Taylor's autobiography. McKenna had a house at Nyungwe, on the north bank of the Zambezi close to where Taylor had built his prewar camp. Harry happened to visit McKenna a few days after the C.O.'s fears materialized, and World War II was indeed carried into neutral Portuguese territory.

> When Taylor arrived back in Tete, he moved in with his old friend McKenna while the arrangements were made to store his equipment. One evening to repay the hospitality, he invited McKenna to dine with him at Hotel Tete, a Continental establishment on the opposite bank which was owned by Herr Paul Schots, a German with a certain resemblance to a large and somewhat unrefrigerated *blutwurst*. Schots was a huge man and his awesome German wife and big, burly son assisted him at the hotel. That night Taylor and McKenna joined the Germans for dinner, as they had often done.
>
> Under the circumstances, it was not a good mix. The friendships of the two groups had been somewhat eroded by patriotic feelings on both sides. Hotel Tete, however, was a neutral establishment standing on neutral soil. Portugal had remained neutral throughout the war. While on the surface everyone was friendly and enjoying one another's company, God alone knew what really seethed under those sweat-stained khaki shirt fronts.
>
> The evening continued cordially enough, until sufficient bottles of Schots's excellent Madeira red had been opened and drained. Then McKenna, rather foolishly as he himself later admitted, brought up the subject of the war and proceeded to comment in less than delicate terms about recent Allied successes. This, of course, intensely annoyed the Germans, and Schots Senior rose to his feet.
>
> Giving the Nazi salute, he roared like a wounded bull, "Zoon our fictorious armies vill push you English piks into ze zee!" Taylor responded by leaping to his feet, knocking his chair over and taking a hard swing at Schots. The German ducked. Schots instantly straightened and in less than a blink loosed a returning haymaker at Taylor. Taylor ducked, but Schots's burly son entered the fray. He jumped from his chair and dived for Taylor's back, intending to pin the Irishman's arms while Schots pummeled him to rubble. But it didn't work out that way. When Taylor ducked, the son took the full force of his father's Westphalian ham-sized fist flush on the jaw and was knocked cold.

A MAN CALLED LION

Taylor and Schots then began slugging it out. Taylor was younger and no doubt fitter, his muscles hard-honed from elephant hunting, but he was considerably drunker and by no means got the best of this spontaneous display of patriotism. Schots's lard absorbed the punches and the German's weight was in his favor. He got in several hard blows to Taylor's face, which would have sobered up a lesser man. They hammered away at each other to the considerable detriment of the hotel's dining room furniture, and they were still trying to batter each other to death when the police arrived. Taylor was arrested, charged with bringing his war into neutral Portuguese East Africa, and deposited in the slammer. Once again his zeal for rising to the defense of Britain had cost him dear.

Schots ran Hotel Tete for the duration of the war, the joke being that a considerable number of his clientele were British travelers plying between British Rhodesia in the south and British Nyasaland to the north. Tete is exactly midway between the two countries and Schots controlled the only game in town, the only hotel along the entire route through central P.E.A., and any Englishman who arrived too late to catch the last ferry across the Zambezi was Schots's prisoner for the night, unless of course, he preferred to sleep in his car, vainly trying to fend off the squadrons and armadas of starving, man-eating Zambezi mosquitoes.

How Taylor got out of the Tete jail and back to Zomba will ever remain a mystery. Norman Carr continues the story:

> After being A.W.O.L. for a week, we all assumed he (Taylor) had deserted. A few days later, before the battalion left, he returned showing obvious signs of having been beaten up. His story was that whilst drinking in the hotel bar at Tete that contained mostly Germans escaping from neighboring countries to a neutral haven he got into a fight, was outnumbered and beaten up, and put in prison for carrying his own war into neutral Mozambique. He managed to bribe or break his way out and found his way back to Namwera.
>
> He was not very sociable, he avoided the wives and women guests in camp, he was not cooperative and rather aggressive. However, we gave him full marks for breaking out of jail and reporting back for duty.

In his autobiography, Taylor brushes lightly and vaguely over his service record, stating simply and briefly that he had been an "intelligence officer" in East Africa, which was a fabrication by definition alone, since sergeant was his highest rank. Taylor's brother, Charles, told Brian Marsh, however, that John had actually served with the Kings African Rifles in Burma and had been wounded there in 1943, taking a burst of 7.7mm (.311 caliber) Japanese machine-gun bullets in his right shoulder and a single bullet in the upper calf of his right leg. He was sent back to Africa to recuperate and he later did serve in Zomba with intelligence but at the rank of private. The British administration of the day was concerned that the disruption caused by the war might spawn an insurrection. Taylor's thorough knowledge of local languages served him well in his role as interrogator and interpreter. He was fluent in some African dialects—Chinyanja, ChiSena, and Swahili—and in Portuguese.

Taylor had another injury, more mysterious than his war wounds, that cost him the middle finger on his right hand. It is curious that Taylor never in all his writings mentioned exactly what had happened to earn him such a fine collection of Japanese lead. In a letter to his young friend, Alexander Maitland in Scotland, he said it was a sort of negative souvenir of a lion bite. On page 297 of *African Rifles & Cartridges*, he tells of crawling around the boonies in the middle of the night in the act of shooting a goat-lifting lion with his .455 Webley revolver, firing from his left hand. Not too shabby an adventure, shooting a lion left-handed from the hip at night and killing it with such a small weapon as a Webley! However, Taylor writes:

> Altho I had practiced shooting a rifle from both shoulders, I had done practically all my revolver shooting in the past with my right hand. But, thanks to World War II, there isn't quite so much of that hand now as there used to be, and I find I can't manage a big gun like the Webley with it. So I was, perforce, compelled to use my left hand, which was not really such a handicap as it might seem because I have always been ambidextrous.

Why did Taylor, who in truth lived a fantastically adventurous life, have to fly a kite about something so silly as a lost finger, first writing that it was a war wound and then penning Maitland a long story that it was the result of a lion bite? He must have known that Maitland would one day read his book.

Taylor was in Zomba from 1944 until unpleasantries ended in 1945, where for the most part he lived alone in a government bungalow he was allocated. Unbeknown to him, Aly Ndemanga, the younger of the two youths he had helped at Lake Amaramba before the war and no doubt forgotten all about, had journeyed to Zomba to seek work, there being no work for him on the family farm. Aly had been in Zomba for a year. He was now about twenty years old and had taken a job as a kitchen hand to an English civil service family. As Zomba, in spite of being the capital of Nyasaland, was a very small town, it was inevitable that Aly would eventually find out that Taylor was also there and was seeking a servant, since he had moved out of the army barracks into a bungalow.

Aly immediately went to work for Taylor, as he had promised, simply by walking out of his employer's kitchen that night and letting himself into Taylor's kitchen early next morning to make his new master tea. The sleepy Taylor heard some movement from the back of the house and wondered what the hell was going on. Houses were never locked in those balmy days and, as it was already daylight, he could not believe he was being robbed. There was a subdued knock and without further ado, Aly entered with a tray. He nodded a curt good morning to his rather startled new employer, picked up the laundry, and walked out. There had been no discussion about terms. Aly had said that he would one day work for him, and there he was.

Taylor had very little money. In bush terms, a philanthropist and spendthrift to the point of vice, he had given away or spent what money he had made from ivory and buffalo hunting before the war. For unknown and undisclosed reasons, he was not given an army pension, to which he would have been entitled, considering his wounds and his military service. Many years later Marsh's inquiries at the Malawian (formally Nyasaland) Army Headquarters, both in person and by mail, failed to elicit the reason. This leaves the only conclusion that Taylor was either discharged for some offense or that he had deserted by simply walking out. Whatever the case, shortly after the war's end, John Taylor and Aly Ndemanga were back at Nyungwe, in the same camp Taylor had made his base when he first arrived in the country twenty-five years before.

Taylor eventually recovered from the wounds he had received—the physical ones, at any rate. He did not recover so easily from the deep financial lacerations inflicted upon him by the "friend" with whom he had left his rifles and equipment for safekeeping. The "friend" had sold everything out from under him while he was away defending King and Country and had absconded with the proceeds thereof. The "friend" had wounded Taylor in the monetary artery, a felon's slash from which he was never to recover.

Needing a rifle and fearing that he would never be able to shoot right-handed again, John wrote to his brother Charles, who was living in England immediately after the war, to look into finding and buying a .600 Nitro double with a left-handed cant. Taylor was obliged to shoot most of his elephant in very thick cover because this was where the big ivory live. The fact that he was opting for what was the most powerful cartridge commercially made—throwing a 900-grain bullet at 1950 feet per second of muzzle velocity and developing a theoretical 7600 foot-pounds of muzzle energy—indicates his lack of confidence at the time. But meanwhile, as he could not hunt, he set about looking for something else to do to make a living.

He had drafted a book on big-game rifles before the war, which he had reworked while he was convalescing in the hospital. This now seemed his only chance to get on his feet again. He and Aly repaired the camp, finding a letter tucked into the thatch, which he had written to his brother Charles before the war but had forgotten to post. He posted it anyway, penning a postscript on the envelope that although the news was some years old it would still be new to Charles. Then he settled down to write in earnest.

This work became Taylor's first book, *Big Game & Big Game Rifles*. When it was completed, he used what resources he had left to make a trip to England to personally hand the manuscript to his publisher, Herbert Jenkins of London. With the advance on royalties received from Jenkins, he bought a motor launch in Beira on his way back to Tete. This he brought by rail to Murraca on the lower Zambezi, and from there upriver to his camp. He mentions this boat trip in his autobiography, *Pondoro*, recounting that when he broke the shaft of the engine he had to hire polers to make the rest of the way. Aly was waiting on the bank for him, having heard by "jungle telegraph" of his breakdown and pending arrival.

Taylor and Aly then abandoned the old camp at Nyungwe for good, moving upriver to Baroma where there were a large Roman Catholic mission station and other facilities, including a clinic. There was a constant traffic of dugouts across the river. Taylor, after the boat's engine was repaired, taught Aly how to run it and used it as a commercial ferry, carrying paying passengers back and forth across the Zambezi. Taylor, in a newly made camp, spent his days writing. He was then engaged in writing for Thomas G. Samworth and his Small Arms Technical Publishing Company of Georgetown, South Carolina, what was to become the now world classic, *African Rifles & Cartridges*.

A MAN CALLED LION

The ferry, at a fare of only four escudos (ten cents, American) per person per crossing, kept them only meagerly supplied. Without being specific about the actual date, Taylor writes of the extreme hardship he and Aly endured over this period, with Aly never receiving wages and their food reduced to weevil-studded corn meal porridge whenever Aly failed to find a fish in one of his bamboo traps. Taylor wrote:

> Some tribes, notably those of Nyasaland, make splendid cooks and servants; they are clean, honest, entirely to be trusted with the running of the house. Once you show them what you want done, you can thereafter leave them to it; you don't have to be eternally following them round to see what they've overlooked, deliberately or otherwise. As cooks they are second to none. I had a Yao cook for some years–Johnny, from Fort Johnston on Lake Nyasa–and never before or since have I eaten so well in the bush.
>
> My good lad Aly, also a Yao, is just the same in that respect; he made me sack two other lads who were sitting around eating their heads off and doing nothing else, and he said he would look after everything himself. That was years ago, but he's never changed. Although he's my head boy now that I'm back in the bush again and have other men on my payroll, nevertheless, he still keeps an eye on my food–which he shares with me–and generally supervises the work of all those in any way attending to me personally. If we get some of our favorite ingredients for a meal and he's afraid the cook may make a mess of things he doesn't hesitate to do the cooking himself. I'm very fond of Aly. When times were lean he worked for me for three years–three solid years–without drawing or even asking me for a single penny of his pay. It's true that I didn't have it to give to him, and he well knew that, but the vast majority of natives would have asked all the same. Once I did get a handful of cash one time, from the sale of a magazine article, I suggested to Aly that he take what was owing to him and, if he had any sense, go look for another job. He scoffed at the notion of leaving me, and when I tried to point out that it was only for his sake that I suggested it, that I certainly didn't want to lose him, he said he was hurt that I should be capable of believing he would ever desert me–especially when times were hard. And mark you, that was a long time ago, when Aly didn't know me as well as he does now.
>
> But then Aly is really exceptional. I've had some excellent and very conscientious servants in my time but never another to compare with him. Maybe some of them would have proved equally as good if they'd been with me as long and gone through as much with me as Aly has. Well, I wonder. God knows there was little enough to laugh about during those three lean years, but Aly always found something; he'd wake up with a laugh; all day he would sing and give that gloriously infectious chuckle of his; he'd fall asleep still laughing. When he'd prepare our two meals a day, and frequently only one, of sour weevily meal for porridge and beans that were full of borers, and I'd turn up my nose but eat it because there was nothing else, Aly, bless him, would pretend he was thoroughly enjoying it, had never eaten anything more delicious, and hoped for nothing better. He'd frequently spend the entire

night fishing to get something better—I was a mighty sick man at the time, after those military doctors had seemingly been unable to put things right. And, like all sick men who have never been sick before, I was captious and querulous, hard to please, never done with grumbling and bellyaching. Aly must have had the patience of Job to put up with me, but he did. I surely did not pull my weight in the boat that time.

It would take a hard person, indeed, not to appreciate the real regard and affection in which Taylor and Aly held each other, despite the obvious implications. They were loyal to each other and even though times were hard and Taylor sick, they made their way in the African world, which is as cruel as they come.

As an elucidation of Taylor's comments, should he seem a bit patronizing when referring to Africans mainly as servants, remember that he wrote his observations nearly forty years ago in the bush and about bush Africans. Their prospects of becoming anything other than servants were very small, this being before a great deal of social progress came to the Continent. Whatever the case, few whites appreciated the African as did John Taylor, and his motives were a great deal deeper than the obvious ones.

* * * * * * *

Taylor spoke to Brian Marsh at some length concerning his conversion to Islam. Marsh naturally presumed that he had become enchanted with it because of the care and loyalty he had received from Aly, the devout young Muslim Yao, during the "lean times" he told about when he was disabled and broke. Harry Manners, however, says this was not so. Harry's and John Taylor's mutual friend, McKenna, told Harry that Taylor was already a Muslim zealot by the time he moved back to his Nyungwe camp after the war, and would parade around Tete dressed in a *thobe*, a white cotton ankle-length shift, with a copy of the Koran tucked under his arm, trying to convert anybody who would listen to him. McKenna opined that "the Arabs had got to him during the war," but Taylor had already been living before that among the Yaos.

Taylor was raised in a strong Presbyterian faith in a religious household, so it might be difficult for the average non-Muslim European or American who has not lived in Africa to comprehend this switch. To those who have not spent time with Muslims, the two faiths seem far apart, but actually they are not, even though a fair number of Crusades were fought over the real estate and principles thereof.

The Prophet Mohammed did not bring a new religion to Arabia. He brought the Word of God as revealed by the biblical prophets—Abraham, Noah, and Moses, plus the same message brought to Christians by Jesus Christ. The differences are really a sort of a theological point of order. Five chapters of the Holy Koran are entitled: Noah, Jonah, Joseph, Abraham, and Mary (mother of Jesus). Jesus, "the righteous prophet" as he is called, is discussed in no less than fifty verses. There are other well-known biblical names as well in the Koran: Adam, David, Goliath, Job, Lot, and Solomon. There is extremism in many of the world's religions, which does not reflect the true nature of the creed any more than the Spanish Inquisition reflected the teachings of Christ. With a few exceptions, for which the Muslims can offer logical arguments indeed, they accept the Old Testament in its entirety.

Islam in Africa dates back to the time of the Prophet Mohammed himself, who died in 632 AD. Because of religious persecution, Mohammed sent his son-in-law and his daughter with some of their followers to Abyssinia (Ethiopia) for their safety. There they commenced to spread the "word," and within a hundred years of the Prophet's death, Muslim rule and religion extended over the whole of North Africa, with the exception of some parts of Ethiopia where the Coptic Christians held sway. The northern Africans welcomed the Muslims as saviors and liberators from their Byzantine oppressors. Islam spread south when the Arabs colonized the east coast of Africa in the year 700. They established their main trade center on Zanzibar Island, which is not far to the north of the Ruvuma River, the border between modern Tanzania and Mozambique. There was absolutely no racial or religious barrier between the Semitic Arabs and the black Africans; not that there was in Christian doctrine either, but Arabia is a lot closer to Africa than Europe is, at least ethnically. This gave Islam an edge.

The Arabs journeyed up the Ruvuma into the African interior to trade, where they came into contact with the Yao tribe. The Yaos were then established in the Ruvuma Valley, with their tribal center at Yao Hill on the south side of the river. It was not long before the Yaos were converted to Islam and, turning to a life of trade, they absorbed the Arab culture.

The Yaos spread into the African hinterland in search of ivory, slaves, beeswax, and tobacco which they traded to the Arabs for guns and powder, cloth and beads, salt, copper, and iron, all of which were regarded as currency. A man's wealth was measured in the traditional capitalist manner by his possessions. The well-armed Yaos preyed easily and heavily upon the surrounding pagan tribes for slaves, using them as domestic servants and laborers to tend their livestock and farm their grain of finger-millet and sorghum. The Yaos also used them as beasts of burden to carry Yao barter goods to the coast. Slavery, which possibly even more than religion "opened up" Africa to the Europeans, was intricately and intrinsically bound to the ivory trade. In fact, because newly captured slaves were used to carry tusks gotten in the interior to the coast, the only form of transport available well into the nineteenth century and even part of the twentieth, these slaves were commonly known as "black ivory."

One of the Yao groups splintered off and moved south along the Lugenda River where they settled at Mandimba Hill, where the border town of the same name stands today, not far from Lake Amaramba. They became known as the "Amachinga," which roughly translates to "the people of the Serrated Mountains," since they settled into the saw-toothed Mandimba range. From there, they indulged in such lucrative practices as slaving and trading into the interior as well as farming the fertile Mangochi Plateau overlooking Lake Malawi. The Portuguese Jesuit, Dr. Francisco de Lecerda, met them when he ventured up the Shire River in 1798 and he advised the minister of state in Portugal that he considered the Yao a serious threat to the development of Portuguese trade in the area. Right he was. . . .

Actually, the Yaos were originally by no means a warlike tribe, but became reliant on the generally accepted pagan method of plundering the neighboring tribes for cattle, women, and grain when things were short, certainly not unlike the medieval Europeans. They did not indulge in open warfare but used their superior weapons normally only in slave raids. The Yaos had a highly advanced culture, relative to that of the pagan Bantu, and they had the very necessary connections for trade. They welcomed the Portuguese when they arrived on the scene as further trading partners, as they did the arrival of the Christian missionaries, at least at first. The Universities Mission to Central Africa was founded on the western side of Lake Nyasa in 1861, on the recommendation of Dr. David Livingstone himself. Its primary and specific purpose was to put an end to the slave trade, which gave the Yaos second thoughts about their new bedfellows.

The Yaos, as firmly established Muslims for almost a thousand years, didn't think much of the principles of Christianity, which, let's face it, was ill-suited to tribal Africa compared to Islam—especially in the concept of monogamy. The missionaries were, of course, rabidly against polygamy, which is one of the most deeply ingrained of African traditions, and this stance probably did more to slow down the rate of conversion than anything else, especially among the pagans. The Muslims, naturally, were not receptive to religious conversion; they had already known a single God, which permitted multiple marriage, for nearly a millennium. Due to tribal warfare and, no doubt, also due to the depredations of the slave trade, African women generally outnumbered men by quite a bit, so practical polygamy was a longstanding institution in that part of the world. For much the same reasons polygamy was sanctioned by Islam in Arabia to the extent of a man being permitted four wives. The only recourses open to an unmarried woman were either prostitution or semi-starvation. The concept was not only sensible but socially necessary. The Christian missionaries did not see it that way, however, but the pagan tribes largely finally came around. Christianity meant protection from being enslaved by the Yaos, even if it did mean—technically of course—one wife.

Things are not so religiously hidebound in southern Africa today. A girl normally has several children before marriage, often by a variety of fathers, to prove that she is fertile. She might then be taken as a wife, or a second or third one, or not become married at all. There is no social stigma concerning wedlock or the bearing of children out of it. Women cost money or goods, either coin of the realm or livestock, based upon the concept of *lobola* or bride price. Girl children are of huge social and economic importance as they represent a family's financial security for their old age. Today, it is certainly not unusual for a "Christian" African to have several wives. Social accommodation usually wins out against religion as Catholic missionaries learned in such places as Ecuador when they tried to proselytize the Indians there. One glance at an Ecuadorian cathedral shows that Mother Church was wise to compromise on a few points or there would have been few converts.

The first act of the Christian missionaries in Nyasaland, in their God-given but not very practical wisdom, was to harbor runaway slaves. Traditionally for the slave, had he been caught again, this meant death. The Yaos took considerable umbrage at this interference, seeing it (quite correctly) as a political action quite outside the mission's scope, and a ferocious struggle soon developed, obliging the missionaries to leave posthaste and the mission to close.

A second attempt to establish a mission, this time by the Church of Scotland, was made in 1876, with a mission station being built in the Shire Highlands. Again, its principal objective was to stop the slave trade. But, once again, the Yaos ensured that it could not operate, and a civil authority was appointed by Britain in 1883 that applied a predominantly military policy to the slavers. The Nyasaland Protectorate was proclaimed in 1891, and by the turn of the century slavery in that country had ceased to exist.

The disciplines of Islam and what they had absorbed from the Arab culture had given the Yaos a long lead over the rest of the still-primitive tribes of Central Africa. A constant and better supply of food, plus an advanced way of life had turned them into an industrious, intelligent, and progressive people. That they are still looked up to and envied by some of the other tribes of the area is evinced by the fact that individuals of these tribes will often claim falsely to be Yaos when asked, so much so that when Brian Marsh first went to Nyasaland he received a completely erroneous idea of where the Yaos came from! Certainly, the Yaos' aversion to gambling and drinking alcohol, very prevalent traits in the other tribes, and their five-times-daily commitment by prayer to Islam, gave the Yaos a feeling of superiority. This gave them a noticeable strength of character that most impressed Taylor.

Having had two opportunities to observe the barbarity of white Christian "tribes" fighting each other, first among his own people in Ireland during the "troubles" and then during the Second World War, and then coming back severely wounded to find that he had been robbed of everything he had by another professing Christian, could have turned Taylor into a newborn, dyed-in-the-wool, practicing cynic. Perhaps living among the Yaos and being able to observe their way of life made it easy for him to believe that theirs must be the better way.

A MAN CALLED LION

The cementing of the friendship between the erstwhile Presbyterian, and ex-Irishman, John Taylor, and his Muslim, Yao friend, Aly Ndemanga, occurred during the lean period between 1945 and 1947 when Taylor was writing his second book, *African Rifles & Cartridges,* for Tom Samworth of South Carolina. A friend of Brian Marsh's, and well-known figure in Rhodesian hunting circles, Gus du Toit, met Taylor at this time. Gus had gone to P.E.A. on a hunting trip with his father and wrote in a letter to Marsh:

> I met *Chimpondoro* in 1947 at Baroma Mission on the Zomba/Tete road that runs along the Zambezi. We stopped at Baroma and I left Pop to make camp while I went to the Zambezi to catch a fish, being very surprised on arrival on the river bank to hear the clickety-click of a typewriter. A short investigation revealed *Chimpondoro* sitting in an open-sided thatched-roofed hut typing his first book while the ever-faithful Aly Ndemanga plied a ferry across the river at four escudos a time.
>
> *Chimpondoro* directed us to the Barui *jess,* which is near Mokassa and where he had previously hunted elephant himself, and gave us the names of the guides he recommended. This was the thickest *jess* I have ever been into, and the guides showed me the very old remains of six elephant *Chimpondoro* had shot. The *jess* was so thick it was impossible to see an elephant at a greater range than four feet. *Chimpondoro* had to pull off perfect brain-shots so that the elephant would collapse upright on its belly or, as the elephant always falls on the side it has been shot, it would have fallen on top of him.

Taylor's African name before the war was *Chimpondoro,* which can mean either "The Lionlike One" or "The Roaring of a Lion." The word for lion in ChiSena, the language of the lower Zambezi, is *pondoro.* Taylor writes that the prefix of "chi" fell away after some years and the "m" is for euphonic value only. Whether Taylor himself decided to shorten the name to *Pondoro* for the sake of his writings or whether it just became abbreviated by time and familiarity is anyone's guess.

The word *jess* Gus du Toit used to describe the thorn tangle he was hunting in is a uniquely Rhodesian term and apparently coined by the early hunters there. Taylor never uses it. This is how du Toit refers to the *jess:*

> The thorn, of the hawk's-bill variety, rises in a dense, matted, utterly impenetrable mass to an average height of about twelve feet or so. You can only get along by following one of the paths beaten out by the big gray ghosts themselves. These paths are more or less clear for a height of maybe three-and-a-half or four feet from the ground, but from there up they are draped by the overhang of thorn. The big fellows can merely brush through this, but the

hunter in his gray or khaki drill and the naked trackers and gunbearers have to struggle along, hour after hour, all doubled up in the sweltering heat, because not a breath of cooling breeze can reach him in there.

That is not an exaggerated description. It is popularly supposed that the name *jess* was derived from the falconry term "jesses"—being the leather restraining straps affixed to a falcon's legs. *Combretum celastroides*, the savanna bush willow, which primarily makes up the *jess*, is not itself thorny. It is merely a tangle of creeperlike bush of very large and dense proportions. It habitually grows with thick concentrations of *Acacia mellifera*, the "hawk's-bill" hook-thorn. This is what places the "restraint" upon the hunter who ventures into it.

But there is another, and probably more likely, name source. The name for any particularly dense thickets in some African dialects is *muchesa*, and the name could have been derived from a corruption of this. Wounded elephant and buffalo will always make for the nearest *jess*. Most of the misadventures along the Zambezi where the hunter has come off second-best have occurred in the *jess*.

The three years of privation that Taylor describes while he was writing *African Rifles & Cartridges* proved worth the effort. The book paid off. This book, although on the same subject as its predecessor, was double the number of pages, featuring numerous illustrations and photographs supplied by Crawford Fletcher Jamieson. This time the advance must have been enough for Taylor to buy some heavy rifles and he went hunting on the Zambezi again. There he was met by Dan Landrey, a fellow professional hunter friend of Brian Marsh's, who wrote to Brian:

The first time I met John Taylor was in 1949. I had been hunting elephant on the Panhame and Angwa Rivers and had visited a coloured chap, by the name of Antonio, who was reputed to be the son of one of Salisbury's white businessmen by a Nyungwe tribeswoman from Mozambique. He had a village on the Panhame. John Taylor, plus his retinue of porters, arrived bringing news that the *chefe de posto* from Macaque was on his way upriver.

We moved back into Rhodesia to the Hunyani Mission, and John Taylor came as well. I can remember him dressed rather like a cross between an Arab and a Kenya coastal native, i.e., turban or cloth around his head, and a lion cloth switched every other day for the old classic 'Bombay bloomers' or shorts K.D., as they were known in the army of the time, and sandals. He was accompanied by his tracker or companion whom he spoke to only in Swahili, which was the first time I had ever heard it spoken. This was a fairly young chap and unlike most of our trackers at the time who were old 'bush types.'

A MAN CALLED LION

I cannot be sure but I think his name was Ali, in which case it would have been Ali Ndemanga. The rest of the group were all local Tete men.

[As we know that Taylor always spoke to Aly in Swahili, which is not used at all along the Zambezi, the young chap referred to as "Ali" was undoubtedly Aly Ndemanga.]

I remember finding Taylor a rather reticent sort of person who did not seem pleased to have other white company. He, however, had a thorough knowledge of the bush and particularly buffalo and elephant and seemed to know most areas along the Zambezi that were good elephant haunts. He also spoke of areas in the north to which I had never been.

Of his guns he had a double .450 No.2, a cartridge of which I still have today in my collection. [Taylor traded it with him.] I cannot remember the maker at all. He also had a .450/.400 3¼-inch, which I do remember was made by Williamson Green of London. As far as I recall, he also had a Westley Richards .318 and, although it may have been at a later meeting, a .375 Winchester.

Taylor was obviously what we would refer to today as a 'gun nut' and had used almost every type and calibre. He spoke very highly of the .400 (.450/.400 3¼ inch), which was the flanged version of the .404, and the .375 magnum, and I remember him warning me not to make a mistake and buy the old .375 rather than the magnum. He further discussed the merits of the .500 (unreliable, as bullets were inclined to 'fishtail' in an elephant's skull, a fact I later found out for myself), and .470 Nitro and various other calibres in the days before the American .458.

Taylor was apparently quite well known to all the local chiefs and headmen and I think he shot quite a few buffalo for meat for them during his visits. This ensured 'news' of the local authority's whereabouts, from which I gathered not all his hunting was covered by licenses. His tusks went to Tete.

One instance that I clearly remember was camping by the Panyani under a big baobab tree and I had to camp on one side of the tree and he the other, which I felt was very antisocial, even allowing that I was just a youngster at the time.

It was also apparent that Taylor lived off the land while in the bush and traded buffalo for meal, chickens, and whatever else was available. I remember also asking him where he lived and his reply was, 'Where I happen to be!' I think he used Beira as a base quite often but seemed to know the whole of Mozambique right up to the Ruvuma River, being the border with Tanganyika.

From what we know of Taylor, it is likely he had chosen to stay on the Zambezi, in spite of the pressures of other professional hunters like Dan Landrey and casual sport hunters like Gus du Toit, because he had an available market for poached ivory, the Chinese at Tete. As soon as he could afford it, however, he once more left the Zambezi and headed north again. He and Aly got a lift back through Nyasaland to Mandimba, and from there went back to Taylor's prewar camp on the Lugenda River just below Lake Amaramba in Northern Mozambique. Many of his old team were still there to welcome him.

It was now the closing weeks of 1949. Taylor had last seen this area in the early days of 1940, nearly ten years before. Things were changing. The wild edge of this part of Africa was also becoming blunted. Taylor did some hunting, but for the most part he was back at his typewriter, working at becoming a full-time author. He had seen the writing on the wall. He was well aware that ivory hunting was not going to last forever.

CHAPTER FIVE

Besides Aly Ndemanga, another good friend of John *Pondoro* Taylor was Fletcher Jamieson, the Rhodesian professional. In order to try to explain the quirky psychological mixture that was John *Pondoro* Taylor, it is necessary to relate a bizarre episode that occurred after Fletcher Jamieson's death. That Taylor and Jamieson were good friends, there can be no doubt. They hunted together, and Taylor's first two books were illustrated with photographs supplied by C. Fletcher Jamieson. *Big Game and Big Game Rifles* has one of a buffalo, the only photograph in the book, and *African Rifles & Cartridges* has twenty-five. Had "Fletch" lived to write the books he had planned, there can be no doubt that he would today be just as well remembered as Taylor, but *kismet* had laid other plans.

That Fletch had planned to publish "wild Africa and hunting" photographic works of his own from the first days of his hunting career was a well-known secret to his family, works that today would surely have ranked with the African classics. Along with his first battery of big-game hunting rifles, was the best camera money could then buy. From the very beginning, wherever he went in the bush, Fletch was accompanied by a large and cumbersome Graflex plate camera, a horribly awkward tripod-mounted affair. It was the type that was focused through the lens with the photographer wearing a black hood over his head. It was the sort usually only used then by the press or seen in professional photographic studios. The Graflex produced a 7x5-inch black and white negative of the very best quality available. With this camera, Fletch quite literally took thousands of photographs of an Africa that was then almost unrecorded and which is now long since gone forever. His was truly a graphic legacy.

Fletch had a specially trained bearer to carry the camera, which was fitted, most fortunately for posterity, with a rubber bulb release. This he taught the bearer to use so he was therefore able to include himself in many of his own photos. But most unfortunately for posterity, Fletcher Jamieson was not to live to produce his planned literary photographic works and practically all his photographs were stolen by a writer who "conned" Fletcher's widow with empty promises of a lucrative biography he was to produce of her late husband.

Fletcher Jamieson was one year and a bit younger than John Taylor, who was destined to become one of his greatest friends. Fletcher was born on August 17, 1905, at Largs in Ayrshire, a coastal town in the southwest of Scotland. His father had come out to Africa ten years earlier, landing at Cape Town were he got a job on the South African Railways. Like many of his pioneer-spirited countrymen, Jamieson Senior had responded to the promise of opportunity in a newly founded country. His destination was Rhodesia, which had only a few years before been opened by Cecil Rhodes and the British South Africa Company.

Paid in smooth, solidly clinking gold sovereign, as was the custom of the day, Jamieson hoarded his money in a waist belt in the manner in which his ancestors would have approved. When the belt was fairly weighty, he bought a .32 caliber revolver for protection against the native hordes, and he also bought a donkey. Upon the latter he loaded his worldly possessions, which didn't exactly threaten to break the critter's back, and then, without a backward glance, he strode off into the sunset to walk the 1200 miles that separated him from Bulawayo.

Some weeks later Jamieson and his donkey arrived in Plumtree, the border town between Rhodesia and the British Protectorate of Bechuanaland. He was undoubtedly footsore and probably rundown from deprivation and fatigue, because immediately upon reaching Bechuanaland, he succumbed to a severe bout of malaria. Obliged to remain in Plumtree while recuperating and regaining his strength before starting off on the last sixty miles of his journey to Bulawayo, he had a chance to look around the area. He liked it and decided to farm there if he could raise sufficient cash.

This actually wasn't a very good idea. Unknown to the newcomer, Plumtree was in a low-rainfall area, much better suited to cattle ranching than general farming, but the inflexible Scot had made up his mind. It was a decision that was not destined to make Jamieson Senior rich, but it was to sharply chisel his eldest son's career.

Arriving at last in Bulawayo, Jamieson found a job and settled down to save money, squeezing every last shilling until it squealed in agony. When he decided he had made enough, he returned to Scotland to marry the sweetheart he had left behind and start a family. Fletcher was born and his mum pregnant with Norman when Jamieson Senior left Scotland to return alone to Rhodesia. There he bought the 7200-acre farm, Hillocks, situated some miles north of Plumtree where the little Matengwe River flows into the Nata. Jamieson paid two shillings and sixpence an acre for it, heavily mortgaging himself, and he remained there alone, building the place up until he brought the family out in 1911.

Young Fletch was then six years old. Playing all day with the farm workers' children, he learned to speak Sindebele, the language of the Matabele people, and began the lifelong learning process of bush craft. He went as a boarder to the Boys School in Plumtree and had just reached his teens when Hillocks went belly up. Jamieson Senior was broke. If he wanted to keep the farm going, he would have to leave to find work in South Africa to raise the money to start again. At the tender age of thirteen, Fletch found himself as "man of the house," in charge of a drought-stricken, bankrupt farm.

While her husband was away working to build up more capital to wash into the hard, red earth, Mrs. Jamieson kept a few dairy cows and chickens and grew vegetables to make a few pennies to buy the basics of life. Fletch, meanwhile, shot antelope to keep the family in meat and to help feed the farm labor. The farm was situated close to the border and the famed game lands of Bechuanaland. It was not too far from where the southern boundary of Zimbabwe's Hwange National Park is today. Fletch resided in a hunter's paradise and the life he was leading beat school any day.

Trouble always seems to compound itself. That same year, Fletch responded to a thirteen-year-old's impulse to climb to the top of a *marula* tree growing in the implement yard. A *marula* tree's branches are notoriously brittle and the one Fletch was standing on suddenly snapped. He plunged down onto the hard angles and sharp cutting-edges of the farm's three-disc ox-plough outspanned below. He dislocated his elbow, shattered his left wrist into spaghetti strands, and broke the bones in both his upper and lower left arm.

The nearest hospital was at Bulawayo, 100 miles to the east of Plumtree. The only transport was the farm ox-wagon, but being Sunday of course—most severe accidents seem to happen on a Sunday—the bloody oxen had strayed. Fletch and his mother were unable to leave the farm until the afternoon, only reaching Plumtree the next morning. There was a further wait for the train to take them to Bulawayo. Fletch never forgot that journey of unspeakable agony. When he was finally placed on the operating table at Bulawayo, his hand was described as a "football of blood." That the arm was saved at all in the days before antibiotics says much for his physical fitness and immensely strong physical condition.

The bones of the wrist were wired together but his wrist had to be set rigid, locked permanently in one position. Although he regained the use of his left hand with time, he was unable to manipulate the wrist sufficiently when shooting to grasp the fore-stock of his rifle. Instead, he was obliged to shoot with his left hand palm-open, facing away from him toward the target, fingers pointing upward and the rifle resting in the fork of his thumb. This denied any firm support from that hand, but his strength was such that he was able to accurately fire even his heavy double rifles.

Having to be proficient as a hunter from his earlier teens, with both his family and the farm workers depending on him, cemented Fletch to the wilds. He knew from a very young age what he was going to be. When his father returned to take over the farm again, Fletch went back to school for a short time but left to work as a plasterer for a building contractor. Wages were low in those days, and it was not until 1928, when he was twenty-three years old, that he had earned enough money to set himself up with rifles, camera, and the basic equipment to begin life as a professional ivory hunter.

His first battery of rifles consisted of a .25/20 Winchester, a 6.5x54mm Mannlicher-Schoenauer magazine rifle, a Holland & Holland Royal .500/.450 double-barreled Nitro Express, and a Manton .577 double-barreled Nitro Express. This was almost like starting off a career as a guitarist with a couple of fine José Ramirez instruments and a good Gibson to boot.

Fletch commenced professional hunting in the wilds of the Zambezi Valley, hunting elephant, rhino, and buffalo. His two excellent double rifles did splendid work for him, and he hunted with his two doubles for the first eight years of his hunting career. Because of the locked left wrist, however, he sometimes had a problem with his rifles when hunting in the *jess*. The extremities of heat found in the Zambezi Valley could greatly increase pressures in cordite-loaded cartridges, sometimes causing cases to stick in the breech after firing, which would jam the action closed. When this happened, Fletch would have to clamp the barrels of the rifle under his left armpit in order to get the leverage to break the action open. This was a somewhat time-consuming method of reloading in the face of an animal weighing seven tons barreling down on you with evil intent. Fletch was well aware that it was only a matter of time before a jammed rifle was one day going to get him killed. He had long considered that a magazine rifle would better suit him.

It would seem, in this connection, that by the middle of 1934 he had already decided that he must part with his doubles. A letter he wrote and sealed under the butt-plate of his Holland & Holland .500/.450 Royal, together with the tail-hair of an elephant that he records nearly cost him his life, tends to confirm this. The letter reads:

Zambezi Valley,
14th July 1934

This rifle, No 17892 .500/.450 has been one of my best friends. She has pulled me through many an encounter with Elephants, Rhino & Buffaloe [sic]. She is one of the most accurate rifles in the world & since being in my hands has achieved a very fine record, I am positive that as far as her record is concerned she is second to none. I have shot with her the following species of animals: Elephant, Rhino, Buffaloe, Hippo, Leopards, Eland, Roan, Impala, Warthog, Bush-pig, Crocodiles, Snakes, Hartebeast [sic], Baboons, Duiker & Bush Buck. But I have used her mostly for Elephant, Rhino, Buffaloe & Hippo, & find that she is all that one could wish for.

My battery of rifles consists of one Double barrel .577 Express, one D.B. .500/.450 Express, one 6.5 Mannlicher Schoenauer, & a .25/20 Winchester. This I consider as the most efficient battery of rifles any Big Game Hunter could wish for.

Whoever may be the proud possessor of this rifle after I am finished with it please treasure it for my sake.

C. Fletcher Jamieson. Big Game Hunter.

The letter and the tail hair were to remain hidden for nearly sixty years in the butt of the rifle, until 1992 in fact, when the weapon was bought from a deceased estate by Zimbabwean sports hunter Doug Riddle. Seeing it had been badly neglected—it had probably been stored for years in its case in a damp cellar and rust had already begun its work on the outside of the barrels—Doug stripped it down completely to thoroughly clean it. He removed the butt-plate in the process. The rifle, we can now report, has found an owner who will treasure it as Fletch wanted.

Fletcher's sister-in-law, Mavis, describes Fletch as tall, athletic, very well built, and with wavy, golden hair, exuding a natural charm that made him "easy" with people. The girls loved him and flocked around him like flies to a dead elephant when he came to town, but until he was nearly forty he gave his heart only to motorbikes and the African bush.

Unlike Taylor, Fletch was a seasonal hunter, only shooting in the dry, winter season after the rains, which came boiling and pounding in black sheets between November and April, had departed. During the summer months he helped his brother in his building business. Fletch, also unlike Taylor, was strictly a legal hunter and did not gamble his license as Taylor was ever wont to do. He was very selective in his hunting and consequently his diaries indicate that he averaged very much above Taylor's estimate of thirty pounds per side, per tusk. We have only Taylor's personal estimate on how many elephants he shot, but his claim is about 1500, of which four-fifths were poached. Every animal collected by Jamieson, however, was legal and faithfully recorded in his five volumes of diaries, so we know that his total was a genuine 134. His records show he shot nothing but bulls, all under license, and all good ones at that.

Some of the few surviving photographs in the Jamieson family's possession were taken on the 1938 elephant-hunting trip Taylor and Fletch took together to Nyasaland–Lake Nyasa is clearly recognizable–but there are none of Taylor. There were bound to have been some, but these were no doubt stolen with the rest by Fletch's so-called biographer. There is, however, a photograph from that trip of an African with a flamboyant headdress with the name SADUKU penciled on the back of it. Taylor's tracker before the war was named Saduku, which is not a common name, and there seems little question that the photo (please see photo section) is of him.

It was not long before he was killed that Fletch supplied the photos that went to illustrate Taylor's first two books. It is not to Taylor's lasting credit that the agreed amount was never paid to Fletcher's widow after her husband's untimely death. Taylor had promised to pay £50 for the use of the photos, which would have been a great deal of money to Fletcher's destitute widow in the lean years of 1947 but probably wouldn't have been a great deal of money to Taylor. We don't know the details, except that the agreement was verbal and Fletch told his wife and Norman about it. The likelihood is that Taylor agreed to pay the money upon the receipt of his advance against royalties from his publisher. The debt, however, was never honored.

This really is an enigma. Why did Taylor refuse—or at least neglect—to pay a poor widow with two small children a lousy £50 legally and morally owing to them? It is well documented that Taylor gave money away—at least to anybody who happened to be a black tribesman who had an open hand or an empty pocket—and his boast was that material wealth besides a couple of good rifles and a full ammo bag meant little to him. Precisely what Taylor's motive was to deny such a small sum of money to an almost destitute new widow, literally with a babe in arms, is unknown. The amount would only have represented a single tusk from a fair elephant for Taylor, but it would have made a big difference to the newly widowed Joan Jamieson. Put it down to a strange facet of the soul of a strange man. . . .

That Taylor defaulted on the debt so enraged the Jamiesons and so bitterly did they feel toward him that Norman wrote an exposé of him in 1958, which he tried to have published in the American magazine *Cavalier*, to which Taylor was then contributing gun and hunting articles. Norman, who was a Rhodesian Bisley shooter, was friendly with a fellow Bisley shooter, an American lawyer by the name of Bob Wallack. Wallack read the exposé and advised Norman not to proceed with it, writing in a letter to him:

> Some magazines would like to have an exposé of Taylor, but I think this would be a foolish stunt unless you could be extremely well documented—Taylor is only known among a few serious gun bugs and the article would have little impact.

What Wallack only hinted at, of course, was that without proper documentation, Norman Jamieson might well have been handed his own rear end in a libel suit. And so, the Jamieson family, who had been Taylor's good friends, came to be his most bitter enemies. And it was all over a paltry £50.

* * * * * * *

When the rains drove Fletch out of the Zambezi Valley at the end of the 1936 hunting season, he went to visit Ronnie Mitchell, a gunsmith in Salisbury, the Rhodesian capital and Fletch's adopted town. The two friends tested all the heavy magazine rifles the gun shop had to offer for accuracy and penetration, a vital factor to an elephant hunter. Among them was a 12.5x70mm Schuler on the short Mauser action, which was built by Krieghoff-Schuler Company of Germany. The 12.5x70mm was at that time the most powerful magazine rifle cartridge ever produced.

Fletch was impressed with the cartridge, but not with the rifle. The very long twenty-eight-inch barrel gave it undue "whip" and made it also impractical for use in the thick bush where Fletcher hunted. Back in London, however, W.J. Jeffery & Company had been building rifles to take the most impressive Schuler cartridge. Not terribly shy in such matters, even though they didn't manufacture ammunition for it, it had been dubbed the .500 Jeffery Rimless. Up to 1936 they had built only twenty of these rifles, all with shorter barrels and of much better quality than the Krieghoff-Schuler.

The twenty-first rifle built by Jeffery in .500 Rimless caliber was ordered for Fletch by Ronnie Mitchell. Only twenty-four of these rifles were ever made by Jeffery, which makes them as rare as checks in the mail or true love and much sought after by collectors today. The most desired of them all is Fletch's rifle, serial number 25554. The top of the barrel is engraved: "SPECIALLY BUILT FOR C. FLETCHER JAMIESON BY W.J. JEFFERY & CO. LTD. 9 GOLDEN SQUARE REGENT STREET LONDON W1"

Although Jeffery made the rifles in England, the only ammo for them was from Germany, either head-stamped ".500" (as illustrated in Taylor's *African Rifles & Cartridges*) or ".500 Schuler Gecado," which is the stamp on all Fletcher's surviving cases. The bullets were cupronickel-jacketed, weighed 535 grains, and were loaded with 103 grains of HiVel powder, giving a muzzle velocity of 2400 f.p.s. and an energy at muzzle of 6800 foot-pounds. Despite the phenomenal "paper" performance of the .500 Jeffery Rimless, Fletch found that he had some problems with the bullet construction, since the solid load broke up too easily. Reproduced in *African Rifles & Cartridges* is a picture of a number of distorted and fragmented bullets that Fletch took from elephant carcasses. There are records in his diaries of losing a few elephant, which he put

A MAN CALLED LION

down to bullet failure, and on 10 November, 1945, he wrote to W.J. Jeffery & Co. Ltd. to complain about it:

> On recovering and examining this bullet on scores of occasions, I have invariably found that the lead has been squashed out of the nickel casing, leaving the casing flattened and bent and because of this I am of the opinion that this bullet loses about 30% of its penetrating power. Extreme penetration is most essential always, especially in the killing of elephant. The core of the solid bullet seems far too soft in relation to the terrific driving power. Would it not be possible to improve this by increasing the hardness of the core? I imagine that to increase it to at least three times its present hardness would prove ideal.

In the letter above, Fletch ordered 400 rounds of full-metal-jacket and 100 rounds of soft-nosed cartridges, which Jeffery had been importing before the war with Germany. By 1945, the Third Reich was certainly not making any sporting ammo! Unfortunately, the reply from Jeffery could not be found no matter how diligently Marsh rooted, either in the old Jeffery records (now at Holland & Holland) or in Fletch's correspondence.

Fletcher and his now famous rifle are mentioned on a number of occasions in *African Rifles & Cartridges.* Taylor describes Fletch as "a real hunter and a country bloke ahead of all the other professionals in Rhodesia." Taylor, who did not much like magazine rifles compared to doubles, had high praise for the .500 Jeffery Rimless, writing that although he had never owned one, he had used three in different instances. He would certainly have tried out Fletch's rifle when they were together in Nyasaland. In addition, the 12.5x70mm Schuler rifles made in Germany were quite popular among the Portuguese hunters, so it is likely that he used one. But he, too, was critical of the ammunition.

Fletch had been commissioned by the Rhodesian Government in 1944 to shoot out the elephant in the Sabi Valley as a tsetse elimination measure. Such "schemes" to get rid of the tsetse fly so that domestic stock could take over their areas was a terrible error and one that would not have been sanctioned if we had known then what we know today. Tsetse are, of course, the greatest friends of the game of Africa, and professional hunters won't even swat them, simply releasing them with a whispered prayer that they may multiply and prosper.

Fletch's control area was sixteen miles long and five miles wide and was used by the elephant as a passageway or corridor between the Sabi River, where they came to drink at night, and Portuguese East Africa, where they spent the long, hot days. Fletch's task was to catch them in between, but as they mostly moved at night, he had only a short period each day when he stood any chance of cutting them off from either direction. Among the many interesting accounts of this period of his life is one that shows how thickly vegetated some of the country was and what is really meant by "thick bush." He writes:

Not until October 26th did we see the spoor of elephant again. This turned out to be eight bulls, which crossed the Sabi. With much hope and excitement we took up their tracks and discovered they were making for one of the crossing places up the Sabi, near my northern boundary. They were travelling slowly however, and by midday we came upon them in fairly dense bush, feeding, and still heading for the Sabi, which I think they intended recrossing late that afternoon. Again the country proved most difficult. I decided to perch on the top of an antheap, hoping to get a better view of them, but this did not prove the case—I was only able to see the tops of their backs and the tips of their ears. I waited for some minutes, when two of them approached me from different directions and decided to feed quite near me. One of these moved forward to feed on young leaves almost above my head.

I realized the position was now dangerous. He was still covered by the thicket, but I had to shoot, hoping my bullet would penetrate and prove fatal. He only stumbled, and was soon following the others. We followed him, and found he had separated from the herd. This was a good sign—he was bleeding badly having a mortal wound. Again we came upon him and I dispatched him with my next shot.

Fletch was a cool customer. Not many people would simply note that "the position was now dangerous" with a wild bull elephant plucking leaves from a couple of feet above his head! And another account, on Chimeni Island in the Sabi, which is four miles long by a half mile wide:

With little delay I was on my way to the island, a distance of three miles from my camp. At this time of the year most of the Sabi was dry, and to get to the island I had only to walk on the sandy riverbed. Considering the denseness of the bush there, I realized the difficulty that lay ahead. Before taking up the chase, I was amused at my natives who, with much laughter and talk, began shedding their clothes, leaving only the bare necessities. They decided clothes would hamper them in the bush. We were soon attracted by the noise of breaking branches, and after studying the wind, cautiously made our way in their direction. One elephant came into view at about twenty paces, an eddying breeze must have given him our whereabouts, because he suddenly turned, facing us with ears spread and his trunk lifted. This position offered an easy target, and with one shot he dropped dead. The remainder of the herd moved off in the direction of the only native village on the island, which was not far distant. Their progress was slow, as the herd was large and the bush thick. The natives of this village knew I was hunting nearby and heard my shot, and they heard the elephant coming towards them. In haste they collected tins, or anything that would make a noise, and, with much beating and shouting frightened the herd, which turned on its tracks, travelling a short distance and stopped.

We were not aware of this happening then, but thought the herd had left the island, and travelled in the direction of my camp. Little time was wasted before we were on their tracks again, and to our surprise we heard them only a few yards ahead, discovering them to be moving in our direction. We halted, and suddenly, without warning, a large bull broke cover about six paces from me. A hasty but well-placed shot at that short range killed him. The herd stampeded, but I managed to get in another two shots, killing two more elephant.

When the Sabi contract with the government was finished, Fletch went back hunting elephant in the Zambezi Valley, and now Joan, Fletcher's wife, went with him. There are some surviving photographs of their well-equipped camp, some showing Joan cooking at the open fire and ironing the laundry with a charcoal iron. Joan went regularly on safari with Fletch till the arrival of their first child, Phoebe, after which mother and daughter stayed behind at their home at Hatfield, a suburb of Salisbury. Not long after, their second child was on the way.

Then Fletch must have gotten a bad batch of that German ammunition for his .500 Jeffery, as he records several frightening misfires. Consider the following entry in his last diary volume, the date being 12 August, 1947:

"I took a side shot for the brain, the rifle misfired—second try dropped him." Two days later he wrote: "My first attempt at this bull was a misfire, this being the fourth misfire I have had."

A month later, on September 17, Crawford Fletcher Jamieson was killed. But he was not killed, as would have seemed likely, by an elephant. Taylor had this to write about the death of his friend:

Destiny, kismet, fate, call it what you like—when you come to look around the big-game hunting world and see the things that can happen, you are compelled to the conclusion that there is no such thing as chance. You will come to believe, as I came to believe many years ago, that when your bell rings, you go, and until it rings it doesn't matter what you do—you won't go.

The late Fletcher Jamieson said in a letter written to me immediately before his death that he'd just returned from a short safari after elephant, during which he'd killed six good bulls, and out of seven shots at elephant had experienced no less than four misfires. Yet it wasn't an elephant that got him, as you might have expected–he was accidentally electrocuted down his own well! Had he continued after elephant, it would have doubtlessly been one of them that settled his hash, but his number wasn't up, though on its way. By the time he got home and went down his well, it was.

On that fatal September 17, 1947, Fletcher had come back home from safari. He parked his pickup with its load of ivory in the garage and went into the house to greet Joan. He had a cup of tea with her, then went to inspect a well he was having sunk in his backyard with the aid of a well-sinking contract gang.

They had made some progress while he had been away and it was dark at the bottom of the hole. He unloaded his pickup, putting his ivory in his storeroom, then drove round to his brother's house to borrow a long-cabled lead-light, but Norman was out. Impatient, Fletcher then drove to the home of a friend who had a lead-light that he could borrow. This was a homemade affair with a short length of metal piping for a handle. Fletch's friend loaned him the light, completely unaware that it had a deadly short inside the handle.

Running a length of cable from the wall plug in the kitchen, Fletcher then joined the wires onto the lead-light wires, and removing his shoes he climbed into the windlass bucket and instructed the well diggers to lower him down the well. Suspended on the nonconductive hemp rope, Fletch called out to his domestic servant to switch on the power in the kitchen. He was now charged with 240 volts of electricity from the handle of the lead-light, which required only to be grounded to electrocute him.

The men on the surface wound round the handles of the windlass, inching Fletcher deeper down the well and closer to his death, now lurking only a few feet away. As the bucket reached the bottom, Fletcher Jamieson stepped out into the water.

Taylor wrote in the "Author's Note" in *African Rifles & Cartridges*:

> I regret to say that my friend Fletcher Jamieson of Rhodesia joined the Silent Majority just as this book was about to go to press. His untimely death is a real loss to the big-game hunting world, as his magnificent photos, which go to illustrate this book, clearly show. There are so few genuine hunters left, that we can ill spare him. One can but hope that he has found his Happy Hunting Ground wherein the breeze is always favourable and the tuskers all big 'uns.

A MAN CALLED LION

One week after his father's death, Fletcher Junior was born.

CHAPTER SIX

Aly was shooting hippo illegally in Lake Amaramba (1950-1952) with one of Taylor's heavy rifles and selling the meat to the tribesmen so they could earn money to live on, while Taylor was in camp on the Lugenda working on his third book, his autobiography, *Pondoro: The Last Ivory Hunter.* By all accounts Aly's poaching was sufficiently lucrative to keep Taylor and his men supplied with the basics of life and it seems they even made a profit from it. Aly was both hunter and salesman. With him as his butcher's assistant, was his brother-in-law, Samson Kazembi, who had married Aly's sister. Brian Marsh was later to track down and get to know Samson, who supplied details of this period of Taylor's career. Samson remembers that these were good days for all of them, plenty of fat hippo meat for the pot and enough money to go round from the sale of the balance for all their needs. Taylor wrote most days, went hunting when it suited him, and was living an idyllic life.

The rifle that Aly was using to poach hippo was the double-barreled .450 No.2. This has since been established as a box-lock action by John Wilkes, a fine and expensive rifle. They had been back at Lake Amaramba for only about a year, living a life of peace and tranquility, when out of the blue Aly was caught, quite literally red-handed, up to his elbows in dead hippo's guts, by the Portuguese police from Mandimba.

The tiny border town with a *boma* was only twenty-odd miles from Taylor's camp, too close for an illegal industry of that magnitude to go unnoticed. The police no doubt knew what was going on right from the start, but it seems it was not Taylor they were after. They set a successful trap and Aly was nabbed but released after the police got their hands on "Bwana Two-Pipe," the affectionate nickname of the double-barreled Wilkes .450 No.2.

Taylor had then gone himself on a borrowed bicycle—he had no other transport—to the police at Mandimba to find out what was afoot and to see if he could get his precious rifle back. The police refused to play ball. They told Taylor that they were only waiting for the papers to come through authorizing his arrest. He was to be taken into custody and prosecuted for blatant hippo poaching. This rocked Taylor right back on his heels, but in spite of this, he was allowed to go.

Any way you look at it, it does seem strange that Taylor was allowed to go free immediately after being warned of his impending arrest. If they were just waiting for the papers to arrive, which sounds flimsy, to arrest him, why didn't they ensure he stuck around for a while? Hadn't he saved them the trouble of having to go to fetch him? Why they didn't grab him there and then, if they were serious about the charges, remains a mystery. Instead they let Taylor return to his camp without his rifle.

Of course there may have been a lot more to the matter than a few poached hippos. Other stories of a spicier nature had probably reached official ears. The Portuguese authorities may have been looking for an excuse to pack up Taylor and deport him. There was a whiff of rebellion in the soft African air. The Porks were even more conservative than the Brits at that time. What is of interest was that the Wilkes was later sold in South Africa to an American collector as being Taylor's personal property. The deal was negotiated through a well-known South African lawyer, which would indicate that the Mandimba police officers who confiscated the rifle were rather "negligent" about handing it over to government ordnance!

Taylor knew the options if he was arrested. He would certainly not have had the funds to pay a large fine. As he would undoubtedly have been found guilty, a jail sentence would be mandatory. He had tried jail before, so there was only one option. He hurried back to his camp and ordered all hands to pack and, abandoning the rifle to the police, he fled to Nyasaland, which he entered without benefit of the usual immigration formalities.

Taylor must have had *some* money, possibly the loose change left over from hippo sales, and he now set Aly up in a small general store, which was run by a relation of his. He and Aly then built a camp in the bush on the Nyasaland/P.E.A. border, ready to jump either east or west, depending on the nationality of his persecutors, a fugitive from one country and an illegal immigrant in the other.

Meanwhile, Taylor stoically continued working on his autobiography, which called for a certain amount of will power while living under these difficult conditions. He was obviously determined to make it as a successful writer. It was here that he was found by the Australian sportsman, John Dawkins, then a tyro in the African bush. Dawkins went on to shoot over fifty elephant, many buffalo, and several rhino in various parts of Africa. He wrote of this meeting in a letter to Brian Marsh:

Here in Australia in about 1950, wool prices suddenly began to rise owing to the Korean War and soon reached a pound per pound. Suddenly I could plan to do hunting in Africa, which I had ever dreamed of doing. I was already a big-game hunter by Australian standards, having hunted buffalo for their hides, but I realized that our buffalo were not very dangerous, for there is no known case of anyone being killed by one in Australia to this day.

Over the years I had been able to collect some African hunting books, and it was plain from these that I would be facing much more dangerous animals in Africa, and would need something more powerful than the 9.3x62mm that I used for buff. The problem with these books I had was that they did not give any detailed information concerning the weapons they were using. Nor could I find anyone in S. Aust. who knew anything about African hunting.

Then one day when I was shopping in Adelaide, I saw in the window of a book shop *Big Game and Big Game Rifles* by John Taylor. So I rushed in and bought it. As I read the book, I was quick to realize that this author really understood his subject, and the "Knock-Out Values" that he had himself worked out answered all my questions. To my mind, this first book of John's was just as valuable for a beginner to Africa as was his *African Rifles & Cartridges*. I wrote to Taylor telling him how much I liked his book and asked him about hunting areas, explaining that I wanted to hunt as the old hunters like himself did and not with an expensive safari outfitter and P.W.H. John replied promptly with useful information, and with an invite to visit him should I ever get that far south in Africa.

Next I wrote to the game departments of Tanganyika, N. Rhodesia, Nyasaland, and P.E.A. Of these four, Nyasaland was by far the more reasonable; though they did warn me that game was not very plentiful there. Meanwhile, one of the local gunsmiths located a rifle for me, being a .450 D/B Rigby Nitro Hammer, that an ex-Indian civil servant had just arrived with in Aust. and no longer wanted. John told me it would be quite powerful enough for Africa. I was also fortunate enough in having forty cartridges available with the rifle. Now with all the important matters settled, I booked my passage to Africa via India, which was the only way to get there in those days.

In due course I arrived at Dar es Salaam, bought a vehicle and supplies, and then headed off for Nyasaland. I did not see much game on the way even though I detoured off the main road now and then, and in due course I arrived in Nyasaland. This looked much more like hunting country, so I stayed there for a week or so in Katumbi's country, shooting some lesser game with the chief's help. He was quite a likeable chap and let me have some tomatoes, etc., from his garden. I saw signs of big game here but decided to go and look up John Taylor and see what the game was like down there. So I said goodbye to Katumbi and was once again on what passed for a road. The country was very picturesque for the first day or so, and I had one adventure when I just managed to rescue an Englishman who had run into and killed an African woman. However, from here on the land became more arid and much less interesting.

Eventually I arrived in Namweras district where he [Taylor] had informed me he was operating from, although he had not been very explicit. I began to search for him at the Portuguese Border Post at Mandimba, where the *chefe de posto* was very helpful. No one at the *posto* knew his whereabouts, so the *chefe* sent out runners into the district to see what they could find out. As this was going to take time, he made a hut available for me to stay in, and it took them two days to decide Taylor was not in P.E.A. The *chefe* asked me why I wanted to hunt elephants, because he was of the opinion that only such mad men as Taylor hunted them, and he seemed to know John very well and considered him the best of elephant hunters.

I then went to the Namweras post office, but they could not help me much. All they knew was that Aly came in to collect John Taylor's mail, but they did not know where he came from. Next I began asking the Indian storekeepers at the Mandimba River, as they spoke English. Eventually one of them found an African who knew where Aly and Taylor lived. He said we could reach there with my vehicle, so off we went across cultivated fields for about a mile, eventually coming to a halt in front of a largish African hut. A heavily built white man came forth from the hut followed by some Africans. I alighted from the vehicle and walked up to him.

"John Taylor, I presume?"

"Yes," he replied. "And who the divil may you be?" he almost snarled. Whereupon I introduced myself, and as we shook hands he exclaimed:

"My God! But you did give me a fright! I thought that you must have been an official coming to arrest me!"

With that introduction over, I suggested that we get better acquainted over a few whiskeys, so he invited me to sit with him at a table that was under the veranda of his hut, and before we sat down on the rough African chairs he introduced me to Aly Ndemanga and his tall African wife. He told me the reason I had so much trouble finding him was due to his being *persona non grata* in both P.E.A. and Nyasaland, and that he and Aly had set up this village right on the border of the two territories hoping it would be a safe retreat, and so it proved. Towards sundown I produced another bottle of whiskey, and also dragged the Rigby over to the table.

"Oh! what a peach!" he enthused. "You will never regret buying that rifle, John." And of course I never did.

He told me that he no longer had any weapons as he had sold the last two, a couple of Winchester .375 Magnums, to buy food, etc., so he could continue writing. During the following days he had Aly take me around the likely areas for game in P.E.A. and Nyasaland, while he remained in the village working on his third book, *Pondoro*. There were, however, no fresh signs in the area, though I did shoot some lesser game. During pleasant evenings under the veranda, sipping our whiskey and watching the baboons getting ready to bed down for the night on a tallish kopje nearby, we came to know each other better and better. So one evening when John told me he was finished in Africa, it did not come as a great surprise. For a start he was not making much money out of his first book, and he had made the mistake of selling the rights to his *African Rifles & Cartridges*, worse still, he sold it too cheaply, and sadly he did not get paid in full. He said that the complete settlement consisted of the two Winchester .375s (which he did not like) and none of the cash promised. After this he used an agent, and I used this agent also, their ten percent is preferable to being robbed of the lot.

One of the first things that I learnt about Taylor in these early days of our friendship was that he had lost all real interest in hunting, apart from writing about it. There were several reasons for this, partly because of his experience in World War II where he fought the Japs in Malaya and was wounded. Then he came back to begin life again in P.E.A. only to find that the Portuguese authorities had sold all his possessions that he had left locked in a shed pending his return. The Portuguese claimed that they thought he had been killed. In any event, they did not pay him any compensation for the loss of his vehicle and his hunting equipment. About a year before I met him he decided to get himself another religion; already being a Moslem, he now became a Rosicrucian, becoming deeply absorbed with this religious order, and remaining so until his death. Another factor for his demise as an ivory hunter was the low price of ivory and the difficulty of being able to get a suitable rifle and ammo so soon after the war. One of the reasons that he sold his Winchester .375s was that he was unable to get full metal jackets for the .375 ammo.

Regarding your enquiry about Taylor and Aly speaking Swahili to one another, yes, they in fact did so. I gather from what John told me, it was so the local Africans did not know what they were saying. Aly took a working holiday in Dar when he was a lad, and learnt to speak Swahili, but I do not remember where John learnt. Aly only spoke a few words of English.

Taylor told me one evening that there seemed nothing left for him to do but turn himself over to the Nyasaland authorities so that they would have to treat him as a D.B.S. [Displaced British Serviceman] and send him back to England. I realized that he must have been desperate to consider such a humiliating act. I continued to sip my whiskey in silence for some time, and I felt it would be a poor show if I could not do something to help. After considering the situation for a few minutes, I made one of the best decisions I ever made in Africa. I offered to take him and Aly with me back to Katumbi, where they could teach me the art of big-game hunting and help run the camp. In return, I would pay all John's expenses to come to Australia, where he would be my guest and do some writing, until we went to the N.T. [Northern Territory] to shoot buffalo. Taylor agreed with this enthusiastically, but wanted more than the ordinary gunbearer wages for Aly and went on to explain that Aly had a store near the village that he had himself set Aly up in. This was one of the things that had made him short of money. So I agreed to pay the extra 100 pounds so that Aly could have some relation run the store and to buy in more supplies. We shook on the deal, and a few days later we were on our way. In the long run, it cost me more than I had reckoned on, but I never did regret it.

In a couple of days we reached our destination and set up camp close to the N. Rhodesian border. As you have my book, you will have read some of our adventures. Naturally I did most of the shooting, but John sometimes used the 9.3mm to shoot some meat or to back me up when amongst elephants, and he seemed quite at ease with this high-quality German rifle, perhaps because while in Dar I had been able to get hold of some British steel-jacket solids. In every way he measured up to what I would have expected of an ivory hunter. He was always the master of all situations whether hunting big game or lesser game and shot well with both my rifles. Now, after years of big-game hunting I would still choose the same man as my teacher. It is not that I am suggesting that many of the other hunters I have met over the years were not the equal of John; it is just that I was very happy with John and Aly. You mention something about "X" saying unpleasant things about John Taylor, but he has always, like most great people, had his critics; not that he would have been in the slightest interested in "X's" opinions. John's name and books go from triumph to triumph, while his critics just disappear into the mists of time.

Anyone who knew John Taylor and also understood ballistics soon realized how well he understood the subject as it had applied to him in Africa. He never claimed to know much about all the other masses of weapons used in other parts of the world.

Some critics want to know where all the photos are to prove that he really did do all he claimed, and this included the publishers of *Pondoro*, Simon & Schuster. They wanted some photos of John in action or no *Pondoro* would be published by them, so John showed me their letter, as he was staying with me at the time. I had warned him while we were hunting together that something like this might happen and had insisted on him having some photos taken on safari, posing with big game. It is more the pity that I did not take more photos of him, but in any case they satisfied his publishers, and the book went to print.

Taylor was like nearly all the old-time hunters in as much as he was not interested in photography. Some drew their own pictures, as did Bell; Oswell and others had artists do their pictures, but times had changed and the readers now wanted photos as proof. Of course it is easy for modern hunters to mouth off about a lack of photos on some of the old-timers' books, but these old timers had no motor vehicles; everything had to be carried on porters' heads. They would be in Africa through the wet season with only a tent or a primitive native hut for shelter, and it did not take long for photos to deteriorate under these conditions.

Yes, I have read Taylor's *Shadows of Shame* very well, because I helped him write it while he was staying with me. It is all his ideas but he had never written in the third person before.

You ask if I remember Ivor Jones, and after thinking for some time, I remember that there was a party of whites hunting near us in Nyasaland, and from memory I think they came from S. Africa. I remember they did visit us once or twice, and I may have taken one or more photos of them posing with Taylor, but this would have been with their camera.

There are, as can be seen, some "furry bits" and inconsistencies in what Taylor told Dawkins and what others told Marsh. Time blurs, or perhaps for his own reasons Taylor decided to mislead Dawkins—particularly about only receiving two .375 Winchesters as full payment for *African Rifles & Cartridges*. We know he had other rifles, some being very good ones, so where did the money come from to buy these? Ivor Jones was indeed in the hunting party John Dawkins mentions, but he was from Northern Rhodesia, not South Africa. Ivor wrote about their meeting in a letter to Marsh:

It was while I was on one of my annual hunting trips that I met John Taylor and John Dawkins in Chief Katumbi's area in Nyasaland. The area I was hunting was called Rumpi, and a dry weather road was the "agreed" border between Northern Rhodesia and Nyasaland. The Northern Rhodesian side of the road was the Luangwa Valley Game Reserve and the Nyasaland side was a hunting area. One had to get licenses from the district commissioner at Rumpi, for which we were charged ten pounds and which allowed you four of each of the bigger animals—roan, sable, kudu, hartebeest, eland, buffalo, etc., plus six each of the smaller species—impala, bushbuck, duiker, etc.

One afternoon I walked into a herd of eland. I was using a Westley Richards .318. I managed to knock two of them down and wounded a third, and owing to the time factor, returned to camp without finding it.

The third day after this episode I heard a vehicle approaching. The van stopped and two strangers entered our camp. The younger of the two introduced himself and "Mr. Taylor" to us. Mr. Taylor was quiet and unassuming and virtually stood in the background while we were talking. At the time I had a copy of *Big Game and Big Game Rifles* with me by John *Pondoro* Taylor, and I asked if he was perhaps the author, and much to my surprise he said he was and that the natives had given him the name *Pondoro*. I fetched the book and asked him to autograph it for me, which he did, and then we took some photographs.

He then asked if I was using a .318, which I confirmed, and he then told me that they had found my eland that I had wounded. After finishing it off they dug out the bullet, which Taylor recognized as a .318! I was amazed and felt this man must really know his rifles if he could recognize a flattened bullet!

He mentioned that he was not married and had not slept in a house for many years. I asked him how he lived. With a giggle he mentioned that he had taken up his Africans' religion and was a Mohammedan, and when times were good he looked after the blacks, and when times were bad they looked after him.

I told him that two years ago I had a spot of bother using a 9.5 Mauser on buffalo in the Luangwa Valley. He politely told me the folly of my ways and suggested I should invest in a .375 magnum.

Taylor was quiet spoken, with the occasional little giggle, very interesting when one could get him talking. I paid them a visit to his camp and spent a very enjoyable afternoon with him. He was busy with another book at this time and one will notice he is wearing the same clothes in my photo as those that appear in *Pondoro,* which Dawkins took for the book, except for the turban on his head. I cannot remember if Taylor had any of his own rifles with him at this time and I cannot remember what vehicle he was using. As for Aly Ndemanga, I never met him at all. Taylor looked in excellent health, but he did have a few veldt sores [tropical ulcers that usually appear on shins and ankles], and showing me these he came out with his little giggle again.

Taylor and Dawkins had made their camp about four miles from ours, right opposite a fairly large village and right in the middle of a lot of high grass. They had cleaned a spot in the middle of it, and when you passed the village you could not see them at all. You had to know there was somebody in that grass.

About three days after Taylor left, we had a white game ranger pay us a visit—looking for John Taylor. He knew his name and that he was with "a chap from overseas somewhere." On enquiry as to what this was all about, he advised us that the elephant they had shot was in Northern Rhodesia and not in Nyasaland, so obviously John Taylor had taken John Dawkins into the Luangwa Valley for his first elephant and poached it!

We all formed an immediate liking for this quiet spoken man with the occasional giggle!

The Dawkins elephant was the last of John Taylor's career. He poached his first jumbo, and he poached his last. After his safari with Taylor, John Dawkins hunted in many African locations, now stalking alone with only trackers. John Dawkins's 1967 book, *Rogues and Marauders,* tells of several safaris together with Taylor when Aly tracked for him. Dawkins had high praise for both Aly and Taylor, commenting on Taylor's reluctance to shoot a wounded elephant so that the Australian could get the experience, and he mentions toward the end of the book: "I had learnt most of my hunting lore with John (*Pondoro*) Taylor."

The following extract from *Rogues and Marauders*, which Mr. Dawkins has kindly allowed us to use, reflects the close relationship between Aly and Taylor, which would not have been considered "normal" in another hunting camp:

"Aly has poured your coffee, John, so you had best drink it before it gets cold," advised my hunting companion, John (*Pondoro*) Taylor.

I sat down again, and added some sugar to the coffee.

"Biscuits, John?" he asked, passing across the tin. Helping myself, I passed them on to Aly Ndemanga, who always shared our fire with us. John and Aly were more than just master and servant. John had a very high regard for this gunbearer of his; he had even dedicated all the books he had written to Aly Ndemanga.

A MAN CALLED LION

"My goodness, we must have walked hundreds of miles and still have not got within shooting distance of one of these marauding elephants," I complained and sipped my coffee.

"Well," began the famous hunter, "I usually reckon that I walk about a hundred miles for every elephant shot, and sometimes a lot more. In fact, I remember some years ago when. . . ."

J. Vance Jr.

CHAPTER SEVEN

The photographs John Dawkins took on his safari with Taylor, which appeared in Taylor's autobiography, *Pondoro: Last of the Ivory Hunters*, are dated 1953. At the end of this safari, the two men saw to it that Aly was left well cared for, and they departed together for Australia where Taylor stayed for three years. *Pondoro* was now all but completed, and between buffalo culling on contract to the Australian government in the Northern Territory, Taylor finished it and wrote two more books: *Shadows of Shame*, a novel, and *Maneaters and Marauders*.

Pondoro: Last of the Ivory Hunters, published by Simon and Schuster, came out in 1955, and *Shadows of Shame*, published by Pyramid Books, came out in 1956. *Maneaters and Marauders*, the last of his five books, was published by Frederick Muller and came out, after the missing manuscript was either retyped or found, in 1959. Taylor must have had good reason to believe by now that he could survive financially from his well-used and lovingly cared for Remington and that he was no longer dependent on his rifle for his living.

Taylor's sixth book, the manuscript he was writing when Brian Marsh met him at Aly Ndemanga Village on the Mangochi Plateau in 1957, was to have been about African witchcraft. Few white men could have been closer to the inner workings of the African mind than Taylor. He was a paid-up member of the Yao tribe, a "white African" who had lived with them for many years as an African and who believed completely in the power of African witchcraft. But, being a practicing Rosicrucian and having had a Western education, he may have seen it from a different perspective. He did for instance believe in the power of "mass suggestion," or "mass hypnotism," which the African saw simply as "straight black magic."

Taylor's book on witchcraft was never to be completed. But he did tell Marsh, during the dark hours of a gusty night when the witches rode by on their haunted hyenas, some of the stories he intended putting into it. These stories he told with extraordinary vividness. To this day Marsh remembers them exactly as they were told. One story in particular, which Taylor called "Ghost Bushman Hill," Marsh regards as the greatest of all Taylor's stories. He had the good sense to record this story on paper while the words were still fresh in his mind and as nearly as possible in Taylor's own words.

A number of Taylor's stories gave a fascinating illustration of the power of "mass suggestion," or "mass hypnotism." One concerned a particularly sane and balanced person with whom Brian Marsh had a considerable amount of contact. This was Oliver Carey, Game Control Officer with the Department of Game, Fish and Tsetse Control, the officer in charge of the area where Marsh hunted crocodiles.

Olley was a highly respected senior member in the department and a very experienced hunter. He was quiet, reserved, and not given to telling exaggerated stories. There was no reason why he should have invented this one. Taylor completely believed in its veracity when he heard it, saying he could very well understand it, which was why he had intended to use it in his book on witchcraft. This is the story Olley told John Taylor:

"I had been called out to hunt down an aged lioness, which had taken to marauding around African villages, goat-napping and such. These lions, either through age or injury, are unable to hunt their normal food and so turn to killing stock. If not dealt with, eventually they eat people. But they are difficult to come to grips with. Always cunning, they never kill in the same place twice and they never return to a kill.

"The call had come from Lake Chiuta, close to the border with P.E.A., and Mbobo, my game scout and an old hand with the department, and I had left in the early hours to reach the village about midday. While Mbobo was brewing a pot of tea, I sat down with the village headman to hear the story. I listened to a string of the lioness's latest felonies against society and asked the usual questions, expecting a lot of blank stares concerning where I should start and when. I was startled by the unexpected reply:

"'You can start right here and now,' said the headman. 'We know exactly where the lioness is and you can go and shoot her right away.'

"This was not par for the course with stock-killing lions, and my suspicions were immediately aroused. I had expected to be pinned down here trying to winkle her out for weeks. But the headman said the lioness had killed a goat near the adjoining village only the night before and she had been tracked to a patch of heavy thicket, where she was known to be lying up, only a mile away. Certainly odd! Stock-killing lions make a habit of getting right away from the scene of their crimes. Still suspicious, I got ready for the hunt. The headman sent out word for the men of the village to gather and act as beaters in a drive to rout her from the thickets.

"'Of course,' I thought, 'this is not going to work.' Driven lions seldom do what you might expect of them, and they can become dangerous, preferring to stand and fight instead of running in front of the beaters. But, when I consulted Mbobo, I discovered the elders of the village had already made a plan.

"'It is like this,' said Mbobo, scratching himself thoughtfully through his khaki overalls. 'Apparently there is an open space to the one side of the thicket where the lioness is lying up. It has a convenient tree with a fork in it in which you can sit. The elders say it will not be necessary for me to take a stand. They are quite sure of the way it will run, but they think I should go in with them with my rifle in case the lioness attacks them.'

"'Well,' I replied, 'That doesn't sound unreasonable. That's if she's there at all of course.'

"'She'll be there. The elders assured me that they have circled the thicket and the spoor tell them she is still in there.'

"At this I'm afraid I gave a snort of disgust. 'If they circled the thicket this morning, then you know as well as I do that the lioness will have scented them and will be miles away by now.'

"'Yet, let us go along,' said Mbobo cheerfully, 'and do as they say.'

"And then, a rather strange thing happened. While I was waiting for the beaters to assemble, one of the elders, a very old man, shuffled out of the crowd to squat down in front of me, taking a large pinch of snuff while he got himself settled.

"'You will see,' the old man told me, 'that this lioness is very old, so old that when she walks it seems as though her hind legs are too weak to carry her. She has the habit, when she is disturbed, of not slinking away through the grass in the manner of a lion, but of running a short distance and then stopping to look back. She does this because she is now very old.'

"This was becoming a bit much, and the attitude of the beaters was puzzling, too. They had all assembled by this time and they were just a little too matter-of-fact about the whole thing. There was none of the usual bravado that always precedes a lion hunt, with everyone armed to the teeth with every bit of hardware they can get their hands on, building courage, all strutting and bragging about what they'll do when they catch up with that lion. Very few of them were armed at all, and then only with light axes. The whole thing didn't add up.

"We set off on foot, the beaters carrying tin cans to rattle and bang, and after a walk of about half an hour, I was directed to a low tree growing by itself in an open space to the side of a thicket. I climbed into the tree while the beaters went round to the other side of the thicket to chase the lioness towards me. The villagers seemed to have the whole thing worked out, but I was not too impressed, as I was quite sure it would not work. This in no way resembled any lion hunt that I had ever been on.

"My shooting position was fairly stable, if very uncomfortable, but I settled down to wait, and shortly I heard the beat commence. Mbobo was with them, armed with his Vickers .404 in case the lioness made trouble. Just as I was nearing total boredom and thinking of climbing down from my uncomfortable perch, a lioness appeared at the fringe of the thicket.

"I was amazed. I watched her as she paused to test the wind, and then she made a run across the open almost towards me. She did not try to sneak away through the grass, which was just long enough to have hidden her, in the usual feline crouch. She came at an awkward canter.

"About halfway across she stopped and turned halfway around to peer back over her shoulder, just as the old fellow at the village had said she would. I could have easily shot her except the beaters were still in the line of fire. While she was standing there, I was able to get a good look at her. She was just a gaunt, old lioness, scrawny and mangy. I watched her as I kept the sights on her, waiting for her to move.

"Then she loped on again, and as soon as she was clear of the beaters, I squeezed off and that was that. She went down like a weevil-eaten bag of beans. And then, a few minutes later, along came the beaters. They just sauntered out of the thicket and wandered over to gather round her. Mbobo was with them. He went over to have a brief look before coming over to hold my rifle while I climbed down from my tree.

"'Are you sure she's dead?' I asked him.

"'She is dead,' he replied. 'And, just as well. It is not good to have an old lioness like that scavenging around the kraals at night.'

"I then walked over to see her myself—and my eyes nearly blew out of their sockets. 'This is not a lioness! This is a bloody hyena!'

"'Oh, no,' said the beaters almost in chorus, looking at me blankly. 'This is a lioness.'

"I looked at Mbobo. He pulled a wry face at me. 'Just agree it is a lioness,' he mumbled, 'and I will tell you about it when we get back to camp.'

"We left the beaters to bury whatever the damned thing was and Mbobo and I headed back to camp. On the way he told me the story: The clan totem of these people is *fisi*, the hyena, so when this hyena became old and started marauding around the villages, killing stock, and even stealing food from the houses, there wasn't anything they could do about it, because to harm it would have brought leprosy and other misfortunes to the village. But, it finally became too bad. The hyena was ruining them. So they had to call a witch doctor to help. What he did was to turn the hyena into a lioness, because only in this way could they have it killed.

"'When you shot it, as you saw yourself,' said Mbobo, 'it was a lioness. But as soon as the spirit left it, as again you saw for yourself, it turned back into a hyena.'

"'Mbobo,' I asked in a serious voice, while all the while I could see his eyeballs rolling round unbidden in their sockets. 'Did you see it before I shot it?'

"'Oh, yes. Indeed. It ran out from right in front of me. I could see it very well.'

"'And what was it when you saw it?'

"'It was a lioness. Very definitely a lioness.'

"'Of course,' Olley concluded when he told John Taylor the story, 'I realized afterwards that what the old fellow in the village was describing to me was a hyena. But, dammit, when I fired, the bloody thing was only fifty yards away. You'd think I'd know a bloody lioness when I saw one!'"

Taylor put this down to "mass hypnosis." Every other human being in the village firmly believed it was a lioness and Olley had become receptive to their vibes. Taylor thought there was nothing unusual about this, and that it was a regular ploy the witch doctors used. He told Marsh a tale from his own experiences, another story he was going to use for his book and which he put down to the same thing, although with a twist, like a negative photo.

Amateur Portuguese hunters used to appear along the Zambezi from time to time when Taylor was hunting there, so it was not unusual for Taylor to meet up with some of them. It was the usual custom with some to employ the temporary services of a comely "camp girl" from one of the nearby villages to do their laundry, wash their dishes, and perform any other service they might have in mind. These hunters were much resented by the village bucks because they could procure with their superior spending power the favors denied to them.

One of these amateur hunters put up his camp not far from Taylor's. He had come up to shoot elephant and he immediately set about hiring trackers and porters from around about. He also took on one of the village belles as his "camp girl," but the girl was already betrothed, her intended having gone to work on the mines down south to get the bride price together. When the two families concerned discovered that she was providing other services besides those applying to laundry and dishes, they strongly objected. There was a row with the hunter refusing to pay the girl what he owed her when he kicked her out.

In those days, every white Portuguese was a king in Mozambique and there was nothing the blacks could do against them. It was futile for any African to report a grievance against a white man to the authorities because inevitably they came off second best. The girl's family knew they couldn't get what was owing by fair means, so they resorted to foul. They consulted the local witch doctor.

A few mornings later, the hunter discovered tucked into his blankets a small bundle of gruesome objects wrapped in a piece of wildcat skin: a puff adder's skull, a dried monkey's paw, and various bits of carved wood and bone, none of which impressed the hunter at all. All he did was crow with laughter at this crude, pagan attempt to place a curse on him, and for all to see, he contemptuously threw the bundle on the fire.

A MAN CALLED LION

This, however, was an ill-conceived move. Knowing what had happened and believing in the curse's effectiveness, his trackers and gunbearers were frightened, fearing to hunt with him in case the evil conjured up by the witch doctor might splash over on them. The whole crew announced they were leaving. Taylor, who had been following the saga from the daily reports of his own crew, was silently congratulating the girl's family for having got back at the man in such a subtle way, but the hunter was wise to that. He refused to pay the men the money he owed them until they had worked for the contracted period. Money was a rare commodity in the African bush, and the disgruntled helpers decided it would be best to stay.

Taylor thought that this would be the end of the story and that the Portuguese had got away with it, and so he was surprised when the hunter's cook came hurrying to his camp a few days later leading a party of agitated men. Would he come? they implored Taylor. The white man had been killed by an elephant.

Taylor immediately went back with them. It was always desirable to get another white man to verify the facts in this sort of incident in case there was a suspicion of murder. The facts sent chills down Taylor's spine.

The Portuguese hunter and his team of trackers and gunbearers had followed the spoor of a lone bull elephant, eventually coming up to him, standing at rest in some fairly close mopane. The wind was with them and the bull was dozing. There was just the right amount of cover to quietly stalk up to within easy shooting range. But, while the hunter's team could all see the bull, the hunter could not. The trackers edged the hunter forward, pointing excitedly with their spears, but the hunter could still not see the bull. They edged him closer, and still the Portuguese could not make the elephant out. And then the hunter, glaring angrily at his trackers, must have decided they were putting him on. He suddenly strode boldly forward—until he found himself right up against the sleeping bull. The elephant woke to find the man standing right alongside. Without moving its feet it lashed out with its trunk, like a long, gray bull whip, and that was that.

Taylor checked the tracks very closely. There could be no doubt about it. He could see where the unarmed trackers had slipped quietly away as soon as the hunter was killed, and that the elephant, as though in contrition for what it had done, had torn down branches and covered the corpse before walking quietly away.

"And, what I saw there," Taylor remarked, "convinces me that this was true. It was ridiculous. The bull must have been standing there as big as a house and yet the hunter's tracks showed quite clearly that he could not have seen it because he had walked right up to stand beside it. And the man hadn't wounded it, either. I checked his rifle and it had not been fired. If the elephant had been wounded, it most certainly would not have stayed to "bury" the corpse.

"The elephant's tracks proved conclusively that it had not moved at all from the place it had been standing before it killed the man. The man's tracks showed conclusively that he had simply walked into it. It seems that he must have been reacting to some sort of mass hypnosis, which was the reason why he couldn't see it—unless of course we accept that the man was bewitched!"

*   *   *   *   *   *   *

Taylor was a Rosicrucian and believed in the power of thought and that thoughts can be transferred through extra-perceptive means from one mind to another—and not only among humans! Taylor once demonstrated something to Brian Marsh that certainly appeared to show that thoughts could be transferred between men and birds.

It was that hot hour of the day when the veldt sleeps, when only the unceasing, mournful cry of the little emerald-spotted wood dove broke the shimmering, indolent silence. The little dove was hidden in a thicket by the stream a long stone's throw away from Aly Ndemanga Village. The dove is a small, smooth creature, sporting emerald spots on its wings, hence its namesake. It has a monotonous but pleasant call, and it is one of the most common sounds of the bushveldt. The lament is interpreted to proclaim: "My mother is dead . . . my father is dead . . . and all my relations are dead . . . too . . . too . . . too . . . too . . . too!"

"D'ye hear that little dove?" asked Taylor, the lilt of his brogue mellifluous on the hot, noonday air.

Marsh nodded. He had not been listening to it but was vaguely aware that it was calling.

"Might not work. These birds that hang around human habitation get too attuned to human thought waves. It should be tried right out in the bush, well away from humans, when I can make it work every time. Anyway, let's try it. Let's see if we can get it to respond and I'll show ye what I mean."

Taylor instructed Marsh what to do the next time the wood dove called:

"My mother is dead . . . my father is dead . . . and all . . . !

At a given signal from Taylor's gnarled trigger finger, Marsh applied all his concentration on the dove, and the call stopped abruptly.

"D'ye see what I mean?" asked Taylor, reaching for a smoke.

"My relations are dead . . . too . . . too . . . too . . . too . . . too . . . too!" said the dove.

"And that," said Taylor, lighting his cigarette, "should demonstrate to ye never to concentrate your thoughts on any animal ye're stalking. I can assure ye, this is ninety-nine times the reason why the tyro has such limited success. He concentrates all his thoughts on the animal instead of concentrating on his stalking, staring hard at it every time he puts his head up to take a peep, which immediately causes the animal to stare straight back at him—even if it doesn't know he's there. Then, with everything else in the fellow's favour, the animal suddenly gets uneasy for no reason that can be seen, and the next time he takes a peep—it's gone."

The next story relates to a mysterious "happening" Taylor tells of in *African Rifles & Cartridges*. The story is about the right hammer of a hammer gun his gunbearer was carrying in front of him that kept inexplicably cocking. Marsh asked him to enlarge on it, which Taylor did. The young croc hunter was so impressed with the telling that he went straight back to his own typewriter and typed it out. Marsh feared that the story would be lost because Taylor had told him that he did not intend to use this tale in his book of witchcraft, which surprised Marsh greatly. As far as Marsh was concerned, this ranks as the greatest of all Taylor's stories. This is pretty much how Taylor told it.

CHAPTER EIGHT

GHOST BUSHMAN HILL
by John *Pondoro* Taylor

There's a big hill on the Southern Rhodesian side, not too far from the border with P.E.A., and a good day's walk from the Zambezi. The locals call it—what shall we say?—Ghost Bushman Hill. That'll do. That's not its real name. I've got its real name and its exact location well tucked away. I last saw it thirty years ago but I'm going back one day to have a real look at it, something I was unable to do the last time I was there.

You can see the hill from a fair good distance on a clear day, before the bush fires start and the whole place hazes over. It's a big hill, much bigger, and I believe much older, than those surrounding because I got the impression from what little I saw of it from the top, from the short time I was there, that it's actually an extinct volcano.

From the distance the summit appears quite flat, but when I got up there I found I was looking right over the tops of the trees, clear over to the far side, because the summit is a basin. The top was a hollow like the crater of a volcano, through aeons being filled in, which of course trapped the rain that can be heavy around those parts. Instead of the open forest I'd expected to find up there, the basin was filled with giant, creeper-hung trees that formed a tangled jungle. From all the elephant trails leading into it, it seemed to be sort of an elephant utopia with a climate all its own.

The trapped water also feeds a strong spring that comes bursting out of the side of the hill. Perhaps there were others. I only saw the one. But this spring runs down through another place of thick jungle, a narrow cleft. With impenetrable cover and permanent water, it was easy to see why this place was favoured by the old elephant bulls.

I had not been in Africa long and at that time I'd not yet learnt to what extent the African's life is ruled by witchcraft, so I'll admit I didn't pay too much attention when I told my men I'd like to go and have a look at it. Even from a distance it struck me as a likely place for big tuskers. But all my men warned me of dire consequences.

I was poaching on the Portuguese side at the time. Occasionally, when the need to lose myself for a while arose, I would slip across the border into Southern Rhodesia. The border in those days was ill-defined, if it was defined at all, because I could never find it. The locals who lived along the river always seemed to know exactly where it was, however. I'd hear them argue as to which side of the imaginary line a certain tree was growing. Not that this was of any consequence, of course. They'd been going unimpeded up and down the Zambezi for centuries and the white man's boundaries were not about to stop 'em. They crossed at will.

Nobody lived permanently on the Rhodesian side along that stretch of country. It was too broken with high hills and rocky valleys. Growing things was out. They couldn't have kept any stock beyond chickens and goats because the place was infested with tsetse fly. We did run across other natives on the odd occasion, visitors like ourselves who were over there hunting. The Rhodesian authorities never ventured near the place, so it was safe enough to be there.

We slipped in along the Zambezi, coming up as far as we could in the dugouts in the hope of picking up a few good tusks, but it seemed all the elephant had moved away from the river. We found no sign of them at all. Due south from where we were camped, I could see the high top of this hill vaguely outlined behind the haze and I made it known that we were about to walk to it.

Now all my fellows at that time, all except one, were Senas from down the Zambezi. They had all said that they were quite prepared to hunt around it, but they were not prepared to climb it. The odd man out, a bright young fellow by the name of Chitali, came from the Nyasaland border way up to the north and had only recently joined us. He had set out with a party of young men to find work on the mines of Johannesburg, intent on trading his honest life in the bush for the bright lights and money. By chance they met up with us. We were camped near a kraal where they crossed the Zambezi and they stopped by to beg some meat.

A MAN CALLED LION

We had plenty of that commodity as it happened. I had just shot a number of hippo that were raiding the *dimba* gardens along the river and young Chitali ate so much of the fat that he got ill. Indeed, so sick did he become that his friends all thought that he'd been smitten down by the tsetse fly. The result was that they went on and left him in my care.

He recovered and without further ado he threw in his lot with us. I gave him the job of kitchen hand and personal assistant, which meant he carried the three-legged cooking pot and my blankets. Apart from my rifles I didn't travel with much else. But he was the only member of my followers who came with me to Southern Rhodesia who did not seem concerned with the legend about this hill. Coming from so far north, perhaps he thought that such things were no concern of his; or being the new broom that was still sweeping clean, perhaps he thought he ought to make a show of siding with me.

Everyone we met in those parts was quick to tell us that climbing this hill was strictly taboo. According to legend the hill had numerous caves allegedly containing rock paintings. This meant that in days gone by the place had been a stronghold of the vanished Bushmen, the true aborigine of southern Africa. They had left the walls of all the caves they inhabited liberally decorated with their long-enduring rock art. These Bushmen lived all over southern Africa but were routed by the Bantu when they came south. What was left of them went to live in the Kalahari Desert. It seems, however, that when the Bushmen were routed, they left their presence behind in the form of evil spirits, and great harm would befall anyone who ventured there.

Only once within living memory had this taboo been broken. The story of this misfortune was told to me many times. It seems a party of native hunters, an elderly man with four of his grown sons, had come upriver to hunt elephant. They had with them a muzzleloader and they camped on the spring where it ran out at the foot of the hill. They found considerable sign of elephant movement, going up and down the hill. They knew the big bulls were spending their days up there, only coming down at night. But they also knew the legend and were disinclined to follow them. They preferred to wait it out at the foot of the hill hoping to catch them when they came down.

They were hungry. They had not yet shot an elephant and they had no meat. Apparently game was short that year. But one early morning an eland bull came to drink at the stream that ran into the veldt from the spring that came down the side of the hill. The old man shot at it, hitting it quite hard, but the eland ran off up the hill. It was leaving a fair blood spoor, and the old man thought he would not have to follow far to recover it. Not wanting to expose his sons to the evil spirits on the hill, he bade them go back to their camp and wait for him. Then he called his dog and set off after it.

I can't imagine a dog ever being in a place like that. The tsetse were the worst I have ever experienced, so it could not have survived long, but there it is. That is how the story goes. Perhaps there had been a bad drought and the buffalo herds had grazed the place flat and pushed off, taking the fly along with them. Whatever, only the dog came back. The four sons found it cowering outside their camp the following morning in a highly nervous state, although there was not a mark on it.

Of course the sons had all been awake the entire night wondering what had happened to their father. The two oldest decided they must follow the spoor to find out, agreeing to go only a certain way. They called the dog, hoping it might lead them to their father, but whatever it was that had frightened it proved too much and it refused to follow. The two sons went off and they never came back. The younger two waited for several days before making their way back to their home with the horrifying news.

I must admit I paid little heed to the story. In Africa stories have a way of getting exaggerated and every untimely human death is always attributed to witchcraft. I wasn't going to be put off on that account. We arrived at the foot of the hill and made our camp on the stream where it ran out at the bottom. I was gratified to find fresh spoor all around it. But all of it was leading upward, which proved they only came down at night.

I liked what I saw. I had the idea that the area around here had not been disturbed for several years. Therefore I could look forward to collecting a good supply of ivory. There was plenty of other game sign around as well. In fact we had no difficulty finding the stream simply because of the number of game trails that all led toward it. We had our evening meal and then I told my lads to prepare for an early start. We were going to climb the hill I told them, but all I received from them was a line of impassive stares.

A MAN CALLED LION

I did not fancy going up the hill alone, although I was quite prepared to. Even a small accident like a sprained ankle could prove fatal if I could not get down and my men refused to come up to look for me. They would have naturally thought the evil spirits had got me so there was nothing they could do about it. I offered young Chitali a good bonus on every elephant we shot. This made him forget his fear and he agreed to come along. I was quite sure that when we came down again unscathed that the rest of the crew would follow us up the next day. We took only some dried meat with us in a knapsack, both of us having had a substantial early breakfast. Since I intended to follow the spring, there was no need to laden ourselves by carrying water.

The sun was not yet up when we departed. I told my men not to expect us back much before dark. I could see from the bottom that the spring ran down through a very thickly wooded cleft and that is where I expected to have some sport. It seemed a likely place for elephant to want to spend the day.

I was carrying my hammerless Jeffery .450 No. 2, with 20 spare rounds of ammunition in my belt, while Chitali carried my other rifle, a double-hammer .500. This was an old weapon, which I did not keep for very long. It was rather heavy, weighing about twelve pounds. He also carried twenty spare rounds of ammunition in a belt, but in his case he was obliged to carry it as a bandoleer, because my waist was several sizes too large for him.

There was a surfeit of elephant sign. The trees had been freshly broken and pulled about. It was clear that it was a favorite haunt of the old bulls and that they probably stayed there the whole year around. It was a hard climb. The sides were very steep in places and covered with a loose shale that was slippery underfoot. But we made good going along the well-used elephant paths. I had thought to follow along the streambed in the bottom of the cleft, but there the thickly tangled undergrowth made it difficult to walk. Instead we kept mainly to the shoulder of the cleft where it was open. Several times we heard elephant in the thickets below and I was tempted to go in and have a look. I wanted first to reach the top and resolved not to disturb the place until I had seen what it was all about.

About two-thirds of the way up, the cleft ended. The two sides came together and rounded off at the top. I found that part formed a buttress, which was wide and flat and not too thickly forested. It came before a very much steeper climb to the top. As it happened, we missed the source of the spring, which I knew must have come out of the ground somewhere near the top of the cleft. Thinking to find the source of the spring on our way down again, I decided to carry on to the summit.

And so we sweated and puffed our way to the top, which we did not reach until the early afternoon. I knew we could not linger. But linger we did! I have never been in a more fascinating place. I did not find the top of the hill to be a plateau, as it appeared to be from below, but it was a round basin, like the maw of an extinct volcano, which indeed I am quite sure it was.

The basin acted as a catchment, so the rain water sank down inside it instead of running off the sides, and the rim allowed me to gaze across the top of the tangled canopy of jungle. The numerous trails leading into it convinced me that this was indeed a natural refuge for elephant. Here was a mass of feed, which would last the year out and a perennial spring gushing forth a short way distant. I confess I wondered who the clever hunters were who had propagated the story about evil Bushmen spirits inhabiting the place. No elephant hunter in his right mind would ever reveal the truth of an elephant paradise like this!

I lost no time in following the nearest elephant trail down into the jungle below. Ancient paths led everywhere. It was not long before we came upon their makers. We blundered right into a group of bulls. And then I saw a phenomenon that to this day I cannot adequately explain. It was burning hot, and what air moved at all moved fitfully. When we barged into the lazing bulls, one, a magnificent tusker and no doubt the leader of the group, lifted his trunk and held it out in our direction.

Taken completely by surprise, Chitali and I froze. I slowly dropped my hand and tapped the ash bag hanging from my cartridge belt. The air was drifting straight toward them, so there can be no question. They had winded us and knew we were there. And yet the bull dropped his trunk, shook his head, and blew. Then he relaxed again and continued to drowse!

I was quite certain I could have shot the lot of them, but we backed off, working our way back to the rim. I had the feeling that having found this place I shouldn't do anything in a hurry, rather to look it over and plan the hunting carefully. I was quite sure, when Chitali and I got back safely and told the others what we had found, that the rest of my men would follow, particularly as I now felt I had the secret about the legend of the Bushmen spirits. No wonder that story had been put about, and I wondered again who the clever hunters were who had started it.

I was nonplussed about the behavior of the bulls. They had scented us and yet showed no fear. Could it be that they had lived up here for so long unmolested that they had lost their fear of man? Impossible! Or was it, as I was later to come to suspect, that they had lived there in harmony with a certain group of men who had never harmed them, and so lost their fear of man while in their refuge on top of the hill? It is well known that the Bushmen hunted antelope with their poisoned arrows but never harmed an elephant, which, in any case, they were powerless to do. But, that afternoon, I was to have none of these thoughts. I was simply nonplussed by what had seemed to be a very interesting phenomenon.

The sun had only one-quarter of the sky left in front of it when we set off down the hill again. I felt some misgiving for having dallied so long. I still wanted to find the source of the spring. Night would be upon us before we reached the camp again. We were both suffering from fatigue and thirst. The way poor young Chitali kept changing that old double-hammer rifle from shoulder to shoulder convinced me he was tired of it. But the way down was not much easier than the way up had been. We slipped and slithered on the loose shale and the sun had not much more to go when we finally reached the top of the cleft. We followed it down, the work of storm water over the aeons having worn a pebbly watercourse. It was not long before we found the spring and we lost no time in sinking our faces into it.

The spring was not in the watercourse itself. It was to one side where a pool of water stood beside an ancient fig tree, through the exposed roots of which the water bubbled. It was a strong flow, but further down it was joined by several other springs, some running out of open fissures in the rocky sides and in other places bubbling up within the watercourse itself until it became a fair-sized stream.

It was now quite clear that Chitali and I could not reach the bottom or our camp in daylight, but I was not too concerned. The moon was at the full. I had reservations about going down in the complete dark. But as soon as the moon came up, which we could expect a short while after sundown, it would be light enough within an hour or two for us to seek our way and to ensure that we did not blunder into any elephant. Elephant are always active in the early part of the night, so I knew we would hear any that were about. We carried on down the stream when I noticed that it continued to increase in size as other springs joined up with it. I was just about to leave it and make my way through the thickets to the shoulder of the cleft, when we came upon a waterfall.

There was a large, level, and perfectly flat shelf of rock covering the entire bottom of the watercourse, curving gently downward toward a rounded lip over which the water spread out evenly and fell in a thin veil, covering what appeared to be a hollow behind. I clambered down, to find the hollow behind the veil was actually a small cave. Putting down my rifle I ducked through the spray of water and went inside. The gloom in which I found myself took me back in time.

The walls were of smooth stone and covering every inch of the exposed surface was the most splendid exhibition of Bushmen rock painting that I have ever seen. In my time I have discovered and seen a fair amount. There were paintings of all the antelope, cows and bulls, rams and ewes and juveniles, and all in perfect proportion. There were elephant and rhino, and even hippo, which means that at some time the artists must have gone to the Zambezi. There were men hunting with bows and arrows and women with camel-hump behinds. The paintings must have been there for centuries and yet, perhaps because of the constant humidity of the cave, the ochres looked as fresh as if they had been put there the month before.

I called out to Chitali to put the rifle down and to come and have a look. I wondered what he would make of it and so stood back to watch. I was surprised that he hardly glanced at them. His gaze was fixed instead upon three objects which till then I had not closely observed. Hard against the back of the cave there were three large mounds of clay, almost square except where the edges had crumbled and perhaps about three feet in height and width.

"Graves!" exclaimed Chitali. "Three people have been buried here. This place is evil." And in no time the lad was back out again.

At that I went forward to look at them. It was dark and gloomy at the end of the cave, but I saw sure enough that they were indeed graves. Three people had been buried there by the unusual method of placing the bodies in a crouching position and plastering them over with clay. Some of the covering had broken away to reveal human bones. One had most of a human skull protruding. If the paintings were centuries old, the graves were not. I cannot imagine that the human bones showing could have been equally old. I believe the exposed bones would have rotted away in that humidity.

Although the sun had not yet set, it was nevertheless growing dark in the cave. It was deeply shaded in the cleft, with the large trees overshadowing on either side. I resolved that when I came back the following day I would take some time to examine the Bushmen paintings and the graves. Regrettably, this was never to be. My chances of going back there were completely obliterated by the extraordinary events that were to follow, which to this day I cannot explain.

We made our way out of the cleft as quickly as possible. We needed to collect sufficient firewood to give us comfort while we waited for the moon to rise to give us enough light to guide us back to our camp. We had no trouble collecting the wood. The elephant had broken down sizable branches for us to drag or carry. We had a good blaze going before full darkness fell. Chitali was acting very nervous, throwing many an anxious glance out into the surrounding gloom. I did not think he would rest at all, but I was mistaken. We shared the dried meat we had been carrying. We were both hungry and had not eaten during the day. As soon as Chitali was replete, he curled his legs up close to the fire and was soon snoring loudly. He was only a lad and he'd had a hard day.

I was also dead beat, but I felt no desire for sleep. Too much of interest had happened for me to have a tranquil mind. I sat with my back against a nearby tree, staring into the fire, while I smoked a long-looked-forward-to pipe full of Magaliesberg.

It was a fine night and very quiet. I had expected to hear the squealing and trumpeting of cow herds, although I had not seen any cowherd spoor, but I heard none of it and began to wonder if it was only the old bulls who came up here. The only sound was the occasional crack, like a rifle shot in the darkness, of an elephant breaking down the branch of a tree. I was feeling contented. I knew I had found the place of the bulls. I was sure, when my men saw our safe return and heard what I had to say about the origin of the legend of the Bushmen spirits, that they would come back with me. I was contemplating some excellent ivory.

I knocked out my pipe. It had long gone cold. My calico Magaliesberg tobacco pouch was nearly empty, so I opened the top and placed the bowl of my pipe inside it and pulled the string tight. I knew better than to leave a pipe in my pocket when about to lie down. If I dozed off and rolled over, the stem would break. Then I got up and walked to a leafy bush that was some six feet in height and was just across the clearing where we had built our fire. I hung the tobacco pouch near the top on a twig, reminding myself to collect it again before we left. Then I pulled the branches up in the fire to get a hot blaze going and lay down opposite the sleeping Chitali.

The moon was just up, throwing a small light around us, but I intended resting until it was higher in the sky. I did not intend to go to sleep. I put my pith helmet over my eyes to keep out the light of the fire, which was flickering on the leaves of the bush where I had hung my tobacco bag and pipe. I felt very much awake. I lay there musing about the diminutive Bushmen people who had painted the walls of the cave behind the waterfall and wondered how long ago it was that they had been driven from here.

Suddenly I felt I was being watched. Living in the bush where there was always danger had sharpened my perceptions. I always had a strong premonition, a sixth sense when danger was at hand, which I have always instantly acted upon, but this was not the same feeling. This was the little prickle you get when sitting quietly and you suddenly become aware that a stranger behind is staring at you.

Slowly, I brought up my hand and pushed back my helmet and I received a jolt. I was quite sure I had not been asleep and yet the fire, which had been blazing merrily, had now died right down. The wood on the hillside was of a soft variety that burnt down quickly without leaving a bed of coals. And the moon, which a short time before had been just above the horizon, was now almost vertically above.

I lay for some moments without moving. I had no fear, but the strong feeling that I was being watched persisted. My rifle lay comfortably against my side, the muzzle upon a piece of wood pointing past my feet. All I would need to do was to grasp it and snap off the safety catch. I moved my head slightly so I could see the bush where I had hung my pipe and tobacco bag—only to receive a second jolt, which was considerably greater than the first! Below the lower branches of the bush I could clearly see the lower portions of a pair of human legs.

For those who have never experienced a moonlight night in the tropics of Africa, it would no doubt be difficult to imagine just how bright it can be. All the colors of the veldt show clearly, although in subdued and pale hues. And there was no question about what I was looking at! The legs were very slim, although well formed, and I judged them to belong to a man of small stature. Their apricot sheen reflected the moonlight so that the skin glistened. The man's torso was hidden behind the bush, so I could not see it. I fancied I made out a wizened face peering at me through the leaves. But whether I did see a face as I supposed, or whether the face was just the tricks of light and shadow, I knew without doubt that what I could clearly see were the legs of a Bushman.

I also knew there were no Bushmen here and had not been for centuries. I lay for sometime staring at the legs, which did not move, then I slowly turned my head to examine the other side of me. I saw nothing and turned slowly back towards the bush. The legs had vanished. I sat up quickly and looked around, wondering now if it had been a dream or if I had imagined it. I stared back at the bush again, trying to reconstruct the wizened face I thought I had seen peering through the leaves at me, but that too had gone. I resurrected the fire and sat by it, now perfectly sure I had seen a pair of Bushman legs. Could it then mean that a group of the ancients who inhabited all of Southern Africa had remained hidden in these remote hills until this modern time? That seemed so unlikely it hardly deserved a second thought. Yet, that could also explain the unusual behavior of the elephant bulls we had encountered in the afternoon.

I thought of smoking my pipe again but changed my mind. The dried meat we had eaten at sundown had been very salty and had left me with a considerable thirst that I thought a smoke could only aggravate. I was to regret it! One of the many mysteries of that day and night might well have been solved if I had gone then and there to get my pipe and tobacco. I built up the fire again and lay down, resolving to stay where we were for the night. I soon went to sleep. A chill came up in the early hours that woke Chitali and I heard him rise and make up the fire. When I awoke again it was dawn.

There was still a walk of a good few hours down the hill ahead of us and my thirst had increased. I told Chitali I was going back to the stream for a drink and asked if he wanted one, but he shook his head. I don't think he fancied that place very much. I left him sitting by the fire while I made my way back down through the thickets to the stream. When I got back, Chitali was on his feet waiting to leave. He had the knapsack which had contained the dried meat upon his back and the rifle he was carrying was propped against a tree. But before we left, now that it was fully light, there was one thing I had to see!

I walked very carefully all around that bush where I had seen the Bushman legs the night before, with Chitali wondering what I was looking for, but I was not about to tell him. I was looking for a sign of a human track, but the ground was so hard and gravelly that a bare foot would have left no trace. A glance into the bush had revealed that my pipe and tobacco had been removed. I had no doubt that Chitali would have spotted them and returned them to the side pocket of the knapsack where, when I was hunting, they were usually kept. Then we set off down the hill. I knew my men in camp would be sick with worry at our nonarrival the night before and decided, if we happened on a good bull, that I would shoot it. The sound of my shot would tell them that all was well.

We walked down along the shoulder of the cleft, listening for any sound of elephant in the thickets below us, and close to the bottom of the hill the cleft widened out into a shallow depression. Here the heavy forest and thick undergrowth thinned out. We left the shoulder and walked in toward the stream, thinking we might chance on an elephant.

I confess I was not paying much attention to the hunt. I was thinking about the cave behind the waterfall with its rock paintings and three graves and the events of the night before. I had by now, in the light of day, persuaded myself that my imagination had been playing a trick, although I can still see that pair of glistening yellow legs as clearly now as I could see them then. But I did wonder who had been buried in those three graves. Were these the graves of the old hunter who had followed the wounded eland up the hill with his muzzleloader and those of his two sons? And, if so, who had buried them? And why in such an unusual way?

A MAN CALLED LION

While my mind stayed upon these thoughts I happened to glance at the rifle Chitali was carrying muzzle foremost upon his shoulder, a pace or two in front of me. He was carrying the old double-hammer .500, and much to my surprise, I saw the hammer on the right side was on full cock.

I reached forward and tapped the butt of the rifle which made Chitali stop and look around, and I pointed to the offending hammer.

"Did you feel it cock?" I asked.

I had never experienced this before but concluded that a creeper must have snagged the hammer as he walked by, bringing it into the full-cock position. This would have required a considerable pull and I could not imagine Chitali not having felt it.

Chitali looked surprised and shook his head while I took the rifle and lowered the hammer. I reminded him that it was loaded and admonished him to be more careful. I gave the rifle back to him and went on.

Sometime later I again glanced at the rifle on the shoulder of the youth in front of me. Once again, to my surprise, I found the hammer on the right-hand side was again on full cock! I was now annoyed with him. I could not imagine what he was doing to get the rifle cocked. If a creeper had snagged it again—but there were few creepers in the forest through which we were now walking—he would surely have felt the pull. I blamed him for being stupid and took the rifle away from him, lowering the hammer and giving him my own rifle. I placed the old hammergun over my shoulder in the same way that he had carried it, and we set off down the hill again.

But it was not long before I tired of it. It was a brute of a thing. And stopping I made to give it back to him, telling him the while to observe that when I carried the weapon it did not get cocked. But then I glanced down. The hammer on the right side was again on full cock!

"The rifle has been bewitched," said Chitali.

Completely nonplussed, we carried on down the hill. Around midmorning we arrived back in camp, myself in a very thoughtful mood. I had no explanation for it. We were warmly greeted by the rest of my party who had come to believe that we had followed on the tracks of the old hunter and his two sons. Food had been prepared for us and we ate it with gusto, but I ate mine in silence while I listened with a sinking heart to Chitali as he regaled our companions with every detail of our adventure.

There seemed no point in trying to deny that we had been bewitched. Was it not, I was asked when Chitali had run dry, a fact that the hammer on a single-barreled muzzleloader like that of the old man was always fitted on the right-hand side? It was, I had to agree and saw my prospects of returning to hunt elephants on the hill rapidly diminishing. Then, I was told, it must be obvious for all to see that the old hunter of the legend who had followed the wounded eland up the hill with his muzzleloader, and who now lay buried with his two sons in their strange graves behind the waterfall in the painted cave, was warning us not to venture there again. And how else would one hunter warn another that he was in immediate danger if he could not express himself in words? Would he not reach over and quietly cock his rifle so he was in readiness to shoot?

Of course, I could not bring myself to believe it. Nor could I explain how that old hammergun became cocked on three separate occasions, something I have never seen before or since, although I do believe the hammer could cock if pulled through a vine or creeper. Then I began to wonder if I had indeed seen a ghost, which I wisely did not mention or my men would have demanded we leave the place right then.

Feeling perplexed, I went off to the edge of the stream. Sitting down on a log, I cooled my tired feet in the water. Then, feeling like a smoke, I called out to Chitali to bring my pipe and tobacco.

"Your pipe and tobacco? I do not have them. I have not seen them and thought you had them in your pocket."

"They were hanging in that bush," I told him. "The one you saw me walking around this morning. I hung them there myself last night, and I did not see them there this morning, so I thought that you had taken them."

Chitali shook his head. "I saw you walking round the bush, searching the ground as if you had lost something. But I did not see your pipe and tobacco bag."

Well, I did not see it either, and I had looked for it. Had I just failed to see it? I do not think so. The bag must have been hanging there as large as life. How could I have missed it? If it had disappeared—then I must have seen a man! There indeed must have been a remnant of the ancient Bushmen people living at that place. Was it just a Bushman spirit who enjoyed the odd pipe full of Magaliesberg?

A MAN CALLED LION

Perhaps it was the old hunter of the legend who cocked that old hammergun after all!

* * * * * * *

Taylor flipped his cigarette butt in a shining arc that landed with a burst of miniature fireworks against a glowing leadwood log. "Another touchh of the creature?" he asked, reaching for the bottle.

The young crocodile hunter nodded mechanically, his eyes glazed as he pushed his glass across, pushing it more by reflex action than a conscious effort. Marsh was mesmerized, completely under the storyteller's spell. There had been few nights in his young life to equal this and he wanted to hear more. He was also conscious, although perhaps only vaguely, that it was almost four o'clock in the morning.

Taylor poured two final tots and added a splash of pure spring water. He lit another cigarette, exhaling the smoke thoughtfully into the night sky. Then he sat quietly, drinking his nightcap in silence. He seemed oblivious, obviously still deep in thought about the events all those many years ago on Ghost Bushman Hill.

It was Marsh who eventually broke the silence. "You say you're not going to use this story in your current book?" he asked at last. "But why not? I mean . . . I'd have thought."

"Perhaps in the next one," said Taylor. "When I've had the chance to get back there, as indeed I must. I need to visit that cave again and settle a few things in my mind."

Marsh did not say it then, but he had already made a firm resolve. He would finance the trip himself and take John Taylor back to Ghost Bushman Hill. The very thought electrified him. He tossed off the remainder of his drink and said good-bye to his host. He strode off, perhaps a little unsteadily, to the tree under which the Land Rover was parked, climbed in, and pressed the starter. The motor awoke with a screechy gasp. He turned to wave a last good-bye and saw that Taylor had not moved. This was unusual for him, as he normally saw his visitor to the car. He saw the older man was still staring into the fire, a lighted cigarette between his fingers. He could not help wondering what memories were tramping again through the old hunter's mind.

The dawn was just threatening with a slight pinkish blush over Mozambique. The morning air was so cool and fresh it seared the inside of Marsh's nostrils as he drove back toward the lake. Before he reached the top of the escarpment, headlights were no longer needed, and as the grayish-green rush of the trees blurred by his mind was filled with the words of the strange tale that John Taylor had told so well. When he reached the Palm Beach Hotel, where he was staying at the time, Marsh sent for a pot of coffee. He sat down at his own portable and began typing out the story while the spell was still on him.

In retrospect, the story about the self-cocking rifle does sound improbable. There have been cases of hammerguns being cocked by creepers when carried muzzle forward on a person's shoulder—and others when the hammer was caught by a vine and slipped off before coming to full cock—and the gun firing. A good friend of Brian's, now a well-known Zimbabwean game rancher, was shot from behind and fortunately only in the meat of the shoulder when a .410 hammergun carried by hunting companion did exactly that.

But there may be a completely logical explanation for the human legs Taylor saw protruding below the bush in the moonlight of that eerie night, although he certainly did not see a Bushman. They had long since disappeared from the middle and lower Zambezi Valley by the first quarter of this century, when Taylor had his adventure with their "spirits." But, he might have seen another equally mysterious being. He may well have been the first white man ever to see a member of a hunter/gathering tribe, which at that time in history were completely undiscovered and unknown.

Taylor may very well have seen a vaDoma, one of the "two-toed" or "ostrich-footed" people, as they were originally called, one of Africa's smallest and most primitive groups. And, a vaDoma may well have stolen his pipe and tobacco bag! These hidden people are said to number only a couple of hundred and they have a strange history—and an even stranger foot deformity. Their brilliant bush craft, the ability to "hide behind their fingers," allowed them to remain a complete mystery until quite recent times. The place where they live is inhospitable and remote. The rare visitors to the area had no idea what left the occasional very strange, two-toed tracks they saw. Taylor's "Ghost Bushman Hill," by his description, is in vaDoma country.

A MAN CALLED LION

The vaDoma are purely Negroid and were first heard of immediately after the end of the Second World War when a surveyor working in the remote Luangwa/Zambezi confluence gave a report to the local newspaper that he had surprised a naked savage at a water hole. The man had run from him at considerable speed, leaving behind the unmistakable footprints of an ostrich! Letters to the editor inevitably followed, some wondering what the purveyor of such information had been smoking—and could they get some? Others suggested that the obviously sun-stricken surveyor take a bit more water with his dop. Then other reports surfaced.

A few years after the first report appeared, a prospector panning for gold in that area was told by the locals along the Zambezi that a strange "two-toed" people lived in the hills, a people who had such an ability to hide that they had only to raise their open hand in front of them to disappear from sight behind the hand. In fact, they named them in their dialect, "The-Ones-Who-Hide-Behind-Their-Fingers." The prospector, a man by the name of Victor Strobel had a son, Kenneth, who was a school chum of Brian Marsh's. Strobel also claimed to have seen ostrichlike tracks in the mud around water holes, and had he not known that ostrich do not occur there, he would have assumed that they were ostrich tracks.

Then the story came out. There was indeed a genuine "lost" tribe among whom some members had a strange foot deformity. They avoided all contact with the outside world by remaining hidden in the wild hills of the Zambezi Valley and lived a hunter/gatherer existence. A study was made of these people by Robin Hughes, a game ranger with the Rhodesian Department of National Parks and Wild Life Management who was stationed for many years in the Zambezi Valley. Hughes was a linguist who spoke the local dialects fluently and a man critically interested in all things relative to the valley. He wrote a paper on the vaDoma for the department, which he made available to Brian Marsh.

The vaDoma legend has it that when the Shona-speaking tribes arrived on the south side of the Zambezi River some 600 years ago, one offshoot, under Chief Mutota, moved into the rugged Wadoma Mountains in the Zambezi Valley in order to mine salt.

Till then, the newcomers had been obliged to make do by shaking burnt goat droppings over their *sadza* and *muriwo* (Africa's standard thick cornmeal porridge with a side dish of stewed vegetables and meat), so it is probably small wonder that they headed for the hills. Quite frankly, I would have done the same. These people were given the name of "Makorekore," literally, "Like a Swarm of Locusts," by the Tavara, another offshoot of the newcomers who settled in the Tete area of Mozambique. It sounds as if there were quite a bunch of them out there.

The Makorekore had slaves with them when they arrived, captives from weaker tribes they had overrun on their way from the north. Four of these slaves escaped, two young men and two young women, to hide in the only place that offered refuge–the vastness of the Wadoma Mountains. The four slaves were to become the progenitors of the vaDoma, which translates to "The People of the Wadoma Mountains." There were alleged to be only thirty families, all obviously inbred, when they were finally discovered. Efforts were made to persuade them to come down out of the hills. Some have now been integrated into Zimbabwean society, but it is known that there are still others out there who refuse to abandon their wild, but free hunter/gatherer life in their rocky mountain stronghold.

The vaDoma differ from the Bushmen in their hunting techniques, but otherwise their lifestyle must be similar. They do not use the Bushman poisoned arrows, the only feasible weapon for the open but bushy plains where the Bushmen live today. Inhabiting broken country, the vaDoma utilize game trails upon which bark rope snares are set and pit traps dug. They also lie on low, overhanging branches and stick game walking below with their stabbing spears. They fish with bone hooks and make their line from finely plaited inner-bark twine.

It is considered that their inbreeding accounts for the strange foot deformity that some but not all members of the tribe have. D.P. Abrahams, who studied them in recent years, describes the big toe as a full six inches in length, intersected at ninety degrees at the base by the small toe, which is about two inches in length and points obliquely outward. X-rays have shown that the second, third, and fourth toes are completely absent, not even a vestige. But those who have seen the vaDoma run have opined that the deformity does not seem to slow them down at all, when fleeing across the rugged country that they call home.

From Taylor's description of how he reached the area, Ghost Bushman Hill must be a part of the Wadoma range, so the figure he spied that night might well have been a vaDoma man hiding and observing him behind that bush. Growing nothing, they would not have tobacco, although they may have smoked the wild variety or wild marijuana, known as *dagga* or *chamba*, but the man could have taken the tobacco bag and pipe out of sheer curiosity.

The vaDoma may have killed the three eland hunters, the old man and his two sons, who disappeared in Taylor's "Ghost Bushman Hill" story. It would not have been unreasonable to suppose that in order to preserve their secret hideout they murdered them and buried them in that unique manner in the painted cave. The vaDoma would have had no adequate digging tools, so it is likely they could not have dug graves in the hard, stony ground on the hillside deep enough to bury them.

In African legend "haunted hills" do exist. One in question is Chirambakadoma, which translates to "The Forbidden Mountain," a particularly big, flat-topped hill near the Wadoma range in the Zambezi Valley. A similar taboo exists about this hill. Joe Wright, a young professional hunter and friend of Brian Marsh's, set off to climb Chirambakadoma with a white companion one day, very much against the loud protestations of his African men. Joe and his companion had not gotten far above the bottom line when they were charged out of nowhere by an unwounded buffalo that came within a nick of killing Joe. This is most unusual. Joe was charged from behind and was only able to swing around and shoot it at the last second. In spite of the fact that he says he is still convinced that this mumbo-jumbo only exists in the African mind, he and his companion, perhaps very wisely, took the hint and came back down again!

Coincidence? Very likely. But there seem to be an awful lot of coincidences, besides John Taylor's, like that in the African wilds!

J. Vance Jr.

CHAPTER NINE

Taylor returned to Nyasaland from Australia either in late 1956 or early 1957. Immediately upon arrival he was back in tow with Aly. Together with some other members of his old team, they set about building a new village on the Mangochi Plateau. It was about a thirty-minute drive by Land Rover from Fort Johnston, which was a small town. It was also the administrative center of the area and was located at the beginning of the Shire River at the southern toe of Lake Nyasa. The new village comprised only six thatched huts. In accordance with the custom that villages be named after the headman, this one was named Aly Ndemanga. Although he did not suspect it then, this was to be John Taylor's last home in Africa and his residence at the village was to be of a relatively short duration.

Once the village was completed, Taylor settled in to become a full-time writer, setting up his old Remington typewriter on a rough deal table under the shade of a nearby grove of *brachystegia* trees. He felt secure now in the knowledge that this dream could be achieved. And why not? He already had four books published: *Big Game and Big Game Rifles; African Rifles & Cartridges; Pondoro, Last of the Ivory Hunters* and his novel, *Shadows of Shame*, and his fifth book was on its way to the publishers.

The publication of the fifth book, *Maneaters and Marauders*, had been delayed. The manuscript, which had been posted from Australia, had been lost en route to the publisher. This was either found or retyped and it came out finally in 1959. Taylor was now at work on his sixth book, which was to have been about African witchcraft but, regrettably for posterity, was never finished. This book, together with all desire to continue writing, was to be blown away by the ever-increasing dust storms whipped up by the winds of change.

Who's to know? Taylor might well have continued writing, in spite of the eventual odds, had he known then that his *African Rifles & Cartridges** was fated to become an established classic and was to be reprinted twice in English in two countries. *Pondoro,*

*Last of the Ivory Hunters** was also to be reprinted twice, both times in America, and two of his other books were also issued as reprints. What was absolutely certain was that Taylor's future books need not have topped the best-seller lists to have kept him handsomely in the modest lifestyle of his choice.

His home was a spacious, newly-built, African-style thatched hut overlooking one of Africa's spectacular settings. There were zero rents or utility rates to pay, and his house came with a number of willing servants to wait on him and attend to his needs, to do his cooking and his laundry and to fetch firewood and water, which was there in abundance—free, gratis and for nothing, simply for the taking. He had his own chickens for eggs and meat. They roamed free and lived entirely on insects and what wild seeds they scratched up in the surrounding veldt, so they cost him nothing. Although he had no goats of his own to provide him with "mutton" for Sunday lunch, these were available from neighboring villages and in those days were cheap to buy. He also had a large *dimba* garden down by the stream, which supplied him with vegetables, for which he supplied only the seeds. His men did all the tending and watering on an equal share basis, so he was living a life of plenty on almost as little as the tribespeople among whom he had settled.

Before he could settle in too deeply, Taylor still had one last chore to put behind him: acquiring permanent resident status in Nyasaland to allow him to live and earn his living there. As soon as the village was up and running, he took the Fort Johnston bus to Zomba, the administrative capital of Nyasaland at the time, to present his application papers. This, he was fully convinced, would not present any problems. Nyasaland was a British Protectorate and he had fought for Britain in the last World War and been severely wounded on her behalf. Also, his books would now show that he was fully capable of supporting himself. What possible reason would they have to refuse him? Hmm! What indeed?

The immigration official to whom he was directed was Ricky Philip, Brian Marsh's pal. Ricky owned the beach cottage at Namasso Bay on Lake Nyasa. There was an instant mutual liking between the two men. Both were of a similar age, of the same height and build, and with the same military bearing—even down to the pukka Thin-Red-Line-of-Empiah defoliated moustaches. They both also had the same direct, clipped way of speaking, similar attitudes to life in general, and a very wide experience in Africa.

A MAN CALLED LION

Ricky had originally been a policeman in British-ruled Nigeria. To use a British euphemism, he had been "retired early" for, as the Brits would also say, "blotting his copy book." Ricky's name is recorded in the tomes of colonial history for being the man who fired the first three shots "in anger" that marked the beginning of what were to become the very bloody, continent-wide, African independence riots.

Expecting an attack, Ricky had been sent with his Muslim Hausa troops to guard a remote explosives' magazine on a gold mine. No sooner were they there than a panga-wielding mob of Ibo nationalists arrived to raid the place for the explosives. Ricky, possibly inspired by Col. William Travis at the Texas Alamo, scratched a line on the ground and announced through the loudspeaker to those gathered there that he would cheerfully shoot anybody who crossed it. Three of the ringleaders, urging their constituents on, promptly did just that, and Ricky fulfilled his promise.

The British government, nonetheless, chose to ignore the simple fact that the gang of panga-swingers would have chopped Ricky and his men into hyena pickings if he had not fired. They howled in anguish, accusing Ricky of having acted "with excessive force." Somebody was going to have to pay the political bill and Ricky was going to be it. He was "retired early."

He and Rene then came to Nyasaland, both in their forties at the time, and set about building the beach cottage at Namasso. Not having sufficient funds from his markedly diminished British Colonial Police pension to both eat and build, Ricky went to work for the Department of Immigration in Zomba, while Rene supervised the builders. Ricky lived in bachelor digs all week and drove back to the lake each weekend.

A blooming friendship sprang up between the Philips and John Taylor. Ricky began to make it a habit to pick John up on his way back to Namasso each Friday afternoon. He and Rene would have him stay for the weekend. John would take the bus from Mandimba, which passed by the village on its way to Fort Johnston, the town at the confluence of Lake Nyasa and the Shire River, and Ricky would meet him there. Perhaps surprisingly, because Taylor was reputed to be distant and offhand with women, Rene and John very quickly became particularly good friends. She took to referring to him and Ricky as "my two pirates" and commenting how unfortunate it was for both of them that they had been born 200 years too late.

As it happened, Brian Marsh rented an outside storeroom belonging to a beach cottage at Nkhudzi Bay as his base, which was just around the point from Namasso. Ricky and Rene had been given the use of the Nkhudzi cottage while they were busy building their own and this was how Marsh became so friendly with them. Marsh soon gained the distinct impression that apart from himself, Ricky and Rene were the only real white friends John Taylor had or wanted. Marsh was to learn much later that they knew about Taylor's habits and it did not concern them. They took Taylor as they found him, a person who in many ways was like them, but in other ways was a mile apart.

The winter of 1957 came and went. Taylor continued writing his book on African witchcraft at Aly Ndemanga Village, while his application for permanent residence was "under consideration." He wasn't too concerned about the delay. Government departments always took months to do even the simplest things.

Meanwhile Marsh struggled on to make a living, but in the end was forced to abandon crocodile hunting. The bund across the Shire at Liwonde was still in place, which had raised the water level in the lake even further. The conditions were now such that hunting crocs on Lake Nyasa had become all but impossible. Marsh and his two boatmen, Tawali and Masamba, had to travel long distances by boat and be out for long hours at night for very measly returns. Besides, there was another factor working against them that made the hunting decidedly dangerous, and this was the wind.

Sometimes the squalls would strike in the small hours. Cold and weary, Marsh and his team would be tracking across open water on their way back to camp and there would be no friendly reed beds for them to dive into. Then they would have to lighten the load by jettisoning any crocs they had been lucky enough to shoot and continue fighting the dark to hold the boat into the wind. After one particularly bad night when they came within an ace of sinking and ended up being blown so far off course that they were lost on the lake till daylight, Marsh decided he had had enough. If he was going to live to see the bloody bund blown, he would have to seek an alternative way of making a living until the dawn of that still-distant day.

On the advice of Olley Carey (of voodoo lioness fame and warden in charge of his area), Marsh applied to join the Department of Fish, Game and Tsetse as a game ranger. This seemed to be the only thing going for a young fellow of his qualifications and inclinations. Marsh had the advantage of already being well known to the top brass of the department as Olley Carey had sought their permission to make him an honorary warden (unpaid) when the bund was first built. Olley needed someone to assist with hippo counts and to report any changes in hippo behavior, as well as to carry out general observations on the Shire River on both sides of the bund when the water stopped flowing. Marsh was also given a virtual free hand to assist with any problems in hippo control. His constant presence on the river and on the lake at night saved the department from sending one of their own men to find out what was happening with the river and how the hippos and crocodiles were reacting to the changing scene.

His application was approved and he was waiting only for the official stamp to turn him into a full-blown civil servant when he paid a visit to John Taylor at Aly Ndemanga Village to tell him the news. He received a reprieve. Taylor lost no time at all in talking him out of it.

"Ye'll never be doing any more hunting, my bhhoy. D'ye see . . . they'll be putting ye into an office in Zomba making out visitor's permits to the camping grounds. That's what they'll do."

The indignant old elephant hunter tore the back off an empty packet of C-to-C, his favorite brand of Rhodesian plain, and scrabbled in his pigskin briefcase for a pencil.

"Now look here, let me give ye a map and I'll tell ye what ye should do. Go and look up an old fella by name of Sampson Nyamhoka," he said while he was drawing. "His home is at Dao and everyone there will know him. He's one of my old gunbearers from before the war and he'll be able to show ye around. There's still a living to be made from the buffalo herds that come down onto the plains around Lake Lifumba this time of the year, and ye can make *chakwe* to sell to the sugar estates at Sena."

Chakwe! Marsh had never heard of it. He meant to ask Taylor what it was and how to make it, but he forgot.

"I suppose," his mentor continued distantly, his concentration focused on sketching the map on the white bottom of the cigarette pack, "ye'll be taking along that Cogswell and Harrison .375 of yours." He glanced up for confirmation and Marsh nodded.

"Well then, ye can shoot the lone bulls with it just fine, but don't go taking on the herds or it'll get ye into trouble. The soft-nosed bullets with plenty of blue showing don't penetrate sufficiently on buffalo. The velocity's too high and they set up too quickly. And the solids whip straight through, so ye'll be wounding cows in the herd on the other side of the one ye're shooting at. Wounded cows can be just as dangerous as bulls when you're running through blinding clouds of ash and dust behind the herd and ye're likely to run straight into 'em, particularly when the last thing on earth you suspect is that you've wounded another one. Remember what old Kipling had to say: 'The female of the species is more deadly than the male!'" Taylor said with a wry, impish grin.

"What should I replace it with?" asked the youngster eagerly.

"Ideally, of course, a .450/.400 top-grade double. That's the best there is for buffalo. The soft-nosed bullets will penetrate both shoulders on a side shot, but will never exit. Ye'll find your bullet rolled back into a perfect mushroom under the skin on the opposite side. Unless crocodile hunting has been better than ye've been complaining of, and I guess it hasn't, ye probably can't afford a good double. So my advice is to get yerself a decent single-action in the same calibre. I've used a good number of Farquharson's in the past and they're excellent weapons to hunt buffalo with. Far better than the best magazine rifle any day. Their drop-block action makes them short and compact. With the weight right between your hands, they're as balanced as a fairy on a toadstool stem, and they'll point exactly where you're looking."

Marsh was astonished. "A single shot? On buffalo? Surely if I've got to follow up a wounded one, I'll need a bit more firepower!"

"Aye," said Taylor, handing him the map and reaching for a new box of C-to-C. He slit the wrapping open with his thumbnail. "And there's my point entirely. Never attempt to press trigger until ye're sure of a killing shot. No matter what rifle ye use. But, when ye're using a single-loader, ye'll find an interesting psychological element emerges. Ye're up against the plain truth that ye have to do it right the first time."

Taylor had sucked Marsh in the way a lazy trout takes a worm. He well knew that Marsh could not afford to buy a double and that a single-shot in any modern caliber would be unobtainable about those parts, but he had got two strategically important points across to the tyro: Don't use the .375 H&H Magnum for work with buffalo herds, and always make the first shot count. He went on to advise Marsh to buy the next best, a .404 magazine rifle, which is ballistically identical to the .450/.400.

"Of course," he remarked when Marsh was taking his leave, "a magazine can never be as reliable as a good double or a single-loader, so make sure ye buy a top-grade rifle. It's yer life that's hanging on it, remember. And by-the-by, remember to take a couple of bottles of our friend Johnnie for the *chefe de posto*. Ye'll be needing it to blind his good eye."

Marsh bought a .404 by W.J. Jeffery, as good a magazine rifle as any in the world. It was built on a long Magnum Mauser action and fitted him like a diver's wet suit. He then drove to Tete to take out a nonresident's 2000 escudo (£25) hunting license before following the railway line that runs parallel to the north bank of the Zambezi from Moatize, through Dao to Sena.

The line ran through wild country with almost nothing by way of human habitation, but there was plenty of elephant and buffalo spoor along the road—and tsetse flies. The slowly moving, dust-colored canvas canopy over the back of the Land Rover attracted them like mopane bees to a buffalo's eyes. Soon the inside of the cab was swarming. Marsh brushed them off his bare skin with a leafy switch. He would not kill them. Few professional hunters do. Tsetse fly were put on this earth to shield Africa's soft underbelly by ensuring an equal division between man's greed and the province of the unprotected wild things. The fly guarantees that Africa's marginal areas are not put to uses they cannot sustain.

Sampson Nyamhoka was at home. Marsh found a stocky African well past middle age, who nevertheless looked keen and eager to get back to hunting again. His black eyes brightened when he heard who had sent Marsh and Marsh gave him a letter Taylor had written. He could not read, so he asked Marsh to read it to him, but it was in Chisena, which Marsh did not speak. But Sampson could speak Chilapalapa, the *lingua franca* of the whole of Southern Africa, so he and Marsh could converse. Sampson was to give Marsh even further insight into Taylor's character.

Taylor abhorred the usual Portuguese way of meat hunting: the so-called professional hunter using teams of native hunters, which he outfitted with rifles and trucks, while he remained in camp. The "hunters" excused themselves on the basis that it was more important for them to supervise the making of the *chakwe* than it was for them to hunt. From a strictly financial point of view, they were probably right.

But Taylor was irritated with the whites who strutted around Tete with cartridges shining in the loops of their bush-shirt fronts, parading as mighty professional hunters when in actual fact they had likely hardly ever fired a shot. Taylor did maintain that there may have been some good in the way they hunted. He said the native hunters made a much better job of things and there was a lot less wounded game about. Taylor was referring only to the Portuguese commercial meat hunters and did concede that the genuine Portuguese ivory hunters whom he had met in the past were not of the same breed.

Sampson took Marsh to Taylor's old camp at Lago Lifumba, translated as "The Lake of the Woman's Anklet." Marsh had expected it to be circular in shape, as was the dot that marked its position in the school atlas he had purchased in Blantyre, but it turned out to be "L-shaped" and not a lake but a lagoon. It is connected to the Zambezi by a reed-filled hippo channel. Sampson told him it was not from its shape that it got its name, but from the grisly contents of a certain crocodile's stomach killed there in days gone by. There is a small island in the corner of the "L," where Taylor had his camp. Sampson told Marsh that Taylor preferred to be on an island so the bushbuck and duiker would not eat the lettuce and tomatoes he planted in his *dimba* garden.

It was nearly twenty years since Taylor was last there and the remnants of his old camp could still be seen. There were some mopane poles lying in the forks of trees and what was left of a mound of ancient buffalo skulls. The horns had long since been consumed by borer beetles and only the disintegrating bone remained. Sampson said that "Jack" had collected exceptional buffalo heads while he was hunting and had stored them on the island but had eventually abandoned them. There may have been a market for them at the time.

The open side of the "L" is swampy, but the other two sides are surrounded by almost impenetrable riverine jungle. A number of old buffalo bulls lived permanently in there, coming out only at night to graze. Sampson told Marsh that "Jack" used to shoot them, sometimes following their spoor into the jungle in the hopes of coming up with them, occasionally succeeding, but more often more successful at night with a shooting lamp. All these old bulls carried old bullets and Taylor thought them a menace to his men.

Intrigued that Sampson always referred to John Taylor as "Jack," Marsh asked him the reason. He was unaware then that John had always been called by that name by his family, and "Jack" was the name he brought with him to Africa. Marsh knew him only as John, which Taylor may have changed to when his books were becoming known.

"But that was his name," replied Sampson, looking surprised. "Everybody called him by that name."

"Yes," said Marsh, "but since I have come here, you have called me bwana. Was he not 'Bwana Jack' to you?"

Sampson now looked more surprised. "Not to me nor to anybody. He would not let anybody call him bwana. Not even the smallest children. We all called him Jack. He would say, 'Are we not brothers, you and I? So call me Jack.'"

There was a lot of game on the Lifumba Plains. During the hot months before the start of the rains, the inland water mostly dried and the game concentrated along the Zambezi. Buffalo were there in numbers but they were wild. Out on the open plains they were impossible to stalk, and running after herds was the only way to get a shot. The Portuguese hunters chased them and shot them from their vehicles. The herds showed considerably more fear of trucks than of men on foot.

Because of the competition from the Portuguese and their teams of native hunters, Sampson suggested they move. They packed up their camp at Lake Lifumba and drove to a village where they left the Land Rover and trailer and hired a line of porters. To the northwest of Lake Lifumba was the Marangwe watershed, beyond which was the Nyasaland border. Sampson knew where to find water. He had hunted there with Taylor extensively before the war. As there were no roads in the broken terrain and the tsetse fly were about the worst to be found anywhere in Africa, he knew they would have the place to themselves. And that they certainly did!

Marsh and his party of porters trekked up the Minjova River, which at that time of the year was mostly a dry watercourse with only occasional pools. Marsh was walking now in John Taylor's tracks, hunting as he had hunted, with a line of porters to carry his belongings and whatever trophies might be worth carrying out. If hunting along the Zambezi had changed drastically in the twenty years since Taylor had last hunted here, this place had not changed at all. And no wonder! The tsetse were so savage that it was not surprising that few natives ventured there. The flies were so bad that they would argue whether to eat them on the spot or take them home to feed their young.

Along the way Sampson talked about some of his memories from the old days. That square chopped in the hollow tree, the axe marks still dully showing, he had cut out himself. It was where he and Jack had taken honey and Jack had been stung so badly that his eyes closed up. The memory made Sampson grin with silent mirth, his own eyes creasing like an elephant's hide and his sugar-cube teeth glistening white in the sun.

This was where Jack had shot five elephant bulls without having to move his feet. Sampson and Jack were there one October, the hottest time of the year, and they were looking for the spoor of the old elephant bulls that drank from the pools in the Minjova River, always staying hidden in the hills. Then they walked unexpectedly into the five of them, jammed together under some sparse shade.

The bulls were drowsing, nobody would bother them, nobody ever came up this way. Jack maneuvred his way into a clear shooting position and picked out the leader, who went straight down on his belly to the shot. Then the others just milled about, their trunks up, searching for the source of trouble and waiting for their leader to give them the sign to leave. Reloading silently, Jack quietly and efficiently shot the lot.

Sampson and Marsh walked on, up along the Minjova, walking in a line so the man behind could switch away the tsetse flies on the man in front of him, hunting only for their own meat, while Marsh listened to tales about his friend Taylor in Nyasaland. How much he would have to tell him when he finally went back again. They were approaching a water hole in the dry riverbed, so Sampson told Marsh that when he and Jack had last been here, an old crocodile had lived in it, a croc as long as two men, which Marsh doubted could be true. Why should a crocodile live in such a small pool when it could go down with the annual flood to the Zambezi?

The pool was only about twenty-five yards around, but it was plainly deep, dammed by a shelf of rock and probably fed by an underground trickle. When the porters drew close and threw down their loads and hurried to the pool to slake their thirsts and wash the sweat from their faces, they quickly drew back. There in the mud were the fresh tracks of a large croc!

Sampson told Marsh numerous tales about his hunting adventures with Jack, but he had few stories of Taylor being charged. Following his own dictum of never shooting until sure of a killing shot, Taylor apparently was seldom charged. When he was, it was usually by someone else's wounded animal. When Marsh pressed Sampson to relate a story with a bit more pizzazz than that Jack shot so-and-so here, and such-and-such there, he far preferred to tell about Jack's drinking escapades in Tete.

Taylor apparently did very well at these extracurricular sporting events, too, certainly better than in his tiff with Schots at Hotel Tete a few years later. One night Sampson had witnessed Jack being tackled by five Portuguese men, whom he had no doubt deliberately annoyed, outside one of the bars in Tete. Taylor is alleged to have flattened two before the others managed to wrestle him to the ground, but they took away a hard lesson from a rough-and-tumble with this wild Irishman. Taylor had managed to free himself and made short work of the remainder. Sampson told this story with many, "Ows!" and clicks, and with much shaking of the head. He was obviously impressed.

Marsh did ask Sampson, however, how it was that he had managed to be on hand to witness the fight in question. "Jack," Sampson said, with more clicks and clucks, "was never in a fit state to paddle his dugout back to his camp across the Zambezi when evenings of this nature ended." Afraid that he would either tip over or fall out and the crocs would eat him, one of his men always went over with him to paddle him back again when his evening of good, clean, boyish fun was over.

Taylor was wild and reckless, but he had some unusual and refined facets. Although he had little formal training, he was a gifted piano player. His brother Charles wrote to Marsh that when John left Ireland again in 1928, after his brush with death from the effects of blackwater fever, a large space in his cabin trunk was taken up with musical scores. Muller, the German elephant hunter who had sent for Taylor's mother when he was ill, had a piano in his camp at Nyungwe. When they were both in camp, Taylor would regularly visit and play his favorites from the Russian composers for Muller.

The music never left him in a mellow mood though. It brought out the wild streak of his Irish temperament. When his reverie ended, the evening was likely to close by taking a dugout across the Zambezi to Tete, where he could get drunk and beat up the town's most available and unlucky citizens.

The stories that Sampson told Marsh confirmed to the young croc-hunter's satisfaction that the things Taylor had told him, and much if not all of what he had read in Taylor's books, were true. Most particularly, Sampson was emphatic that Taylor never employed native hunters. Sampson initiated the discussion by asking the white man why he did not use them. The African does not hunt for sport and therefore sees nothing wrong in the system.

Sampson also told Marsh of Taylor's extreme generosity. The wage for a porter at that time was ten shillings a month, equivalent then to $2.50 in United States currency, plus his keep and his rations. But, Sampson said, shaking his head, if Taylor had the money he would sometimes pay £10 a month—twenty times the going rate. Sampson may have exaggerated, but he made a point. Others have also told Marsh about Taylor's polished talent for giving his money away. It seems he only hunted for the excitement of indulging in the oldest pastime. The money was incidental to his pleasure. He never gave a thought to his old age when he would—and did—desperately need money.

One hunting story that Sampson did tell Marsh was about the time Taylor had tried to entice a very elusive man-eating lioness to attack him in the moonlight so that he could shoot her. The lioness had been causing trouble for some time, not killing a great many people but enough to bring the area she operated in to a virtual halt. She had killed only women when they were out in the bush collecting firewood or bringing in water or hoeing in their lands. Not surprisingly, the women had stopped going abroad during the day and none of the essential services required to keep a village going were being done. Taylor was in the area hunting elephant, and the villagers appealed to him for help.

Hearing that her tracks had been seen in the vicinity only the night before, he hit upon a plan. She had not killed, so it was likely she would still be there. He dressed up in a woman's clothes, unwashed so the woman's scent would mask his own, and stationed himself with his back to an overhanging slab of rock close to where the lioness's spoor was seen. He was armed with what Sampson called a "shotgun," but this may have been the Paradox he tells of owning, a smoothbore 12-gauge with rifling in the last few inches of the barrel that would handle both shot and ball ammo nicely.

Taylor was betting that as the lioness had made a series of easy kills she would not charge him, thinking she had the "woman" at her mercy. He spent the whole night giving high-pitched, stricken wails, only to find in the morning that the lioness had indeed come and watched him but was not fooled. She had lain in the grass for a while, as indicated by her distinctive spoor, and then slipped away suspiciously. Taylor made a lucky connection one night a few weeks later and killed the lioness, but this time using a flashlight clamped under the barrels of his double rifle.

According to Sampson, Jack did shoot a number of man-eating lions when they hunted together before the war. He maintained that it was largely the fault of the native hunters with their muzzleloaders that there were so many man-eating lions around. The native hunters would shoot at the lions hoping to get the skin, but would not follow with their "old gas-pipes" as Taylor called them, to finish off any that were wounded.

When they reached the crocodile's water hole in the Minjova River, Marsh and his retinue put up a semipermanent camp just far enough away not to disturb the game that risked its life drinking there so close to that toothsome behemoth. Sometimes at night Marsh would walk down to the water hole, following the feeble, yellow finger of the torch, to watch the croc. It always lay in the same place, in the shallows at the edge of its pool like a greenish-black missile, the light reflecting its near eye like a huge ruby. He could get quite close to it by walking on rocks, but as soon as his feet crunched on the sand the croc would slip backward into the deep with hardly a ripple on the smooth, black, oily surface. Watching it would remind him that he had his croc hunting equipment and his crew waiting for him in Nyasaland, and he wondered if they had blown the bund.

Then the rains came and they moved back to the Zambezi. One day Marsh had to journey to Tete to renew his hunting license and buy supplies. Sampson directed him along the rough track that ran beside the Zambezi, crossing the washes and dongas on mopane-pole bridges, which was a shorter route than going back along the railway line to Moatize. On the way, Sampson showed Marsh the small brick store at Benga that Taylor had once rented. Taylor had had an African storekeeper run it while he was away hunting, returning from time to time to collect the money and to replenish it with more stock brought downriver from Tete in his freight canoe. It is likely, knowing Taylor's reputation as a businessman, that the only person to make anything out of the venture would have been the storekeeper.

Benga is close to Nyungwe and Taylor wrote in *Maneaters and Marauders* of shooting three man-eating lions near his Benga store. At that time, this part of the north bank of the Zambezi was still wild and overgrown with few African habitations, so to have three man-eaters setting up shop there would not have been unlikely.

What Marsh had been doing in Portuguese East Africa had been good, clean fun, but hardly tailored to making money. He decided quite early in the new year that it was time to return to Nyasaland to see if the bund had finally been blown. He needed to get back to croc hunting again. He returned Sampson Nyamhoka to his home at Dao and Sampson's wizened, but eversmiling, wife gave Marsh a chicken to present to Jack, her old friend of long ago. The chicken was imprisoned in a small cage made from thin wands and bark string, supplied with a rusty, cutoff jam tin for water and a small packet of crushed maize so it could drink and be fed along the road.

Apart from looking forward to delivering the chicken and relating the many words of greeting from the old hands who remembered him, Marsh was looking forward to seeing John Taylor again himself. He had a great fund of stories to tell him, of the places he'd been to, and what he'd seen and what he'd done. He wanted to show his mentor the .404 Jeffery rifle that Taylor had advised him to buy.

He spent the night at Sampson's village and after heartfelt and warm good-byes, Marsh turned the Land Rover back along the railway line toward Moatize the next morning. On reaching the Great North Road to Blantyre and beyond, he turned south toward Tete. He wanted to buy a five-liter demijohn of Portuguese red wine as a present for Taylor. He knew this would make the old hunter smile!

As ever, the historical aura of the old town captivated him, and he spent the day wandering around it. All the old hunters had stories to tell about Tete, not all of them complimentary. Harry Manners had often stayed there and knew it well. Manners called it "a heat-blasted hell-hole," and many of the famous Mozambican ivory hunters and safari hunters whom Brian subsequently got to know, like "One-Shot" Araujo, José Simoes, and Baron Werner von Alvensleben, had their own stories about their times there. F.C. Selous was there in 1889, but records little of his impressions of the town, saying only, "Tete is too well known to need much description," and mentions only that the sanitation department was under the firm control of the pigs that roamed the ancient streets.

Marsh stopped at the Hotel Tete for the night. It was an establishment that throbbed with hunting history. After an early breakfast, he was once again heading north. With any luck he'd be in Blantyre by late afternoon and he'd book into Ryall's Hotel. He knew he'd find some of his Blantyre cronies in the Ryall's pub. Not having been among his own kind for a while, he felt in the mood for a party. Early the next morning he would call on the Philips. They would be interested to know he was back. Then he would head out for Aly Ndemanga Village, so he could spend the evening swapping yarns with *Pondoro*.

(*Both books, **African Rifles & Cartridges** and **Pondoro,** available from Safari Press.)*

CHAPTER TEN

"He's been deported," Ricky Philip repeated, striking a match and touching the flame to his cigarette. "And that's all I can tell you." Ricky looked at Marsh, then looked quickly away.

Marsh was stunned. "But there must be a reason."

Ricky gazed at the young crocodile hunter steadily with no compassion in his eyes. "I don't doubt it."

Marsh was perhaps still a bit tender to realize that a stiff upper-lipped Englishman like Ricky Philip did not care to discuss such matters further. He eased back in his overstuffed chair and listened to the muted sound of suburban Blantyre traffic. The shock he had felt at the unexpected news was beginning to subside. Now he felt only disappointment and anger. He looked at the brass buttons on Ricky's starched police tunic. He hoped that Ricky would relent and volunteer a rider, but that look in Ricky's eyes convinced him that he would say no more on the subject. That seemed to be that.

Just before Marsh had left for Portuguese East Africa, Ricky and Rene Philip had left their beach cottage at Namasso to take a house in Blantyre. The hot winds of change swirling down Africa were now kicking up dust-devils in Nyasaland and the natives were restless. Even the schoolchildren were hurling rocks at passing motorcars. Ricky, being an immigration officer by circumstance but a policeman by profession, had been seconded into the Nyasaland force.

Marsh sat brooding. His annoyance was mainly that he hadn't received the news from Rene. Rene would have told him. Rene was a Yorkshire girl and neither her accent nor her native bluntness had been diminished by the African sun. She didn't call a spade a bloody shovel. Well, if Ricky wouldn't tell him, he wouldn't tell him. He mentally jerked back to reality.

"Did he leave a forwarding address?"

Ricky took another deep drag on his Gold Leaf, cork-tipped cigarette. "My dear fellow, I had no idea that he was leaving. I was surprised he didn't contact me. Perhaps he tried to. It's also possible because of my previous official position that he thought I might have had something to do with it. That's bunkum, of course."

"So you don't even know where he went?"

Ricky fixed Marsh with a hard stare and crushed the half-smoked Gold Leaf in the ashtray, letting it sink in that this was positively all he had to say. "I only know that he was put on a plane to London at Her Majesty's expense. I presume he will go back to Ireland. I know he's got a sister there. Knowing him as I do, he will not be long out of Africa, but where he'll end up God alone knows. He'll never be allowed back into British territory. From what we've heard, the Porks won't allow him back, either. Now what about a beer, old boy?"

So that really was that. In colonial Africa, especially British colonial Africa, the system was everything. End of story. Marsh's expectant return to Nyasaland had fallen flat. In fact, it had broken its nose. . . .

Marsh turned down the beer Ricky offered and said good-bye to the colonial cop. As he walked along the red dirt driveway to his Land Rover, he wondered what to do next. Behind the worn steering wheel, he laced the fingers of both hands over the warm plastic and bent his head forward. How now to find out where John Taylor had gone? Ah! Aly. It was obvious. Even if John had gone, Aly would be sure to still be at the village, waiting to hear about the next move. Aly Ndemanga Village was not far from Fort Johnston and its post office. Taylor would have been bound to leave Aly with an address. He'd go back to the village to ask Aly.

He switched on the ignition and punched the starter button, the engine rattling into life in the shimmering African heat. He drove through the outskirts of town, weaving through herds of goats and women dressed in wild cotton prints, more exotic than the tropical birds. He swung onto the Great North Road, pondering what Ricky had told him. The breeze felt cool on his brown right arm, which he cocked out the sliding half-window of the Land Rover. Patches of salty, slick sweat already stained his light, faded bush jacket. It collected in a slimy pool at the seat of his hunting shorts against the hot gray leatherette of the seat. At least the dirt road, seemingly scattered with diamonds from chips of mica that caught the sun, had been recently graded. Ricky had been right. John would not be long out of Africa if he could help it, and Marsh knew that John would not permit a long separation between himself and Aly. After all, black Muslim Yao tribesman Aly Ndemanga was white Muslim Irishman John Taylor's adopted son.

It was not yet noon when Marsh pulled up at the pontoon cable raft strung across the two shores of the Shire River at sleepy Liwonde. It looked like a child's cat cradle. A quick glance downstream showed the damn bund was still in place. So it had not been blown as promised by the government and the crocodile hunter said a short, nasty word under his breath. Of course, the pontoon raft was on the far side of the river. Why was it always on the far side? Why was it never on my side? Africa. Bloody Africa. He put his fingertips into his mouth against his tongue and gave a piercing whistle. Then he watched the pontoon crew slowly come back aboard. A few red-backed swallows skimmed the greasy, swollen water and a blue-cheeked bee-eater channeled to rest on a slender reed.

At last, the pontoon raft arrived, powered by the boatmen who walked the cable along the side, simply gripping it and walking to the stern. Finally they were on the far side. Marsh flipped the men a pack each of Tom-Tom, "Tickey-for-Ten," cheap Rhodesian fire-cured cigarettes that he used for tips. He started the Land Rover again to the accompaniment of the soft lap of water against the forty-four-gallon drums used for flotation. The eerie shrill of cicadas could be heard from the big green trees ahead. Somehow it seemed a fitting background noise for his troubled mind.

He drove off the pontoon and swung along the road that skirted the reed-bedded shoreline of Lake Malombe, actually a swelling in the Shire River that looked like an aquatic python that had swallowed an uncomfortably large goat. He remembered that several months before he had collected his last croc skin on Lake Malombe and wondered what the shooting would be like now. Everything still looked the same as it had the last time he had seen it. The fish vendors were still plying up and down the road with their palm leaf bales of delicious dried *chambo*, the incomparable lake bream, suspended on long bamboo poles lashed to the carriers of their bicycles. Young pickaninnies waved with shiny black palms at the passing Land Rover and nobody threw stones at him

While he drove, Marsh mulled over the likely reason why John Taylor had been deported. He knew that Taylor was quite a bit more than just another of "those bloody white liberals." His views were the reverse of the prevalent thinking in Africa at that time. He called himself a white-African and lived among the blacks like one of them. Nyasaland was squirming like a black mamba with a broken back under British "protection." The nationalists, led by Dr. Hastings Kamuzu Banda (soon to be president-for-life), were demanding their country back. Taylor had no doubt been a continuous abrasion to the carefully oiled gears of government. The pukka British powers must have finally decided that they didn't need a man like that around—especially during these troubled times. Marsh swerved to miss a spotted pig that could have put the Land Rover's radiator in his lap. Sure, that had to be it, he finally decided.

He crossed the Shire again at Fort Johnston. From here it was only half an hour up the Namba escarpment, glowering with dark, mysterious greenery and overlooking the southern end of Lake Nyasa, to Aly Ndemanga Village. He slipped the red knob of the Land Rover into low-ration four-wheel-drive and whined up the towering, winding ribbon of steep road.

The Namba escarpment was as lush as a New York bankroll, deep green thickets lining the sides of the track and the steep slopes punctuated with feathery emerald exclamation points of huge trees. At every switchback there came a new flash of the lake below, patches of shining blue as deep as a freshly blued gun barrel. Small tribes of astonished black-faced monkeys leaped with their clinging babies shrieking to the tangled vines at the base of the forest giants. Dung beetle scarabs, looking the same color as old, dried, and blackened blood, pushed their balls of bush pig manure backward across the rutted road. Nyasa lovebirds flushed like thrown beryl and rubies into the shadows, screaming like goosed banshees as they disappeared into the tangles. But Marsh noticed it had changed. It was late summer now and good rains had fallen. It had been late winter when he was last here. He wondered what else might have changed as he churned on up the escarpment, the heavy treads of the Dunlop Safari tires now soft against the moist earth.

The village finally slid into sight and Marsh's heart slipped down to the bottom of his chest. One glance told him it was deserted. He slowly turned off and ground to a stop with a tiny squeal of brakes, flipped off the ignition key, and eased with an ache out of the cramped confines of the cab. There was nothing but the dank, close smell of damp cut grass and the rustle of insects in the leaf layer of what had once been a well-swept apron of earth.

In parts, it would still look the same if he had forgotten that the rains had turned the bright urine-yellow of fresh thatch to a deep, nondescript brownish-gray. Dust was whisked and lifted in nervous gusts across the yard. There was no brightly colored native rooster scratching in the dirt for ants, nor the bald-necked vulture-looking hens he remembered with their toddling, scuttling broods of chicks. The whole village was a decaying corpse, a rotting, partial skeleton, the doors missing and the windows gaping like empty eye sockets in a semicircular row of skulls. He thought that nothing could look so abandoned.

He called once, but there was no echo and he really had no hope of an answer. He left the Land Rover and started to move forward, stopping in front of the hut that John Taylor had used. The crepe of his *veldschoen* made no sound. There was a large paw print in the dirt of the doorway, well pressed down at the rear but with the faint impressions of claws in the earth. Too big for a dog. Hyena. *Piri.* And a big one, too. Anyway, as it flashed through Marsh's brain, the local leopards would have long converted any stray dog into hairy, bone-splintered scats. But, he realized, there was something. It was the same sound of a little emerald-spotted wood dove, still calling as if his heart would break in the same shady patch by the stream. His melancholy lament suited the place entirely. Aly was gone and with him Marsh's only chance of tracking down John Taylor, deportee.

Although Marsh had had a bit to do with Aly, it had never crossed his mind to inquire where his home was. It had been of no importance at the time and there was no reason why he should have asked. He knew Taylor and Aly had been together after the war on the Zambezi in Mozambique. While there Aly had married a Sena woman from Tete, and later he was with Taylor at Lake Amaramba in Northern Mozambique. So Marsh had no reason to suppose that Aly didn't come from somewhere in Mozambique, which is a mighty big place to start looking for a fellow with crinkly hair and a big grin on a shoe-shined black face. As far as Marsh was concerned, Aly was well and truly gone.

He was not to learn for another thirty years, in 1987 in fact, that Aly Ndemanga's home was, in fact, in Nyasaland, right on the border with Portuguese East, and only about twenty-five miles from where he now stood. Aly's family, his parents, wife, and children, lived in the village of Mwambwajila, just before the Mandimba River, and his brother Kandulu and his family, together with numerous aunts and uncles, lived only a stone's throw away at the village called Nombo. Brian Marsh would only find out what had happened to Aly when John Taylor supplied the key to the mystery in a book that Marsh believed had never been published, Maneaters and Marauders, *when he described a visit to Aly's home.*

But that late summer day in 1957 on the Mangochi Plateau, he did not know this. With a rising sense of frustration and loss, he turned the Land Rover in a tight circle and drove back the way he had come, down the escarpment and back to Fort Johnston. "What a bloody balls up!" he thought. He had really liked and admired John *Pondoro* Taylor. Listening to him and learning his bush secrets had made him feel much closer to the professional hunter's mystique. Taylor's advice had been damned good. Marsh had tested it. Without any doubt, Taylor had been the one person who had directed the course of his life more than any other—right from the time, in fact, since he had found the copies of John Taylor's first two books at Kingstone's Book Store in Salisbury shortly after leaving school. But now, he was well and truly gone.

Well, so be it. There was nothing he could do about it now, and it was time to look in on the tools of the trade. He had his two croc hunting boats and motors and the rest of his rather exotic equipment neatly stored at his base at Nkhudzi Bay. He turned right at Fort Johnston along the gravel road that ran its potholed length along the western shore of the lake. Everything was as he had left it. As the sun was beginning to slip quietly down over Mozambique to the west, past where long, thin Nyasaland gouged it in a downward, green stab, almost severing the Portuguese territory like a hot dog in its bun, Marsh turned off to stop for the night in one of his favorite places, the Palm Beach Hotel, nestled cozily along the southern shore.

Marsh glanced over the familiar bar as he walked in, blinking to rid his eyes of the glare. The oiled bar top with the rolled ridge gleamed softly across the room, little bowls of salted peanuts and *piri-piri* Cajun nuts interspersed along it. Glass ashtrays big enough to scald a warthog studded the dark wood. The ever-familiar pub dartboard and slate blackboard hung against the wall with three darts stuck in the bull's-eye. He didn't think they had been thrown there. On the planking of the wooden walls there were native fishnets with artifacts looped through their mesh and a few badly taxidermic specimens of Lake Nyasa fish. The same red-topped bar stools were neatly staggered along the elbow space and, as always, the brass foot rail was immaculate. It was as bright as it only could be in Africa where labor was plentiful and cheap, by any measure.

As his eyes accustomed themselves to the welcome, cool gloom, he saw two youngish policeman at a table, their ties loose and their heat-sagged tunics hanging gratefully from the backs of their chairs. One of them raised a froth-topped thick glass mug advertising a local beer and waved it at Marsh, inviting him to join them. The two were from blighty Australia, all the Nyasa police were, Marsh knew. They were handpicked, all of a hearty, well-built, and cheery type and generally jolly good fellows, what? They all came out on three-year contracts and were usually invited to stay on when the terms of their contracts expired.

Nyasaland then was hardly what the most optimistic foreign service type would call "bustling." As a protectorate, it was very meagerly developed, and commercial enterprise, particularly by whites, was not encouraged, so the population of that group was small. It was not a British possession to be exploited or developed. Everybody who had been there for even a short length of time was at least known by everybody else and Marsh was anxious to catch up on the local doings.

The barman had just brought him a tall, amber, foamy, frosty relief from the white man's burden, when Pixie Sweetman sashayed in from the main hotel and the three asked her to join them. What a looker, Marsh thought. She had a couple of well-grown kids and a hell of a nice husband, but with her corn-colored hair, wide-set aquamarine eyes, deep, Indian tan and yet-perfect figure, she was still something to see, even at the extreme age of forty, Marsh decided. Hell, she was as pretty as an eighteen-foot croc sound asleep on a sandbank at point-blank range!

Pixie Sweetman owned and ran the Palm Beach Hotel and certainly knew what was going on from one end of Nyasaland to the other. The four of them chatted about various things and Pixie asked Brian what he had been up to since she had last seen him.

"Been hunting in P.E.A.," he replied, after taking a gulp of icy beer. It made his throat ache in joy. "Waiting till the lake level drops again. That bloody bund rather mucked things up for me."

"For us too," Pixie agreed. "Flooded our beach. I wish they'd blow the bloody thing."

"Me too, but it was firmly in place this morning."

"And likely to stay that way." Pixie observed, "in spite of all the noise in the local paper. What were you hunting in P.E.A.?"

"Oh, just having a swan-around, really." Marsh waved to the barman for a round. The black man nodded and bent down to the fridge. "I hunted a bit along the north bank of the Zambezi. Went to look the place over on the advice of a friend of mine. Fellow by the name of John Taylor. He put me in touch with some of his old crew." Marsh felt in his pocket for some money to pay for the drinks. "He used to be a professional elephant hunter there, but moved to Nyasaland to become a fulltime writer."

"John Taylor," said Pixie, screwing up her face and cocking an eyebrow. "Isn't he the man who's just been deported?"

Marsh nodded. "As I've just found out."

"And not before time," snickered one of the policeman unpleasantly.

Marsh shot him a glance. His remark hit a raw nerve and Marsh felt his hackles stirring. "That's uncalled for, isn't it?" he said quietly, turning back to a new beer. "Taylor's lifestyle might have been a bit unorthodox by general European standards, but that's what he chose to do and chose to be and I don't see it had anything to do with anybody else. He wasn't harming anybody and kept himself to himself, and I think it bloody unfair that they would kick him out just because his political beliefs and his liberal ideas don't fit into the scheme of things." Marsh was just that little bit angry that he could feel his gut twitching.

"Whoa!" said the policeman. "Hold on a bit. There was a little more to it than liberal ideas and political beliefs."

"Really! Like what?"

The young Brit glanced at Pixie, not quite sure what to say. He sank his nose into his beer rather than having to say anything at all. She came to his rescue.

"Well," she said evenly, matter-of-factly, "there were some rather ugly rumours. . . ."

"Rumours! What did he do?"

The second constable leaned over to him and whispered quietly, "Every black boy he could lay his hands on."

Marsh was stunned. Blood roared in his ears and he felt a deep flush creeping up his face. He had never heard anything like this about Taylor. He looked to Pixie for confirmation, but she turned away and wouldn't catch his eye. John Taylor one of those? He flat didn't believe it. In 1957 and at the ripe old age of twenty-nine, Marsh had never knowingly met a homosexual in the flesh and his only contact with them had been when they were the subjects of barroom jokes. The little he did know about them suggested that they were everything that John Taylor wasn't.

"That's a load of tripe," he said, flustered and embarrassed now.

The second policeman gave a few guffaws to hide his own embarrassment in front of Pixie and offered his opinion. "I, for one, happen to know it's true. He's as queer as they come and the government was quite right to give him the heave-ho. We don't want fellows like that around at any time and we certainly don't want that sort around right now." He had lisped the word "fellows" when he spoke.

"But how do you know it's true?"

"I did a few patrols around his kraal on top of the escarpment. You only had to go there to know it was true. He always had a whole string of young boys hanging round the place."

"Good God!" Marsh thought. "That's proof? How little these young Aussies knew about rural Africa and how quick they were to pass judgement on things they knew absolutely nothing about. They'd be better off sticking to their cold showers."

If either of these two had ever visited one of Marsh's camps in East-of-Nowhere, in the virgin bush where he always camped, they would have found a whole string of young boys hanging around there, too! This is something every white bush dweller in Africa knows all about and it is normal and natural. A white man was still an oddity in such places, something very different that attracted a lot of attention from the local people, if there were any. Even today in the more remote parts of Africa if you pull your car up on the side of the road, a group of youngsters will quickly surround the car to stand and gawk. It is, after all, free entertainment!

Marsh had strange things among his gear that were then completely new to the tribal African—a canvas tent, folding camp bed, outboard motors, rifles, but, above all, a portable radio. In those days, even the adults who had not strayed far from their villages had neither seen nor heard a radio, and when Marsh camped near them every man, woman, and child would come to look and listen. The young boys were the sons of the fisher folk who lived around the lake shore. Too young to help with the nets and canoes, and having no stock to tend or fields to hoe and no school to go to, they had the day on their hands to go adventuring. One of their favorite haunts was around his camp. No, sir, that was hardly an argument!

"And you know," continued the policeman confidentially, "he even had one of his black fellows sleeping in the same hut with him."

Oh boy, thought Marsh. There had never been any sort of master/servant relationship between Taylor and any of the Africans who worked for him, and none of them ever referred to him by the general colloquial tag of "bwana." The black Africans were all his friends and equals as far as he was concerned, and he treated "his" people as such. Taylor was, by his own admission and brag, a "white African," preferring to live among the Africans as an African. He spoke their language as well as they did and had rejected the Presbyterian faith he was born into in favor of Islam, the faith of the Yao tribe he lived among. He had completely adopted their culture. Marsh well knew that Aly Ndemanga did share his hut with him, but he also knew that Aly was John's adopted son.

To be fair, he had to admit that he had thought the arrangement unusual when he first met Taylor, but he had put it down to his ingrained colonial viewpoint (Marsh was a Southern Rhodesian, a citizen of a British colony) and certainly not because he suspected anything funny going on. He had a young friend called Roy whom he had met in Blantyre and who occasionally visited him at the lake. When he did, the two shared Marsh's tent and neither of the young policemen would have thought this unusual or in any way smacking of immorality.

For Chrissakes, when they were on patrol together they might well have shared a tent themselves, and no one would have thought that unusual. Even the American army used the shelter-half system in which each man would carry half of a two-man tent! Taylor, after all, came from a country where racism was entirely unknown, if for no better reason than that there were very few black Irishmen. The same did not apply to Marsh. As a child before World War II in Salisbury, the capital city of Southern Rhodesia (later Rhodesia and then Zimbabwe), the blacks he encountered walking the streets were not even allowed to share the sidewalks with him. Certainly, this two-men-in-a-tent-business was hardly an argument, either. And, it certainly wasn't proof. That—or he was talking with two deviate policemen.

But, the constable persisted, "Of course he's queer. Everybody says so."

Well, maybe "everybody" was saying so, but none of the people who was smearing Taylor with these stories knew anything at all about him. In fact most had never laid a naked eyeball on him. "Crap," Marsh said to himself. "This was typical malicious gossip by a bunch of saber-tongued old mother hens. Everyone indeed!"

Although he had been looking forward to a night's stop at the Palm Beach, Marsh finished his drink and said his good-byes. He didn't want to listen to any more of this claptrap. He knew why John Taylor had been deported. It was because he had been a particularly long, festering thorn in the flank of the establishment. And, they had hung this other thing on him like the star on a Christmas tree to justify their action.

He drove through the night, a night spangled with sequins like a woman's formal evening dress, back to Blantyre. He had many good friends there, friends whose opinions he valued and respected. Yet, it came as a shock to him when he found that the rumor persisted. There was, however, an Asian medical doctor in Blantyre whom Marsh had gotten to know through Ricky and Rene Philip. In fact he had met him first at their beach cottage at Namasso Bay. As Taylor was also a good friend of the Philips and had often visited them at the lake, he thought the doctor might know something about Taylor. Marsh found the occasion to visit his rooms on some pretended medical matter so he could question him about Taylor.

"No, no, no," said the doctor shaking his bespectacled head. "I myself cannot believe that. Of course, you know, I had nothing to do with Mr. Taylor personally, so I cannot really speak for him, but for the Africans I can. I was brought up here, you know, and I speak their language just as they do, and of course I know their customs. For the bush African to indulge in, you know, ah, homosexual practices—never. It would be against their culture and their traditions and, of course, there is no reason for them to turn, ah, that way."

The doctor stirred his tea thoughtfully and poured a small streak of milk into it. "Homosexuality, you know, is really a product of civilization. To the bush African, sex is just an every-day thing, as it were. They start at an early age and they have absolutely no hang-ups about it. Perhaps among workers on the mines and in big cities, when they are parted from their families—perhaps. But in the bush? Positively no. I hope this answers your question?"

It was answer enough for Marsh. John *Pondoro* Taylor a homosexual! Taylor was a professional hunter and a living legend, not a mincing fairy!

CHAPTER ELEVEN

Taylor was deported from Nyasaland in December 1957, having been put on a plane for London by the British authorities. Prior to his departure from Aly Ndemanga Village, his last home in the relative wilds, he received a letter from a young Scot, Alexander Maitland. Maitland was a distant relation of the famed light-rifle hunter, Walter Dalrymple Maitland Bell, best known in the swirling mists of African hunting history as "Karamojo." Alexander Maitland had apparently inherited some of the kinsman's desire to be a big-game hunter—a desire that had probably made Bell the world's most famous elephant hunter and rifle field shot extraordinaire. The young Maitland wanted desperately to join John Taylor in Africa as an apprentice hunter. In that first of forty letters he penned to Maitland over the next eleven years, Taylor wrote, "I expect to be here through another week or possibly ten days, but nothing is certain, so don't leave it too late."

Taylor, at that point, had firm plans to get back to Africa as soon as he was able to raise the wherewithal. It seems apparent from subsequent letters that he looked upon Maitland as the financial springboard that could hurl him "home."

When he first pitched up in London, he moved in with old family friends, sisters Grace and Dorothy Dow, at Iverna Court in Kensington. The then middle-aged sisters were from Howth, near Dublin, and it was Grace who had accompanied John's mother when she had journeyed to Portuguese East Africa on that terrible trip of 1928 to rescue her malaria-stricken son from his camp along the Zambezi.

Although the young John Taylor was recovering from recurrent malaria and blackwater fever when his mother figuratively grabbed him by the ear and put him aboard ship for Ireland, he was apparently well enough to at least dabble in a shipboard romance with Grace. Knowing his preference for his own gender, it is most interesting that he and Grace even became engaged to be married before the boat reached Southampton! But, the betrothal was not to last for very long, seeming to dissolve into romantic ectoplasm shortly after the ship docked. Neither Grace nor Dorothy Dow ever married, but Grace held an affection for her old beau all her life and was protective of him right to the end. She even tried to talk him out of any thoughts of going back to that dreadful Zambezi.

As Taylor never returned to hunting after he was deported from Nyasaland, Maitland's plans to become a professional hunter under his tutelage fell flat also. According to Maitland, he and Taylor saw each other "fairly regularly though infrequently" during the ensuing eleven years, and they kept in contact by mail. Brian Marsh is mentioned in one of Taylor's letters to Maitland, but not by name. Maitland does recall Taylor talking about Brian. In a letter dated 11 June, 1958, Taylor wrote:

> In PEA and Nyasaland they had started serious professional croc-hunting shortly before I sailed for Australia. I met several of the hunters at that time from both territories, and whilst things were still good in Nyasaland, they had so thinned out the crocs in most parts of Portuguese East Nyasa [a P.E.A. Province] that they were quitting—the comparatively few survivors having become altogether too sly. When I was in Nyasaland shortly after returning to Africa and shortly before coming over here, I met a friend of mine who had been croc-hunting for several years on Lake Nyasa and he was quitting because he did not figure it was any longer a commercial proposition. He had quit some months before I left.

Knowing that he would not be readmitted to any of the British or Portuguese territories in Africa, Taylor was scheming to go to French Equatorial Africa—today's Central African Republic and formerly the French Congo—and travel up the Bahr Aouck River to Lake Mamun where there were reputed still to be substantial stocks of toothy elephant. To reach the lake, he proposed to travel up the river in light Canadian canoes of the same type used by Karamojo Bell in an earlier year. Taylor was generally scathing in his regard for most professional hunters, but he ranked Walter Bell as "the greatest elephant hunter of all time."

Karamojo explored and hunted along the then-virgin and completely unknown banks of the Bahr Aouck, an area so remote that few if any whites had ever been there. But Bell never did reach the lake, which is the river's source, and this was where Taylor wanted to go. Bell's account in his classic book, *The Wanderings of an Elephant Hunter* (1923, Country Life), of his search even to find the river makes daunting reading for the adventurer wanting to paddle in his wake:

A MAN CALLED LION

> To reach the watershed [he wrote] to which our mystery river belonged—
> if it existed at all—it was necessary to travel many hundreds of weary miles.
> First 500 miles against the current. Then a land portage of 80 miles. Then a
> descent with the current of 200 miles, and then an ascent again against the
> current of 450 miles.

That excursion over, it was only then that Bell's party finally poled their canoes into the river they sought. But Bell was diverted. He found the hunting so rich along the Bahr Aouck's fabled and untouched banks that both canoes were fully laden with ivory, rhino horn, and other trophies long before they reached the lake. They had little option but to turn around and return.

Bell's Canadian Peterborough canoes, the only kind that Taylor was interested in buying, were described by him as "the freight type," eighteen-feet-long and nearly four-feet-wide, and were able to float "an enormous amount of stuff" while the canoe itself only weighed 150 pounds. They were constructed of light spruce frames over which canvas was stretched. Apart from their extreme lightness they had the added advantage that they could be speedily repaired with patches and glue when inadvertently holed on submerged rocks and stumps. Bell claimed that they proved the cheapest form of transport he had ever used.

Taylor was also used to canoes, but his experience was with the heavy native dugouts of the Zambezi, which were hewn with adzes and fire from the straight trunks of huge trees. Even these cumbersome dugouts, in spite of their own weight, are capable of carrying incredible loads. Taylor wrote of his own "freight canoe" that was able to carry a three-ton load and eight polers, which he used to transport stores down the Zambezi from Tete to his trading store at Benga. Light spruce and canvas designs in a modern age, when polers, who took up valuable space, could be replaced by small outboard motors, offered not only cheap transport, but especially to Maitland, an extremely adventurous and exciting trip. He was bursting with unalloyed enthusiasm when he traveled from his home in Scotland to meet Taylor in London. There it was agreed that they join forces. Maitland had heard none of the rumors winging around Central Africa about Taylor's somewhat bizarre habits and, like Brian, would not have believed them if he had.

Taylor had arrived in London with very little money, only £200 in fact. It was immediately necessary for him to find a job before his belly met his backbone. It was left to Maitland, a tender seventeen-year-old at the time, to write off to inquire about the canoes. Maitland was also expected to finance the safari. Had the project come to fruition, certainly the way to go would have been to use canoes, but the entire Bahr Aouck project disappeared into smoke, much to Maitland's dismay, as did all of Taylor's plots and plans during the last years of his life. It was discovered that the elephant hunting permits for the region had been hamstrung by the authorities, only available on a sport-hunting basis, and very expensive at that.

Throughout the next few years, Taylor worked on other ideas of getting back to Africa, but they all came to nought. The cost of outfitting kept them a tantalizing dream. It is suspected but not confirmed that Taylor attempted to land an advisory position with Holland & Holland, Ltd., one of the top London gunmakers and the sort of establishment his commanding presence and good breeding might well have suited. His intimate knowledge of top-grade rifles and African hunting could have well served potential clients, but Taylor never disavowed his reputation as a poacher and renegade. A firm as steeped in rich tradition, like an old tea bag, as was Holland & Holland, could likely not be seen to support a man of Taylor's past misdeeds and supposed character. Not done, Old Boy.

Detractors of Taylor have used the fact that Holland & Holland would not employ him as proof that he was a fraud. If he knew so much about rifles and African hunting, how could any firm of gunmakers refuse to put him on the payroll? But, this is topspin logic. Taylor's reputation denied him access to many places and people where he might have otherwise been welcomed for his knowledge. As a result of his reputation as a poacher—and perhaps a few molecules concerning other matters had wafted over from Nyasaland—he was forced to accept menial work very much below his background and status.

Being a financial prisoner to his empty pockets and having to work a full day just to keep himself in a beggarly existence, Taylor was robbed of the leisure he might have used profitably at his well-loved and well-used Remington typewriter. He could have been creating the books he wanted to write, which he was well equipped to do. Presumably, he would have taken with him to London the incomplete manuscript of African witchcraft on which he had been working. It would not have been beyond the bounds of possibility, had he been able to complete it, that he could have succeeded sufficiently with his new book to make enough money to finance his trip back to Africa. There is no doubt that he would have been accepted back into Nyasaland with open arms when the country became independent Malawi. There, under the new government, his liberalism and his known affection for his black friends would surely have been seen as a positive, not a negative, factor in any decision.

But, alas, he was reduced to earning a hand-to-mouth pittance after leaving the Dows and setting up residency by himself. We can only surmise that he had exhausted all avenues of congenial employment and found all the doors bolted and locked against him when he finally took a position in London. We can also only assume that he took the best available job: that of a night watchman at a kennel, the Battersea Dogs Home. For those who admired him for his courage and extraordinary talents, this was truly a bitter twist in the hand of fate for The Last of the Ivory Hunters, The King of the Elephant Trails.

The cultural shock must have been enormous. Taylor's background, both before and during his time in Africa, had not equipped him for anything like this. Taylor had been born into the privileged class; he had servants to wait on him from the day he was born. Even immediately after the war, when a financial and physical derelict in Africa, he always had at least one servant, Aly Ndemanga. He regarded himself as a gentleman, lived as one, at least so far as his conduct was concerned (except of course when he was loaded), and was always treated as such.

To those who knew him, he kept up a cheerful front, but inside he was numbed with despair. He was spiritually crushed like a rotten *marula* fruit, and the desire to continue writing could no longer survive in the bleak mental landscape that had been formed from the desertification of his mind. In later years he wrote a few magazine articles, but his books were finished forever. Even the half-finished manuscript must have been discarded in a fit of melancholy.

He became cynical, at times moody and not talkative, and much of his income went for gin and whiskey, which alternately cheered and depressed him. Soon his eyesight began to weaken and his hearing fail, which often noticeably irritated him.

Taylor, however, prospered at the kennel. He was promoted to the dizzy post of Night Supervisor. His duties were little changed but it did entitle him to a small raise in pay. He smoked a pack of cigarettes a day, but after he finished paying for his meager groceries and his rent, there was not much left for luxuries.

Maitland describes the accommodation in which Taylor lived in London as a succession of cheap rooms in houses owned either by Irish or West Indian families, some reasonably clean and others fit to make a cockroach gag. His room was usually a bed-sitter, with a sink and a small gas cooker in one corner, and a bathroom on the landing of a walk-up, which was shared by the other tenants. Certainly his rooms were very different from what he had enjoyed in the bush, especially at Aly Ndemanga Village, his last home in Africa.

Taylor had owned no firearms at all during his last days in Nyasaland. Brian Marsh had found this surprising, as he could have augmented his fare considerably with what he could have shot in the veldt. There were game birds aplenty in the nearby forest: guinea fowl and several species of francolin, as well as kudu, bushbuck, warthog, clipspringer, and duiker roamed the bush-furred hills. Taylor obviously could not have afforded to buy a firearm then, but he told Brian that he had plans to buy a shotgun and a 7x57mm Mauser rifle, his favorite light caliber, and no doubt would have done so as soon as his books had started to pay. A man like Taylor would have lived well in the situation he had chosen . . . had he not been deported.

Shortly after his arrival in London—despite the fact that he professed to abhor East Africans with military ranks prefixing their names—Taylor contacted Captain C.R.S. Pitman, who was then living on Sloane Street. The former Uganda Chief Game Warden had made something of a name for himself with his own writings, *A Game Warden Among His Charges* and *A Game Warden Takes Stock*, and was a fairly powerful colonial figure in London. Pitman appears to have snubbed Taylor and certainly avoided him. Taylor's reputation as a poacher—Pitman's job in Uganda had been to catch poachers—as well as his aggressive liberalism in a still-conservative England caused many doors to be slammed on his figurative foot, and Pitman's was one of them. Taylor got his own back—not that anybody especially listened—by disparaging Pitman's writings. In a letter to Maitland he says, "I read several of his yarns in different magazines, and it seemed to me that he was overwriting, exaggerating, so as to squeeze the last drop of thrilling effect out of his descriptions."

A MAN CALLED LION

Concerning his poaching enterprises, Taylor boasted volubly in his autobiography about "The Great Tana Raid" of Kenya, devoting an entire chapter to it. We have spoken before of this escapade that Taylor referred to as "the largest, most highly organized, and most successful poaching spree that Africa has ever seen." Certainly, in the years when this was supposed to have taken place, poaching didn't have the same sort of stigma that it does now, poachers being thought of rather like romantic pirates of the Spanish Main. The general public looked upon it with more interest than abhorrence, never dreaming of the critical consequences that organized commercial poaching could have in the future, and perhaps more old hunters than not were guilty of some indiscretion in this area. Africa was wide open. They ran little risk, if any, of getting caught by a very thin line of enforcement officers. The Great Tana Raid as described by Taylor was not in the category of casual lawbreaking. It was an assault, mythical or not, planned with military precision and executed upon one of Kenya's great game reserves. A massive number of porters were supposed to have been employed and a huge amount of ivory and rhino horn was said by Taylor to have been poached.

Taylor reminisced with Brian Marsh about this "raid" with almost a schoolboy's pride. The raid was supposed to have taken place in 1936, when there were no four-wheel-drive vehicles or helicopters for pursuit, and Taylor openly ridiculed the efforts of the Kenya Game Department to catch him and his party. Taylor said he had catered for every emergency in his planning, and when a game ranger with a group of game scouts was observed and reported to be following them, Taylor sent out a decoy party and the pursuers were easily led off on the wrong tracks. The raid makes interesting if not very convincing reading. We have said before that we consider the logistics involved with the enterprise prohibitive. Perhaps there was some sort of raid into the Tana, but we very much doubt that it could have been on the grandiose scale that Taylor described.

Remarkably, for a hunter of such experience, Taylor's excuse for the raid was that he could see no reason nor justification for the colonial governments of Africa, whom he deplored, to manage their game by placing restrictions upon it. Was this simply his aversion to any sort of authority, particularly from white governments, or did he really believe such restrictions were unnecessary? Certainly, no thinking person even then would agree with him and support his view, and African history has proven just how wrong he was.

Uncontrolled poaching in many parts of Africa has put a number of species onto the endangered list and one of the problems that legitimate hunting must battle is the ignorance or reluctance of the general public to consider the obvious difference between poaching and licensed sport hunting, which is actually beneficial to game population management. This obvious difference is tantamount to referring to your local pharmacist as a "drug dealer" (which, of course, he is) or suggesting that a person who goes to a bank to cash a check is a bank robber because he has removed money.

Maitland commented to Brian Marsh that unlike outstanding hunter-naturalists, like C.H. Stigand, Blayney Percival, and F.C. Selous, Taylor's attitude to wildlife seemed almost exclusively to be that of a rifleman/hunter, rather than that of a conservationist/observer. This was an obvious gouge in the veneer of Taylor's "old pro" image, and one that is quite significant. His consuming interests associated with the profession were almost exclusively centered on fine-grade rifles and the hunting he could do with them, certainly not the prevalent passion of today where hunting is practiced more as a subset of the whole experience of "being there." So far as we know, Taylor of course knew the dialect names of the common birds, trees, and grasses, but he does not mention any interest in the natural history of the creatures about him in the bush.

For most professional hunters whom Brian and I have known, the wild places and all they contain are the overriding reason why they are professional hunters in the first place. Hunting itself, or at least the logical conclusion of a successful hunt, is the shooting of the prey animal and is only a justification for earning a living in these wonderful places. Yet for Taylor, it seems that his primary motivation was the hunting itself, the ability to cleanly kill an elephant or a buffalo with a best-quality, precision-made, perfectly-fitting double rifle as beautifully and lethally produced as any famous Samurai sword, rather than a profound appreciation of his surroundings.

Being in the wilds to him, it would seem, was only a means to that end. But, and let's be candid about it, the question still remains whether Taylor was drawn to Africa by the possibilities of hunting big game or those of an extended homosexual liaison with young Africans boys. It is hardly a secret that some adventurers of an earlier era journeyed into the interior primarily to seek the favors of native girls, whose charms were available at a time in recent history when those of the girls back home were not.

Taylor's lifestyle and his outspoken manner on many topics were unpopular at the time, and even now. They brought him many detractors and there are some that label him an out-and-out fraud. I had read all Taylor's books several times over the years before I met Brian Marsh, yet except for his hunting and shooting observations I knew little about the man himself, except that he died in London under tragic circumstances and that he was reputed to be somewhat odd. I knew from my reading that Taylor obviously, shall we say, embellished his stories. But, Brian is certain that he was no fraud, and in a taped conversation with Brian that led to this book, he makes the following comments when I asked him how genuine Taylor was:

Sure, Peter, there is no doubt about it. Taylor did think it necessary to "fly a few kites" and I know he certainly "flew" them, which was probably directed at keeping his reader's interest, but then so did other famous hunting authors—such as Marcus Daly. But, I've met enough people who knew Taylor, and some who have hunted with him, people who had no reason to exaggerate Taylor's hunting experience and ability, to be convinced that behind the Irish blarney there was a genuine experience and also deep knowledge. I have also spent considerable time with two Africans who worked for Taylor, Sampson Nyamhoka, his old gunbearer from before the war with whom I hunted for several months in Mozambique in 1957, and Samson Kazembi, Aly Ndemanga's brother-in-law and sidekick in the Lake Amaramba hippo-poaching episode, whom I spent some time with in Malawi in the late 1980s. Neither Sampson nor Samson had any reason to exaggerate about Taylor, yet both told me stories with sufficient sincerity about Taylor's hunting ability to convince me that they were true.

Brian is undoubtedly right. Nobody could come up with such technical data and practical experiences that Taylor wrote about without being a boffin on rifles and African hunting. John Dawkins had more opportunity to observe Taylor in the bush than any other white man, and his comment that "in every way he measured up to what I would have expected of an ivory hunter" is of obvious significance as Dawkins became a most proficient hunter in his own right. He made this comment many decades after he had first met and learned from Taylor, so it was not a case of a novice being awed by an "expert." The person described as "X" in Dawkins's letter, whose identity has been deliberately deleted, is an internationally known professional hunter who admitted meeting Taylor very briefly only once, in 1958, when he himself would have been a young man. One night at the dinner table of Brian and Jillie Marsh, at which this gentleman was a guest, the subject of Taylor came up.

"An absolute fraud!" he said immediately. "I met Taylor in London and as soon as he opened his mouth I knew that he knew nothing at all about firearms or hunting. I don't believe he shot more than a couple of elephant in his life. He got all his photographs to illustrate his first two books from Fletcher Jamieson, and it is quite obvious that he stole all Jamieson's work on ballistics. After all, didn't *African Rifles & Cartridges* come out the very year of Jamieson's death?"

Actually, this is a very good argument for the opposing view. If Jamieson died in September of 1947 and the book came out that same year, it would already have been long submitted and in the printing process. As an author I can assure you of this. In fact, Taylor seems to have gone to some trouble to get Samworth to inject the news of Fletcher's death when probably that part of the book had already been typeset and had to be rearranged. Jamieson did not die of a long illness. He was electrocuted when he went down a well to make a repair.

Even if Taylor had started the day Fletch died to completely "steal" Jamieson's ballistic work, he could not possibly have gotten the book edited, typeset, and published in the same year—let alone in the last three months of the same year. Just consider alone the delays in the international mails of that year, 1947, and you'll realize the absurdity of "X"'s accusations.

Brian Marsh is an old friend of the Jamieson family and he confirms, through explicit questioning of Fletcher's widow, Joan, and his brother, Norman, also a most knowledgeable rifleman on such subjects, that Fletcher did not produce any work on ballistics. Norman was emphatic, in fact, that Fletcher's interest in ballistics did not extend beyond the few particular rifles that he owned, and if Norman could have attacked Taylor on any front—

he considered him a cheat and a brigand because of the £50
debt—he would have done so. There is no doubt that Taylor
embellished his adventures, none at all. However, equally certain, on the positive side of the equation, is that his ballistics
investigations leading to his printed conclusions and the research
and premises that produced his "Knockout Value" tables were his
own and nobody else's.

Toward the end of 1958, Taylor was again taken with the
idea of marriage. We don't mean to be cynical, but it does appear
this was more for financial reasons than any other . . . although
Alexander Maitland insists that no matter how bad Taylor's life
was during his years in London Taylor would not have married
for money. To back up his claim that Taylor was simply not that
bad off, Maitland states that Taylor received a bit from his royalties—enough even to be able to buy a moped. Maitland further
suggests that Taylor was looking for nothing more than companionship. Be that as it may, the whole approach by both parties
was hardly an example of classic romantic love in which boy
meets girl, ad nauseam. Taylor had set his sights on her even
before they met. A friend told him that a young Jamaican with
whom he was acquainted had expressed the sentiment that she
would like to marry a white man. Taylor wrote of his intentions
to Alexander Maitland.

> You may be interested to hear that I am hoping to marry a very lovely
> West Indian girl from Jamaica—though it is just possible that she may feel I'm
> a mite too old. We'll see. But it is strange how these things work out: You
> must know my feelings about Negroes and I have always known that the only
> woman I could marry must either be full Negro or at least have a lot of Negro
> blood in her, and here is this girl who says that all her life she has known that
> she could only marry a white man. I heard that from a mutual friend before
> I met her and immediately asked him to arrange a meeting. She is a very
> clever girl employed in some government scientific research department—one
> of those with security guards on duty both day and night. We have become
> very friendly and all who have met her are enamored of her beauty and her
> quiet way. So am I. . . . But this in no way detracts from my wish to return
> to my beloved Africa.

The marriage never took place.

On several occasions in his writings, Taylor firmly states that
he never interfered with native women, roundly condemning the
white man who did on the grounds that such practices always caused
friction. The bush African does not object to a white man marry-

ing one of their women, but he does object to the unfair competition when it comes to casual affairs with the local village belles. Just look what happened to that Portuguese hunter, mentioned earlier, when he didn't treat his "camp girl" properly! A white man does not need much to be considered "rich" in the African bush, and Taylor would have been easily able to inveigle favors in exchange for small gifts—gifts that would have been well beyond the means of most young African men.

In his novel, *Shadows of Shame*, Taylor tells of a half-breed woman (the mother of the twins that "Jack," the hero—of course—adopts) who was free with her favors, especially to "Bwana Jack." Is there a biographical connection with Taylor's own life and that of this character? Who knows? The male bush-African tribesman, whose very way of life depends for its survival on the cooperative labors of an adequate woman, cannot choose a wife for her beauty. He picks her strictly for practical reasons and looks for somebody who will fit snugly into his customary scheme of things, so he would not tend to marry anybody out of the ordinary, such as a half-breed woman.

Brian and I are not playing at being amateur social anthropologists when we observe that a "colored" woman, which is the African term for someone of mixed blood, usually cannot get married under tribal bush conditions. She might also have a problem if she is not of mixed blood but happens to be an incredible beauty. She may be far too handsome for a husband to want to take the trouble of keeping other men away, dooming her to a single life, which is truly a doomed condition in the African bush. The usual course of existence for a female colored under tribal conditions is that of prostitution, for she must grant favors to eat if she doesn't have a husband. It's a tough life out there!

There were many shades of color represented in the old Mozambique, these people being the offspring of careless and carefree white fathers who produced half-breed children they never thought of again. Certainly, such a conservative, traditional establishment figure as Fred Selous, whose father was Chairman of the London Stock Exchange, made no bones about his colored children and several of his offspring live today in Zimbabwe and have kept Selous's surname, of which they are proud.

Since he considered marriage twice that we know of, it is highly likely that Taylor was bisexual rather than homosexual and it is indeed possible that he may have consorted with native women, especially when he first arrived in Africa. Brian even went to a psychologist to research if this was a feasible premise. The opinion of this professional was that Taylor may have been heterosexual until initiated into homosexual rites of the Sena tribe with whom he lived for a time. Granted, homosexuality is hardly common among Africans, rural tribesmen in particular, but it would seem that the Senas do have a drift this way.

Perhaps the best person to explain to the reader the sexual intricacies of Sena culture would be John Taylor himself. The following paragraph appears in his erotic novel, *Shadows of Shame*. The person speaking is "Dumba," an African Sena tribesman who, by the strangest coincidences, just happens to be "Bwana Jack's" adopted son:

> Listen! We Africans never sleep alone if we can possibly help it. If we have no women then inevitably, since we are strong and healthy and full of vitality, the pressure mounts up until it begins to interfere with our thoughts and our sleep. When this happens we relieve it—alone if we are alone—or for each other if we are two together. We thereupon put it out of our minds until the pressure again mounts unduly. We do not indulge just because it is pleasant, we do not make an orgy of it. We take pride in our bodies and like to have them fit and ready for anything at all times. We like to have our eyes bright just as we like to have our teeth white and clean. This applies to practically all African tribes, but we of the Asena go just a little bit further. It is a recognized custom of ours to invite a stranger who has just joined us to come and share our sleeping-mat and indulge in this small and harmless operation in order to remove any feeling of being outside our circle. In the same way if one of us has been away for a period, perhaps working elsewhere, then when he returns he will as a matter of course sleep with one or more of us so that this little indulgence will bring him right back into the same intimacy as he shared previously. Otherwise he might take weeks to regain the same footing as he had before. You will see from this that we can only regard it as fantastically narrow and ignorant to describe as "vicious" a custom that is the very basis of which is friendship and affection. But just because we indulge in this manner on occasions it most certainly does not mean that we are homosexual in preference to heterosexual.

Clearly, this is John Taylor himself speaking through Dumba, and it is, perhaps, his explanation of why he was the way he was.

* * * * * * *

Taylor left the kennel position as night supervisor to take a post as a security guard elsewhere. The job fell through, however. Taylor said that he didn't like working inside anyway, but this might have been sour grapes, considering London winters. The last job of his life was that of a park keeper at Clapham Common in South London. It was menial in the extreme, but at least he was out in the open air. According to Maitland, Taylor was less concerned by the low pay than by the restrictions on his time—feeling that he would miss seeing his friends and couldn't return their hospitality if he were chained to a job with restrictive hours.

By then, Taylor had resigned himself to the fact that he would never again see Africa. Photos of the period reveal that although only a few years had elapsed since he had left Africa and its relatively healthy life, the bronzed and virile fifty-three-year-old whom Brian had known was already becoming an old man. His face had become prematurely pouchy and his body, once hardened by elephant hunting on foot, had become white and flabby. He looked years older than he was. The London weather certainly did not agree with him. In 1961, he came down with his first attack of bronchial pneumonia.

Taylor, at this time, in spite of his bluff exterior, showed that he had grown insecure and sensitive. He felt dejected and rejected if Maitland or Sammy Wong, a Chinese acquaintance from Mozambique who was then living in London, failed to keep regular contact, and he would write complaining letters to them. He wanted people to like him and went to great pains to make friends with the children who came to the park. Once, when a small girl fell on a broken bottle and cut herself, the sympathetic park keeper located a medical box and expertly dressed and bandaged her wound. This job, although more congenial than the others he had, was never more than a tedious means of keeping himself alive. From time to time, it allowed him to renew his old acquaintance with Mr. Walker. Nevertheless, it lacked any sort of stimulus or challenge that the old hunting life had given him.

He came to spend most of his time in the fantasy world of escape. He would tramp again the African veldt, hunting elephant once more with a fine Rigby or Wilkes in his brown, tsetse-bitten hands and sit yarning with Aly and his old team of trackers round a leadwood fire that flew bright exclamation points of spark into the black Mozambique night each time he nudged a burning log with his old sandal tips. He could smell the roasting eland steaks with their rim of yellow fat and could still taste the pungency of *tshwala*, African beer, clinging to the back of his throat. But he met few people with whom he could communicate in real life. The other park keepers, mostly cockneys, often stopped by for a chat while they smoked their Players, Craven A, or Gold Leaf cigarettes. He knew that if he told them he was once a famous elephant hunter and the author of five books, they would have laughed at him. "Sure you 'ave, Guv. An' I'm Bonnie Prince Charlie."

One day, as he was chatting away to himself in Chinyanja, as had become his habit, an elderly lady crossing the park stopped to ask him a simple question. He replied respectfully, but so far away were his thoughts that they would have needed a passport. He answered in Chinyanja. The good woman recoiled and threatened to report him, believing he was swearing at her. When he told the story later to Maitland, he laughed, saying he had been accosted by "some terrible female creature."

His eldest brother, Bill, had died, and he had grown apart from his sister, who was also living in London. Taylor then assumed his father's title (a knighthood and the use of the title "Sir" is not hereditary) and started calling himself "Sir John," which became a supporting pillar of the lofty, pink dome of his fantasy world. To his various landlords, and he had many, he became something of an enigma: an apparently titled, completely impoverished park keeper who was sometimes visited by some extremely "different" characters all of whom came to speak of such nonsense things as rifles and hunting and elephants.

As time passed and reality became a lost inconvenience to "Bwana Jack," he began telling his few friends about his regular visits to his old haunts via astral travel, claiming the ability to leave his body and to float off anywhere he wanted. He told Maitland that he frequently went to visit Aly at Mwambwajila village and once had to "dematerialize" because a child recognized him, ran toward him, and would have run into the side of the hut he was standing next to if he hadn't dematerialized. Taylor was clearly afraid that the child would hurt himself. It is interesting to note that Taylor truly believed that if he hadn't dematerialized then the child would have been seriously injured. This was not a case of Mr. Walker talking, but of fervent beliefs.

PETER HATHAWAY CAPSTICK

In *Shadows of Shame*, written in Australia in the middle 1950s, as might be expected the character "Bwana Jack," the amiable professional hunter, was a practicing Rosicrucian. At the village where Taylor was living in Nyasaland, Brian also noticed that he was a Rosicrucian by the books he saw lying around. Brian didn't pay too much attention at the time, but Taylor was a great believer in the Rosicrucian doctrine, something which, no doubt about it, helped to sustain him during his years of misery in London. Taylor also had a great belief in extrasensory perception. He and Brian had had some discussions on the subject of thought transferal or the passing of information from one mind to another through the medium of concentration. Well, if the incident with the emerald-spotted wood dove is any example, perhaps Taylor was on to something!

Taylor believed that he could force any stranger to turn around to look at him simply by concentrating his thoughts upon that person. It would seem that a number of people can do this and, as an extension, Taylor claimed that it was the greatest folly when hunting to concentrate one's thoughts on the animal being stalked, which he maintained was the greatest reason for the failure of inexperienced hunters. Today, I think we would say that the animal "got your vibes." Both Brian and I firmly believe Taylor was correct in this. We have noticed that an animal has a nervous reaction when someone stares at it hard. We're ex-professional hunters with many decades of experience between us. We've seen it too often not to believe it.

Taylor was also a firm believer in the "sixth sense" and often wrote about it. He claimed that he had been so frequently alerted to danger he could neither see nor hear nor smell, that he came to rely on this sixth sense completely. When his hackles went up, he acted in whatever way the sense "told" him. That he died in London rather than in the dangerous African bush hunting elephant, buffalo, and lion shows that his primitive instincts were pretty sharp.

But, Taylor wasn't the only great hunter who claimed this sense of warning. Jim Corbett, the notable hunter of Indian man-eating tigers and leopards and the author of such books as *Man-Eaters of Kumaon and Jungle Lore*, also placed great stock in this warning device. He maintained that he often received alerts that he was being followed, watched, or stalked by man-eaters. The spoor invariably proved him correct. Commenting on this, Corbett said:

A MAN CALLED LION

I have made mention elsewhere of the sense that warns us of impending danger, and will not labor the subject further beyond stating that this sense is a very real one and that I do not know, and therefore cannot explain, what brings it into operation. On this occasion I had neither heard nor seen the tigress, nor had I received any indication from bird or beast of her presence, and yet I knew, without a shadow of doubt, that she was lying up for me among the rocks.

She was, too!

Taylor tells of being alerted to danger in a similar manner in a number of pages of *Maneaters and Marauders*, remarking that this remarkable facility is available to anybody who uses it and has faith in it. The American philosopher, Napoleon Hill, concurs. He wrote in his book, *Think and Grow Rich*:

> The fact remains that human beings do receive accurate knowledge through sources other than the physical senses. Such knowledge, generally, is received when the mind is under the influence of extraordinary stimulation. Any emergency that arouses the emotions, and causes the heart to beat more rapidly than normal may, and generally does, bring the sixth sense into action.

Taylor also, perhaps because of absorbing the superstitious beliefs of the tribesmen he lived among, believed that "supernatural" happenings were a part of everyday life in Africa, which is why Brian and I believe that his unfinished book on African witchcraft would have been so interesting. Corbett, to call on him again, had a very weird experience one night in the Himalayan foothills of northern India that certainly smacked of the supernatural. Being pragmatic (rather than phlegmatic), he simply commented that he must have been mistaken. He tells of having heard the death screams of a dead man, a man who had been killed a few days previously by a man-eating tigress. The village, to add to the eerie scene, was now completely deserted:

> It is best to assume that neither the karker [the Indian barking deer, often spelled karkor], the sambhar [the Indian red deer], nor I heard those very real screams—the screams of a human being in mortal agony.

Corbett was ensconced in a *machan*, a tree-platform for hunting, over a bait he had put out where the man was killed, and when "the moon had been up for over two hours," he heard a repetition of the dead man's screams that turned his stomach to icy putty. However, a thorough investigation by Colonel Jim convinced him that these unmistakable human screams could not have come from any earthly source. They were not imagined, as both a sambhar and a karker reacted violently to them. There is probably no logical conclusion to be drawn from this spooky incident, but it should be remembered that Jim Corbett was an absolute ace at identifying jungle sounds and much of his hunting of the man-eaters of Kumaon was directed by what he heard and correctly interpreted.

This brings to mind that Africa also generates her share of human screams. Perhaps before going into Taylor's weird parapsychological experience with them, we had best explain about Nyasaland's *lintumbu*, the red soldier ants, and tell a few stories to get you in the mood. . . .

A marauding horde of these terrible insects, when they have decided to go on the march, is under normal conditions generally welcomed by housewives, both European suburban and rural African ones. The ants will tooth comb all the nooks and crannies of a house or hut and will only depart after all the rats, cockroaches, and other inhabitants of the pantry, storeroom, or thatch have been removed and eaten. *Lintumbu* have excellent appetites. Should the householder happen to be away when visited by this swarm of formic-acid-smelling jaws, the chicken runs will only contain feathers and raw bones. There will certainly only be the well-cleaned bones of any pets that were left shut in the house. These large, vicious ants are deterred by nothing and will attack anything and everything that moves. They are not quite as numerous as the classic short story *Leningen and the Ants* might have us believe. Man cannot fight them, but they are not dangerous when a person is not incapacitated and can retreat. When he can't, however. . . .

There were a couple well-documented attacks of macabre interest around the time that Brian was in Nyasaland and too well-discussed to have been fiction. One was about a newcomer from England who had left her infant momentarily in the garden of her home while she went indoors. In her absence, a swarm of *lintumbu* swept through. Finding the baby carriage, the ants immediately blanketed the infant. Upon coming back outside, the frantic mother rushed to her child, but she could neither brush nor pull off enough ants before they swarmed, biting, into the child's open, screaming mouth. The child choked and died.

Another attack involved a nighttime traveler who managed to roll his pickup over on a dirt road one night, pinning his

A MAN CALLED LION

African servant by the leg when he was thrown out of the vehicle. Unable to release him unaided, the white man ran back along the road to a village he had passed not long before to get help. You guessed it. The sight that met his eyes on his return was more than gruesome. Few men could have died a more horrible death.

Sea stories? Well, let us tell you of an incredible one that happened to Taylor. When he was an invalid in 1944 in Zomba, the then-capital of Nyasaland and the headquarters of the King's African Rifles, he was befriended by another new arrival, a young officer also recovering from war wounds. The soldier sought Taylor's friendship because of his reputation as a hunter. The young man's family owned land in England and he had been brought up in the sporting tradition. He intended staying in Africa after the war to do some big-game hunting. Meeting Taylor was an unexpected bonanza. Taylor greatly enjoyed taking him for walks around Zomba Mountain. The town stood below. Here Taylor taught him the stalking and hunting craft.

The Mulunguzi River, fed by icy springs high up on the Zomba Plateau, giggles and chortles in liquid glee down the mountain and smack through the town. Before the war, the fly-fishing fraternity of English civil servants had stocked the upper reaches with rainbow trout fingerlings, now thriving as sleek slabs of mango pink and silver. The young man managed to borrow some equipment and a greenheart rod and persuaded Taylor to climb the mountain with him one weekend to tickle a March brown or a gold-ribbed hare's ear in the bright current.

They took groundsheets and warm clothes and proposed to camp for the night, but Taylor, not well recovered yet from his dose of Japanese lead, found the long hike too arduous. He therefore gave his new pal some cautious advice to where and how to spend the night. Then Taylor turned around and came back down.

His friend was an officer with considerable combat experience and although still recuperating, was certainly capable of looking after himself. The Zomba region was fairly well settled since the time of Lyell and Stigand. There was little dangerous game about, but as there were bushbuck and duiker on the slopes— as Taylor had noted from the spoor—he warned that there might very well be leopards. He advised his friend to keep a fire going all night. What he did not know and could therefore not mention, was that there were a number of *lintumbu* colonies in the heights, probably hungry ones at that.

Taylor admitted, when he told this story to Brian at Aly Ndemanga Village, that he had been drinking quite heavily at that time. Professional hunter Sydney Downey, later immortalized as the Downey of Ker and Downey Safaris of Nairobi, got to know Taylor at this time and confirmed that he "always appeared to be drunk." That particular evening, feeling especially tired after his long walk, Taylor had several whiskeys at the club and opened a bottle at his billet before hitting the hay. He slept very heavily, but at some time during the night was awakened by a vivid nightmare.

He found himself sitting on the edge of his cot shouting, "Jump in the stream, man! Jump in the stream!"

Taylor had no recollection of the nightmare and the shouts had no meaning. Nightmares at this time were not unusual for him although he normally remembered them exactly. He lay down and went back to sleep with a mental shrug. The next day, a bedraggled and red-eyed fellow returned from the mountain. He had caught no trout but he did have a fascinating and scary tale to tell—of that there is no doubt. . . .

The young officer made his camp in the forest on top of the plateau next to the Mulunguzi and, after gathering enough dry firewood to last the night, lit a fire. He ate a meal from his rations and, after a few pulls from his hip flask, he placed his Webley service revolver next to his head, rolled up in his groundsheet and began pondering the bright diamond chips of eternity above him.

His fire, sighing and sizzling occasionally, slowly burned down to a glow of embers, and the young officer finally dropped off to sleep. Then he was jerked awake in the cold dark by a sudden wave of *lintumbu* ants, which instantly swarmed over his head and hands, biting hard. They had come up from his feet inside his groundsheet and his clothes were already smothered in them—a crawling, heaving, biting, softly-buzzing mass that felt as if he were being touched with handfuls of flaring match heads. Quickly, they reached his head and found an easy way inside his shirt. Streaming in, they began to rip tiny pieces of his living flesh with their mandibles, while he rolled around in complete panic, screaming his anguish into the blackness as he beat and tore at his clothes, now saturated with his unknown and incomprehensible attackers. Perhaps it was in this brief second that his thoughts may have flashed to Taylor, his much-admired mentor, who was supposed to warn him of such things as *lintumbu*.

He realized in a flash that if he didn't get a grip on himself, he was a dead man. Fighting down his pain and panic, he forced himself to think. His salvation was obvious: He threw himself into the icy water, tearing off his clothes and pinching off the savage insects, which even continued to bite underwater, many leaving their heads with jaws locked in his meat.

Finally, the biting stopped as the last of the ants drowned and the frustrated army quickly left the camp area in search of a baby bushbuck or a careless ground-roosting bird. Cautiously, the young officer, shivering, climbed from the numbing water and revived his fire, using his pocket knife to prize away the remaining heads and jaws of the dead ants. It would be a long and astonishingly cold night.

Taylor had no way of knowing if he had awakened shouting at the exact moment of the *lintumbu* assault on the young man, but Taylor was quite convinced that he had. After all, he maintained, why else would he wake up shouting, "Jump in the stream, man! Jump in the stream!" He in no way thought that the incident smacked of the supernatural. Taylor felt it would be more unusual if people did not communicate by thought waves as he believed animals and birds did. That most humans had let this primitive sense lapse didn't in any way mean that the vestiges of this latent talent had disappeared. Stranger things by far have happened. . . .

* * * * * * *

If Taylor was more interested in mysticism and the hidden faculties of the human mind than in studying the marvels and hidden secrets of the African bush, this was not the case with Aly Ndemanga. For Aly, every tree, plant, fern, and flower were known to him and if any had medical properties, he made it his business to be aware of it. Later in his life, Aly became a *sing'anga*, a traditional healer, which he thought would give him a better and more profitable way of life than that of a peasant farmer.

The word *sing'anga* describes a traditional healer who uses herbs, bark, roots, and such for healing and should not be confused with *ng'anga*, which defines a witch doctor. The latter proscribes and prescribes by "throwing bones" and either cures or causes curses, whether psychosomatically or actually, depending on one's viewpoint.

That there are quite a few herbalists doing reportedly fine work in Western white cultures should be remembered when considering that being a *sing'anga* is a true and licensed calling in many African countries. Jillie Marsh's cook in Zimbabwe, also a Yao, was licensed as a herbalist many years ago by the white Rhodesian government then in power. Aly was licensed to practice by the Malawi government. A photo of his certificate to operate as a *sing'anga* is shown in the photo section. Although somewhat trapped by the hereditary poverty of the African tribal farmer, Aly somewhat bettered his lot by his practice of herbalism.

While Taylor was in London, living his life on a figurative bed of nails, he kept in touch with Aly by means of letters written in Chinyanja. Aly was illiterate, as were most Africans of his place and time, although he could probably pick out a few phrases in the Koran by familiarity. When he would get a letter from John, he would have it read to him by the village scribe who would also write down Aly's reply. One year, Aly wrote that there had been a horrendous drought and that his crops had failed. When the crops failed, Aly's herbalist practice failed, since his patients had no money to pay him. In spite of being broke himself, Taylor went to his bank manager—what we would call in America his friendly loan officer—and put the hard bite on him for a £100 loan, which he sent to Aly.

Obviously Taylor was no fair-weather friend. He must have had a hell of a time repaying the money with interest, but he never forgot that when he was down and out just after the war Aly worked for him without pay for three years. He regarded the bond that he had mentioned to Ivor Jones, one of the hunting party he had met on the Northern Rhodesian border when on safari with the Australian, John Dawkins, as sacred. When times were good, he looked out for the black people, and when the reverse happened, they looked out for him.

Taylor was outspokenly critical of the disparity between African and white farmers in colonial Africa. A seasonal drought affected the white farmers very little. They had sophisticated government measures such as financial support, whereas the black agriculturist couldn't get government loans or other help to see him through disastrous times. The African peasant farmer, who grew only enough to feed his family and with a bit left over to trade for his very basic needs, couldn't dial the agricultural equivalent of "911" and scream for help. In spite of Aly being a *sing'anga*, he and his family were primarily peasant farmers, tied to a peasant farming economy. That was pretty well that.

Perhaps Taylor's comment about the "bell" ringing and all your problems being solved, all your life memberships canceled, rang true as far as Aly was concerned. A staunch Muslim, Aly didn't drink alcohol and we know he didn't smoke. All his life he was in top condition, well-muscled and apparently healthy, but he didn't even outlive his adoptive father, John Taylor, in terms of years. Taylor beat him by a full seven years and a bit. Aly died at the age of fifty-eight and Taylor died at sixty-five.

From the symptoms described to Brian by Kandulu, Aly's elder brother, it seems that Aly suffered a heart attack, probably a coronary occlusion, quite an unusual death for a teetotaling, bush African of only fifty-eight years, living a simple, healthy life, unencumbered by thoughts of taxes, nuclear wars, or cholesterol. Tribal Africans during that period didn't pay any special attention to their dates of birth. Death after a life of accomplishments was what was celebrated, and still is. Pressed, they would say that they were born the year the bridge was built, or the last time locusts came, or marking their beginnings by some such other singular natural phenomenon.

We concluded that Aly was fifty-eight years old when he died by Taylor's remark that Aly had been born around 1925. In the latter part of 1982, Aly began to complain of severe chest pains and a strange tingling sensation down his arms into his fingers. He squeaked by this first probable heart attack by treating himself but was stricken again in April of 1983. While Kandulu was trying to arrange a vehicle to take his brother to the hospital, Aly collapsed and died.

Aly probably never considered that there were photographs of himself roosting in bookcases of trophy rooms all over the world, and surely many people who have read Taylor's works must have wondered who this bush African was who had two books dedicated to him by a well-known white author. Taylor gave Aly inscribed copies of all his books, which would be priceless collectors' items today. This was confirmed by Kandulu when Brian showed him his own copies.

"Yes," he commented as he paged through them. "I remember them. Aly had them all."

The books, and many other relics of their years and lives together, were stored in a wooden box in Aly's pole and thatch hut. One dark night–a very dark night indeed–one of Aly's children knocked over a kerosene lamp, and that was the end of that. . . .

Aly is buried in the village graveyard at Mwambwajila, beneath a low mound set with an ordinary stone border in a grove of *brachystegia* trees, only a short walk from the humble hut where he and his wife had lived. Formally, it was unmarked. It was but one of twenty or so in which rested other members of the Ndemanga family whose bells had also rung.

Had Taylor been able to live out his life in Africa, it is possible that neither he nor Aly would have died prematurely. Being the son of a knighted and famous doctor, Taylor might have recognized the seriousness of Aly's first heart attack and insisted that he be taken immediately to the hospital.

As for Taylor himself, his exile in London was quite literally a death sentence. Taylor's last years were indeed unhappy–perhaps tragic is a better word. He had no goal to strive for or to keep his failing mind active. Had he not had to keep packs of financial hyenas from his door, writing might have provided the outlet he needed. Instead, he was sucked deeper and deeper into his weird fantasy world of astral projection and flying visits to Aly. He had become an outcast to his own class of people with whom he shared a birthright. To many members of his own race, he became a pariah because of his outspoken views. He lived poorly and fed himself poorly, most of what he had left over going for cigarettes and *wampo* (booze). He had nothing left to live for. He was reduced to a burnt-out shell in health and spirit, and an English winter finally killed him.

John Howard *Pondoro* Taylor died in the London that had become his hated prison on March 31, 1969, from "an acute flare of chronic bronchitis." He was sixty-five years old, still five years short of his three-score-and-ten. He looked eighty. The body, which was once so hard and clean, was incinerated at Lambeth Crematorium and his ashes, together with his eight-day gold pocket watch and £35 sterling, all his worldly possessions, were sent to Aly Ndemanga, his adopted son, by Alexander Maitland.

Col. Sir William Taylor, John's father.

John Taylor in 1921, probably just before he was jailed by the Sinn Fein. (Charles M. Taylor, M.D.)

John Taylor in exile from Ireland in 1925, just after he had been court-martiale
by the British South Africa Police (BSAP) for the unauthorized release of
prisoner. (Charles M. Taylor, MD)

much more rakish John Taylor in his tweeds and plus-fours in Ireland in 1929. riously, the pipe he holds in his right hand seems to be missing the mouth-ce. (Charles M. Taylor, MD)

Taylor's Uncle John, for whom the hunter was named. Uncle John was ranchi
in southern Africa at the time that his nephew first went there. (Charles
Taylor, MD)

This picture is thought to be of Saduku, John Taylor's gunbearer before Wo
War II. Note his spears, headband, necklaces, and what appear to be t
carved ceremonial drums. Circa 1938. (Mrs. C. Fletcher Jamieson)

Aly Ndemanga as a youth, about 1942 at age 17. Taylor always spelled his adopted son's name "Aly" but it is more likely that it was properly "Ali" and one reprint of a Taylor book has changed the name to "Ali." (Mrs. Aly Ndemanga)

Aly Ndemanga's certificate proclaiming him to be a Malawian government approved *sing'anga* or herbalist. The right-hand document is his tax receipt for 1982, probably for the levy on his hut. (Brian Marsh)

John Taylor and Ivor Jones, who met on the John Dawkins hunt in Nyasaland.

Fletch Jamieson with a Cape buffalo. He is not posing with the .500 Jeffe
Rimless magazine rifle, but with a double, so this shot must have been tak
before he acquired his very rare Jeffery version of the 12.5x70mm Schul
probably taken early 1930s. (C. Fletcher Jamieson)

Fletch with a croc of about nine feet. Crocs require a perfectly-placed sho
"anchor" them, the best being the brain. (C. Fletcher Jamieson)

etch with his gunbearer and a very fine bull Livingstone's eland, again ken with a double. He probably holds the long spear for effect. (C. Fletcher mieson)

etcher Jamieson with a trophy black rhino. The vertical line down the nimal's side seems to be a mark for a skinner, which would correspond with e proper place to cut for a modern shoulder mount. (C. Fletcher Jamieson)

Camels at Tete in Mozambique in 1904, the year John Taylor was born. Tete the oldest town in Africa south of the Equator, and was originally a slavin center. (The National Archives of Zimbabwe.)

Telegraphic Address: "SCHOTS TETE."
Codes:
A.B C. 5th and 6th Editions.
Mosse.
P.O. Box 52 Tete.

❈

TETE HOTEL
(Paul Schots)

SUPPLY STORES
BAR
GARAGE

❈

ENGLISH   TETE (Zambesi),
SPOKEN.   P.E.A.

The front of a brochure adve
tising the Tete Hotel, the lair
Herr Paul Schots, erstwhile n
tionalist.

hn Taylor with Aly Ndemanga and an unidentified crew member of John
ylor's team (Rt.) in 1953. The animal is a roan antelope and Taylor is wearing
s idea of normal Muslim dress, obvious by the turban. (John Dawkins)

hn Taylor (far right) and Aly Ndemenga (center right) with the elephant
ached just across the border from Nyasaland in Northern Rhodesia in 1953
an unwitting John Dawkins. (John Dawkins)

Aly Ndemanga and John Taylor with a Chevrolet belonging to John Dawki[n]
the Australian sportsman and author who went hunting with Aly and John
1952-1953. Yep. Same shirt. The rifles are Dawkins's. (John Dawkins)

Rene and Ricky Philip, two of John Taylor's rare white friends, at Mlan[j]
Mozambique, in 1959. (Brian Marsh)

rian with his crew hunting crocodiles professionally before he met John Taylor. The canoes are interesting—not that the croc's Ipana smile isn't—as they were made with edges that curved over the top, for the reason that the waves n Lake Nyasa (now Lake Malawi) got very high. (Brian Marsh)

Brian Marsh's 1957 Mozambique Tete hunting license, acquired on the Irishman's advice at the time he first met Taylor through Ricky and Rene Philip. (Brian Marsh)

A member of the extraordinary vaDoma people who may very well have been responsible for Taylor's incredible experiences at "Ghost Bushman Hill." (The *Herald*, Harare, Zimbabwe)

The dreaded Chirambakadoma Mountain with the flat top. This is a feared and revered place as was John Taylor's Ghost Bushman Hill. The vaDoma also lived here and may have a great deal to do with the haunted and evil reputation of the place. (Brian Marsh)

John Taylor four years before his death, at about age 61 in this picture. His three-piece suit belies his terrible circumstances. (Alexander Maitland)

ompare this photo with the previous one taken only four years earlier and you an see what London did to John Taylor. (Mrs. Aly Ndemanga)

A photo of Aly's brother, Kandulu. Aly and Kandulu looked so much alike they were usually taken for identical twins; however, Kandulu was older and outlived Aly. (Brian Marsh)

Kandulu posing at the bridge over the Mandimba River where many years before, two old lions met each other; one *Pondoro* Taylor and the other the bush pig-eating old male who lived on the hill behind Aly's home at Mwambwajila village. The remains of these two old Africans, Taylor and his namesake, probably rest within a mile of each other. (Brian Marsh)

e memorial tablet in place on the joint grave of Aly Ndemanga and John ylor. The people are members of Aly's family and clan. (Brian Marsh)

emorial plaque with (left to right) Kandulu, Aly's brother, Aly Ndemanga's dow, Arina, and Aly's son, James Ndemanga. (Brian Marsh)

Brian Marsh (left) and Peter Hathaway Capstick, old friends and profession
hunters with strangely parallel careers.

A MAN CALLED LION

And so, "The Last of the Ivory Hunters" came back to be with his chosen family in his beloved Africa. John Taylor had been born too late to live the life he would have chosen, hunting in the days when elephants were unrestricted in Africa, and born too early to profit from the books he had written on his well-loved Remington in the heart of the bush and on the banks of the dark-bright, mighty Zambezi. He had become a prisoner of his own times, trapped between yesterday and tomorrow.

Perhaps Alexander Maitland said it best when he remarked to Brian Marsh, "There were very few before him, and most certainly, there will never be another like him."

CHAPTER TWELVE

Brian Marsh did not go back to crocodile hunting again. Being in the right place at the right time and with the right sort of experience, he was awarded the game management rights on the half-million acres of snagged, thorn-fanged mopane wilderness that is Nuanetsi Ranch. The ranch is in the heart of the Rhodesian Lowveldt, and Brian's job was cropping excess animals on a sustained-yield basis, the same basis that is the keystone of the modern conservation theory of utilization of renewable natural resources. Brian had very large quotas of both elephant and buffalo, as well as lesser game. He sold the meat, ivory, and hides and paid the ranch a percentage as royalty.

The following year Brian was offered the game management rights to the 360,000-acre Central Estates, a vast ranch in the midlands, and shortly afterward obtained an area of 44,000 acres at Matetsi, which bordered on the Hwange National Park, then called Wankie. He also got the game management rights to the huge Triangle Sugar Estates next to Nuanetsi, mostly to keep down problem animals, such as hippo, elephant, and buffalo. They are mad for young green shoots of sugar cane and they have to be kept in check. In all, Brian now had the game management rights to over a million acres of central Africa, which, from a business viewpoint, beat croc-hunting all hollow.

Safari hunting became legal in Rhodesia only in 1967. Brian ran the first commercial sport hunting safari in that country the same year. That first safari was a shouting, ringing success and Rhodesia never looked back. Today, safari hunting is one of the major producers of foreign income and local employment for Zimbabwe. John Taylor's advice to Brian not to join the Nyasaland game department and rather to stay in professional hunting had been a shining, solid gold chunk of wisdom.

Rene and Ricky Philip left Nyasaland when it became Malawi after it became independent in 1964 and a republic in 1966. They settled at Uvongo, a seaside holiday resort on the south coast of Natal, South Africa. Brian was able to visit them at their new home from time to time.

"No," Ricky told Brian. "I never did hear from John Taylor again. Somebody said he had died in Ireland in 1960. Can't remember who it was now. But it seems he never got back to Africa at all." Well, one thing we know is that John Taylor did not die in Ireland in 1960!

Brian had Taylor's first three books: *Big Game and Big Game Rifles; African Rifles & Cartridges;* and *Pondoro, Last of the Ivory Hunters*, and he had seen his fourth, his only novel, *Shadows of Shame*. Brian knew there had been a fifth book, the manuscript of which had been lost. He had never found out if it had ever been published. He had never seen a copy. Then, in 1987, a friend of his in New Zealand, of all places, sent him a new reprint copy of this book as a present—*Maneaters and Marauders*. One paragraph from its pages sprang out of the book at him:

> I was camped on Lake Namaramba on Portuguese territory close to where the Mandimba flows into the Lugenda at the latter's source at the top of the lake. My good lad Aly has his home on the British side of the border. . . . There is a big, maned lion that has been living on the slopes of a kopje just back of Aly's home. He has been there for years. He comes round regularly and helps enormously to thin out the bush pig, which come raiding Aly's crops. He never attempts to interfere with man. We often hear his singsong roar soon after dark as he starts off for his night's prowl, and again just before daybreak when on his way home again. He seems to be a confirmed bachelor because we have never heard more than one voice up there, and have never seen any spoor along with his. But although he comes through the lands, which run right up to the village and frequently kills pigs in them, he has never made even so much as a face at any of Aly's folk, much less threatened them. I feel sure that it was he that Aly and I met one night when we came over the border on bicycles en route to Aly's home. We met him on that same bridge I mentioned a while ago, over the Mandimba, about a mile and a half or two miles from Aly's village.

Brian read the paragraph again and again, wondering what the hell he was seeing! It was now thirty years since Brian had seen Aly. How old would he be now, he wondered? He had been a youth just before the last war, so would probably be about sixty-five. No great age for an African. Brian grabbed the first convenient plane to Malawi, as Nyasaland was now called, and hired a car on his arrival in Lilongwe to take him to Mandimba.

It wasn't Fort Johnston any more. It was now called Mango-chi. He crossed the Shire and drove up the escarpment. How it had changed. The top of the plateau was now very thickly settled. Malawi not only has a fast-growing natural population among its own citizens, but it also had then a high refugee population of brother Yoas who had fled the civil war in neighboring Mozambique. He could not even recognize the place where the old Aly Ndemanga Village had once stood.

He drove on, past cluster after cluster of African huts standing close to the side of the road. Scrawny chickens and yellow dogs cleared a way for the car. Young barefooted and raggedly dressed children ran to the roadside when they heard the car approaching to wave as he went by. This much of the old Nyasaland that he used to know had not changed at all. He drove on through the little town of Namwera, the only town between Fort Johnston and Mandimba, where the fish vendors still had their bales of dried bream tied to long poles protruding from the carriers of their bicycles. He drove on till he drew close to the Mozambique border. Then he came to a river. The sign on the bridge said "MANDIMBA." He remembered that it was on the lower reaches of this river, where it ran into the Lugenda below Lake Amaramba, that John Taylor had his camp in Mozambique. He knew he was now "about a mile-and-a-half to two miles from Aly's village." He had to be. John Taylor had told him so.

There was a man walking along the road. He wore the white skullcap of the Muslim. Brian greeted him, "I have come to find a friend of mine. His name is Aly Ndemanga. I know he lives in these parts. Do you happen to know him?"

The man stared hard at Brian. "When did you last see him?" he enquired.

"A long time back. When we were young men."

"I see," he said after some thought. "I will need to guide you. I will take you to his brother." He walked around to the passenger side and Brian opened the door for him. "Carry on this way, please," he said, waving Brian forward.

Brian drove along the road for a short distance and was then directed onto a narrow track, which led to a village. The man got out, saying, "Wait here, please."

Brian's guide disappeared between the neat, rectangular Yao huts and almost immediately emerged with an elderly African walking beside him. The old man also wore the *shehe* skullcap. Brian stared hard. It was Aly. Older and matured, but still the same Aly he remembered. And yet as he watched him approach, he seemed slightly taller. Brian stepped out of the car and walked to meet him.

"Aly? Aly Ndemanga?"

The crinkled old African shook his head and smiled sadly. "I am Kandulu, Aly's elder brother. Even from childhood they said we looked exactly alike."

"I am seeking Aly. I was a friend. I knew Aly when he and John Taylor lived at Aly Ndemanga Village."

"John Taylor and Aly were as father and son when they were together on this earth. Now they are together again. Aly died in April of 1983. If you were a friend of Aly, then his wife and children will be glad to see you. I will take you to Mwambwajila, the next village on, so you can meet them, and I will show you the grave."

Brian felt a wave of sadness sweep over him. For all those bloody years, he thought, he had been so close. How easy it would have been for me to find him!

* * * * * * *

Brian Marsh returned a number of times to Nyasaland/Malawi, first in 1959, the year after he failed to meet up again with John *Pondoro* Taylor and Aly Ndemanga. That was shortly after his marriage to Jillie. But he did not return again until 1987 when he discovered Taylor's clues in *Maneaters and Marauders* to the location of Mwambwajila village. In 1988, with the prospect of doing this book with me, Brian and Jillie made the third of their nostalgic trips back, this time a research mission. It proved to be their most dangerous, going by road through Mozambique where a particularly ugly civil war was then still raging.

Zimbabwe, which was once Southern Rhodesia and where Brian and Jillie are citizens and live, is a penultimate neighbor of Malawi. Getting there isn't half the fun. In 1988 there were three choices: You could take your chances and drive through the war-mangled, ambush-infested, land-mine-pocked dying country of Mozambique with its platoons of teenage rebel RENAMO soldiers who notch their AK-47 rifle stocks with human kills as if they represented defunct impala; you could take the plane to Lilongwe, as Brian did in 1987; or you could drive through Zambia, which, although quiet and peaceful as a golf course, is five times the distance to where they wanted to go. Brian and Jillie decided to risk a couple of extra nostrils from the rebels for the sake of seeing his old girlfriend, Mozambique, once again. They drove. It would be a long time before they tried it again.

When Brian went in by plane in 1987 and rented a car to discover Mwambwajila and Aly's brother, he may have made it sound simple. It wasn't. The car he rented had to be push-started, was supplied without tools or even a spare tire, and generally gave plenty of trouble. In 1988, he checked with the Automobile Association of Zimbabwe and found out that to the best of their knowledge there had not been an "incident" on the Tete road for more than two years. It was the road the Zimbabwean military-escorted convoys of heavy transport trucks used. The Marshes decided to risk it. They took along Isa Vatiwa, their old herbalist cook, who was a Muslim Yao and whose home was not far from Lake Amaramba in Mozambique. Isa had not been back among his own people for the thirty years he had worked for the Marshes nor for the forty-four years he had been away from them.

The major reason of the Marshes' mission for going back to Malawi was to research material for this book, but there was also another reason. This was to erect a memorial to John Taylor, Aly Ndemanga, and their old Africa. Why? Well, it just seemed right. Brian had learned from Alexander Maitland in London, who had wrapped up John's affairs after his death, that Taylor's ashes had been sent to Aly, and he wanted to erect a cairn of stones at the place where the ashes had been scattered. Brian then presumed they had been scattered. Wouldn't you? And he wanted to cement a commemorative plaque onto it. The plaque had been made by Gillespie's Monumental Masons in Harare and it was designed so that it would show no religious symbols. It was of granite and with a simple inscription to the two of them, the chiseled writing flanked on either side by a pair of elephant tusks. Brian wrapped the plaque in an old blanket to keep it from chipping on the rough roads he would be using. He stowed it under the front seat of the station wagon in the hope Mozambican customs wouldn't find it and decide it must be made of solid gold.

Brian and Jillie made arrangements to leave on a Monday. That gave them the weekend to pack, but on Sunday morning a phone call revealed that a set of important documents Brian had mailed had gone astray, hardly a rare occurrence in Africa. They canceled the Monday departure so they could duplicate the documents, and rescheduled for Tuesday instead. By doing so they unwittingly may have saved their lives from a fatal land-mine "incident."

Mozambique is a vast country with irregular borders. To the east there is a major length of the African coast where it meets the Indian Ocean. Because of the narrow "waist," the borders of Zimbabwe and Malawi are only 300 kilometers, about 190 miles, apart, with the ancient town of Tete almost exactly equidistant between them.

There were two military convoys, one running north, which Brian and Jillie joined, and another coming south. Each left their respective borders at 7:30 in the morning, presumably when it was light enough to return fire should there be any ambushes, and met at Tete a few hours later. That was theoretical of course. Then the armed escorts of armored cars, supplied by Zimbabwe and manned by Zimbabwean troops to the FRELIMO government, turned around at Tete. Each assumed the job of guarding the long line of heavy trucks for the continuing journey on the gauntlet to both the Zimbabwe and Malawi borders, which were supposed to be reached in early afternoon.

Brian, Jillie, and Isa crossed the border into Mozambique at Nyamapanda in northeastern Zimbabwe. This was the same border post John Taylor would have used when he came to Mozambique in 1928, sixty years ago. It was the same one Mrs. Taylor must have used when she came that same year to cart her son back to Ireland. The convoy was ready to start on schedule. Brian had been told by the Zimbabwe Automobile Association that he could expect a number of other light vehicles to be joining the convoy, but this did not prove the case. This day they were alone. He slipped in behind the last truck and concentrated on driving exactly in its tracks, paying particular attention to avoid any potholes in which mines might be lurking–those flat and deadly flying saucers with that cute little detonator on top.

Immediately behind them came "Tail-End Charlie," the last armored car, a v-shaped hull built on a Land Rover chassis to dissipate and deflect any blasts outward and upward. Brian was not anxious to see if the principle worked. Grim black faces stared out with cocked automatic weapons. Brian and Jillie felt like plucked chickens at the butcher's. At first, the convoy commander, a cheerful black officer with an easy grin, had directed them to the front of the convoy. Nice guy. Thanks a lot. Brian demurred.

"If it's all the same to you I'd rather one of the heavies ran over any land mines first," he said.

"Won't make any difference," was the cheery retort. "They're using the delayed-action ratchet type that can let the whole convoy pass and still blow with the last car. At least in front you can make a run for it if we get into a shootout."

Brian still said thanks but no thanks. He had decided that land mines presented the biggest possible invitation to dine with the angels and, ratchets or no ratchets, he'd stay at the back. He did concede that the commander had a point. One stray bullet in the radiator and he would have to kiss his now uninsured Toyota station wagon good-bye; he had just discovered that his insurance didn't cover "acts of war." He might also have to throw in their collective tails in the bargain.

He had been promised by the commander that, if they were hit or broke down, the rear, armored car would take the three of them in. The station wagon, though, would have to be abandoned right where it stopped. After all, there was a genuine fifteen-year-old war going on. There were already tens of thousands of people dead, most of whom weren't combatants. Neither were they! RENAMO'S teenagers, it seemed, liked to shoot people for the sheer joy of it, sort of a deadly competition among its best marksmen.

The road was tarmac, a relic from the Portuguese colonial era. It would not have been tarmac in Lady Taylor's day. We do not know what car she was driving but it was then the era of Henry Ford's Model T. Rubber tires were particularly unreliable in those days. Fixing punctures was an ongoing event. As Brian looked at the road, his admiration for Lady Taylor jumped several notches. She, like her son, showed rare courage.

The tarmac was now in shocking disrepair since no road work had been possible because of the war. It doesn't require a degree in engineering to understand what the twice-daily traffic of eighty heavy trucks had done to it over the years. All Malawi's traffic to Zimbabwe and vice-versa had to come this way. One of the first things destroyed by RENAMO had been all the rail links. Long stretches of the tarmac were completely broken up, leaving heavy sand beneath. What wasn't torn up was badly potholed. Brian thought it would be an easy cruise behind those heavy trucks, but he bent the hell out of the steering just struggling to keep up.

The trip from Nyamapanda to Tete was eerie, but not because they were on tenterhooks expecting to be blown up or shot. The very veldt itself had become a casualty of war. The whole expanse appeared to have died in lonely agony. There were no animals and no people, and it seemed from their dusty place at the rear of the convoy that there were no birds, either. They saw nothing and heard nothing living. The feeling was of a total, deafening vacuum, a void.

Here and there along the road Brian and Jillie came to places where small settlements had been, a burnt-out country store with accompanying buildings like a bedraggled, singed hen with sooty chicks. There was what may have been a petrol pump and over here a water trough that had burnt down to the level of the liquid. Even the light-fingered vervet monkeys who should have been stealing the fruit of the abandoned mango groves were missing. They didn't much like the war either.

Halfway to Tete, the convoy churned through the ruins of the town of Changara. Thirty years back, on their way to revisit some of Brian's old haunts in Nyasaland, the Marshes had stopped here for breakfast. They remembered it with an advanced attack of nostalgia. Those were the days: a salad bowl full of french fries with three fried eggs and crisp bacon on top, served with mouth-puckering black olives and a bottle of chilled red wine.

Changara, in that happier time, was in the heart of the game lands, and then the road on either side of it was strewn with elephant and buffalo sign. This was where Fletcher Jamieson had made his base camp in the early 1930s. It was where Norman and Mavis Jamieson, Fletch's brother and sister-in-law, used to drive their three-ton Chevrolet to bring in the supplies that Fletcher needed and to return laden with Fletch's ivory. Fletcher did not own a vehicle when he first started professional ivory hunting. He could not afford one, but he also did not need one for hunting. Like John Taylor, Fletcher's mode of hunting was to walk out with porters, hunting elephant in the immediate bush. It was here too that he and John Taylor had first met and where they had planned their safari together to the Elephant Marsh on the Lower Shire River in Nyasaland.

Now Changara, or what was left of it, was a theoretical army base. There were some military-type tents and a large number of rusting, mine-blasted trucks scattered about like rhino carcasses, and a few sweat-stained FRELIMO troops, but little else. Changara had become a ghost town.

Right on time the convoy snaked into the town of Tete. Brian noticed that the countryside on the approach hadn't changed at all. It still looked like a moonscape satellite photo or the surface of Mars, as it had been when he had last seen it. The descendants of the same goats still roamed the rock-strewn vacant expanse, still picking away at seemingly nothing.

Brian felt the same small stirring that had tingled in the pit of his stomach all those years ago, seeing this romantic, blood-washed place again. He wondered how much it would have changed. He deviated from the convoy route as soon as they reached the outskirts of the town. He circled twice to get his bearing, and then turned down the old road he remembered to the river to see if the old Hotel Tete was still where it used to be. It wasn't. It had been pulled down and every trace of it had disappeared.

Brian wanted to drive across town to see if the Chinese shop where Taylor sold his ivory and skins was still open. He had been there once, out of curiosity, after Taylor had spoken to him about it. The old pigtailed man and his unsmiling wife had lived in attached rooms at the back of the store. Faint whiffs of incense had emanated from their quarters, mingling with the specific odors peculiar to all tropical African general stores: fresh bread, dried fish, old leather, the sharp winter smell of oiled steel, and the fusty pungency of long-baled blankets. Behind the store had been the windowless shed that Taylor had seen when it had been filled to the ceiling with all kinds of wildcat skins. Perhaps, if there was such a thing as a credit side, the skin trade would have paid for the war.

They turned back to join the convoy. Now there was a high-level skeletal bridge across the smooth, brown hide of the Zambezi. The last time Jillie and Brian had been here they had to use the old pontoon ferry and they couldn't help wondering how long it would have taken to get the entire convoy across on it. Probably days. In those days, that would not have bothered them much. They would have taken a room at Hotel Tete and enjoyed Paul Schots's excellent food and hospitality and possibly endured some of his patriotic Nazi songs. But now that was gone, replaced by the more centrally located Hotel Zambezi. Brian and

Jillie wondered if the Laurentino beer, unpasteurized in those days and at its best when the beer truck from Lourenço Marques hit town, would still taste as good as it used to.

They crossed over the bridge, the Zambezi slipping below like melted chocolate. Being at the back of the convoy ensured that most of the trucks were already across by the time they arrived. Because of their weight, they would only allow one truck to cross at a time. Brian and Jillie drove up past the long line at the marshalling point, looking for someone in authority who could tell them what was next. They finally reached the front.

Parked there was a white Land Cruiser pickup with Mozambican number plates. They pulled in behind it and just then the driver got out to search for something in his suitcase on the back. He had the stamp of one of their countrymen and so Brian went up to speak to him, a young, clean-looking white man with a trimmed red beard.

"What happens now?" Brian asked him after they had chatted a while.

"Usually, we're getting ready to move about this time, but its anybody's guess what will happen today. The convoy from Malawi isn't even in yet."

"What's so special about today?"

The young man glanced at Brian quickly. "Didn't they tell you?" He gave a snort of disgust. "They never tell anybody anything about what's really going on up here. A truck went up yesterday afternoon. Land mine souped up with plastic explosive. Blew most of the front end off the truck and killed the driver. They must be giving these fellows an awful lot of danger pay. But, I guess it's the old story. You never believe it can happen to you. It'll make the escorts cautious for a day or two. They'll be pussyfooting, which is why they're so late."

"So, there's been another incident," Brian remarked, remembering with a small chill that they'd originally planned to be with that convoy. "First in two years, isn't it?"

Red beard regarded him soulfully. "Who told you that?"

"I checked with the Automobile Association."

"Then please don't blame them. They're not told either."

"So things have suddenly escalated?" Brian asked.

"Not at all. Same as usual. Simply situation normal. The previous land mine to yesterday's was just two weeks ago, and in between, two young hitchhikers from Holland got killed in an ambush. They were riding on the back of one of the trucks."

Brian thought this over most carefully. "And what are you doing out here?" he asked.

"I'm with a Christian organization. The Lord called me. So I came. I'm based in Tete, and at the moment I'm driving around the outlying areas distributing free maize seed so that the starving peasants out there can grow some food."

"Isn't that a bit dangerous?"

"The Lord called me, so I have no doubt He will look after me. I've been ambushed on three occasions. Fortunately they're rotten shots, and so far I've never been land mined."

Brian admired his faith while envying his luck.

Brian turned back to his vehicle. During the short time he had been away from it, it had become surrounded by a tight pack of raggedly-dressed, starved-looking urchins. They all had their hands out, begging. Brian pushed his way through them and managed to squeeze back into the car.

"What did he have to say?" asked Jillie.

"Nothing much," Brian lied badly. "He seemed to think the convoy could pull out at a moment's notice." Brian swallowed. Tete is always hot and dusty.

Most of the starving ragamuffins surrounding the car were half-grown boys, and shortly they were reinforced until they were about fifty strong. Those who had first arrived were flattened against the side of the car by the jostling press of those behind them. They were pleading for food, but even if Brian and Jillie had given everything they had to them, it would not have helped. Jillie was overwhelmed by their plight and shortly became agitated. She wanted to give them something at least, but Brian knew better, sitting it out with the unrealistic hope that they would go away. Brian knew there was absolutely nothing they could do for them and very much regretted it. He was born in Africa too.

Time passed slowly and Brian's nervousness grew. Shortly, it would be noon and there was still no sign of the other convoy or their escorts. Noon in November, the heat-blasted month before the rains, sometimes called the "suicide month," makes Tete an outdoor oven. The car was square in the relentless sun, heat waves shimmering off the melting tarmac, and the windows of the station wagon, not air conditioned, were all but sealed by the crush of bodies. The atmosphere, both physically and emotionally, began to grow unbearable. The three of them were imprisoned inside the car like tomatoes roasting in a tin: Brian, Jillie, and Isa sweating rivers.

"We've still got two sandwiches left over in the breakfast basket," Jillie finally said. "I think I'll hand them out to the two smallest."

"I warn you. You're gonna start a riot!"

These hungry children were the sons of peasant farmers driven into Tete from their farms by the war, tribespeople who traditionally lived by bartering a surplus of food for the simplest necessities. Except in the time of severe drought, these young boys would have lived simply and eaten adequately, but now they were starving.

Africa's history was forged in war, but bloody as the tribal conflicts were, they mostly consisted of a single battle, fought with spears. Then the survivors would immediately get back to the business of staying alive, African-style. The war in Mozambique wasn't really an African war, however. It was a European war, being fought by black Mozambican Africans on African soil but with European weapons: land mines, AK-47 assault rifles, and RPG rocket launchers. It was dragging on year after bloody year, the flames of no-quarter slaughter kept alive by surrogate sponsors, like what used to be the Soviet Union and still was at that time.

But, even a declaration of peace and the amicable solving of differences cannot possibly bring peace. The *jeunesse*, the young soldiers who started carrying AKs at ages seven and eight, are beyond help or reconstruction. They were born in war and most will probably die as bandits as they have lost any possible direction in the conflict. They see assault on civilians as a way of life rather than the irresponsible acts of trained soldiers. To them, guns are absolute power and once they have tasted power, they will never be content to be disarmed, relieved of their power, again.

The two leftover sandwich packs were individually wrapped. Jillie placed a pack into two of the smallest and skinniest hands she could find, but they were instantly snatched away. The two packs literally exploded like two limpet mines as dozens of clawing hands grabbed at them and tore them apart. The packs and their contents were mashed into the dirt as the young urchins hit, kicked, and bit over them. At the end of it, Brian saw one of the older boys lick a smear of dirty butter from his thumb. He got the lion's share. It was Africa at its worst, brutal and pitiful.

Long after midday, with a sudden rush, the southbound convoy swept into view. The convoy commander stopped his armored vehicle nearby to advise that his men would first eat lunch before going back. At 2:30, which was the time they had expected to be at the Malawi border, the convoy flexed to its length like a dusty, disjointed python. The trucks burst into life as the starters ground in unison and the big diesel engines revved. They had sat there, dripping grease like bacon in a microwave, for four airless hours.

But, Jillie and Brian were among the lucky ones. They at least could leave. In the middle of the afternoon the convoy passed the spot where the land mine had exploded. They looked at the oil-splattered hole and the bright, twisted shards of metal blasted about the bush. There were dull dark stains beside the hole that lacked the sheen of spilt engine oil.

What had been left of the ruined truck had been towed away by the Zimbabwean Army's sophisticated recovery equipment to prevent the rebel RENAMO forces from looting the goods on board. Food was RENAMO's shortest commodity and the theory was that they blew up trucks primarily to get what they carried. Brian drove around the land mine crater, now more cautious, making sure that he stayed exactly in the tracks of the truck ahead. The convoy now proceeded more slowly than before. Brian wondered what the other drivers thought. The man who had died in the blast of the Communist-bloc land mine had been one of them, risking his life for the danger pay! Well, his wages were aptly named.

In the late afternoon the convoy neared the Malawi border and here, for the first time, they came on signs of human settlement. Fields had been cleared for the new planting season, ready for the rains, and here and there several scattered kraals had been built. They consisted of a few round pole and grass huts, but around them were a number of tiny, raggedly-built, low and open temporary grass shelters.

"What are those shelters for?" Jillie asked Isa innocently. "I've never seen those in the villages before."

The old man clicked his tongue in disgust. "It is like the old days of the slave raiders again. These people are afraid to sleep inside their huts because they cannot get away in time if they are attacked."

"Don't tell me they sleep in those!"

"Even when it rains. And the children have to sleep alone. If there is a raid at night their only hope is to get out quickly and run to hide in the bush."

"What a way to live," Jillie murmured, visibly shocked. And, she's a native-born African, too.

"The people have to eat." Isa continued. "They must risk their lives to grow their crops. As we have seen," he said feelingly, "there is no food in the refugee villages."

Shortly, standing on the side of the road, they came across some occupants of one of the kraals, a group of scrawny children holding their hands out pathetically for anything that might be thrown to them. The boys were clad in the traditional bush apparel of the past, a string of plaited bark around their loins with a few strategic strands hanging down in front. The only girl in the group, a skinny child in her early teens, had made herself a miniskirt from an empty plastic cornmeal bag, having tailored it quite simply by cutting holes for her head and arms.

The young lady's mini was certainly colorful, being bright yellow and decorated across the front with the name and trademark of the miller in large letters of screaming, dayglow red. Being plastic, it was noticeably drip-dry. The hemline was of the Paris fashion of the sixties, barely reaching below her hips, which required her to maintain a pull on the front of it to just, and only just, retain her modesty. But it lifted in the back to reveal her bare buttocks. Isa, a traditionalist if ever there was one, gave another click of disgust.

"She wears nothing underneath," he muttered like a distant thunderstorm. "Where are her aprons? This country is dead. The people have no food and they have no clothes. What happens to the aid they send to these people?"

Well, Brian could answer that too. He had seen the canned fish being hawked in the border town of Mutare in eastern Zimbabwe. "Gift from the people of Norway to the people of Mozambique," the labels read. I also have seen mountains of donated food being sold in Ethiopia and elsewhere, like in Morocco where I was almost mobbed for indiscreetly taking pictures of a huge pile of goodies donated by CARE. When will the West ever learn? This aid is worth far too much on the black market to be given away or distributed properly as it was intended to be. If the African is nothing else, he is certainly a gifted opportunist and a rabid capitalist. To have foreign gifts of food and clothing distributed in stricken countries by profit-hungry locals is tantamount to giving the fox the keys to the hen house and asking him to feed them.

It was 8:30 in the evening before Brian and Jillie had cleared Malawian customs at the border post of Mwanza and nearly 11:00 before they were settled in a hotel room at Blantyre. As they had risen before midnight in order to reach the Zimbabwean border by convoy time, it had been a twenty-four-hour day and they were whipped. Nevertheless, they were up early after a few hours of exhausted sleep, anxious to be on their way again. Fifteen minutes after the bank opened and they had cashed some Zimbabwe travelers' checks for Malawian *kwacha* and *tambala*, they were heading for the road to the lake. From there they would drive to the border of Mozambique. In the late afternoon, they reached Nombo village where Kandulu, Aly's brother, lives.

CHAPTER THIRTEEN

Brian and Jillie headed the Toyota station wagon into the village. They saw Kandulu sitting on a chair outside the shed that houses his Lister, diesel-driven maize mill. Isa went over to tell him that they had returned. Isa took him the photographs Brian had taken on his previous visit and had sent by registered mail to Kandulu's post box at Namwera. Because he doesn't get very much mail and therefore makes the trip so seldom, the envelope had been returned. Kandulu jumped up and hurried over to greet them.

Brian and Jillie had proposed to leave Isa at the village. In traditional African custom, and because Isa was a Muslim Yao in Muslim Yao country, he would have been welcome as long as he wished to stay. They figured on moving to the Mandimba River to make a camp, but Kandulu quickly dissuaded them. He said the children of the nearby village there would give them no peace. Being whites, the Marshes would be something of a novelty value in that out-of-the-way place, and the children would spend their time visiting. Rural Malawi had not changed!

Kandulu most kindly gave Brian and Jillie his kitchen hut as a cooking area and a place to store their surplus equipment against possible rain and directed them to a grove of mango trees nearby where they made their camp. The kitchen hut was thatched and had a circular hard-pounded dirt floor as smooth as linoleum. It had a low wall at the back that acted as a windbreak. A group of giggling maidens appeared bringing buckets of water and firewood almost as soon as the tent was up, and Brian and Jillie were soon feeling like part of the Ndemanga family.

The village at Nomba is traditional Yao, the walls of the houses being a latticework of thin poles plastered with clay and then covered with uncombed, cowlick-studded thatch. The houses were square, in the old Arab design, and with wooden-shuttered windows instead of the usual airless African "beehives."

There are two "permanent" establishments in the village, the one a small brick-under-iron-roof store, which sells only the basic elements of a simple life: maize meal, sugar and flour, candles and matches, cooking oil, beads and feminine knickknacks, and dried fish from the lake. The other is Kanudulu's similarly constructed mill shed, which is the social hub of the area much as a barber shop was in a small American town of the 1920s. Women in flamboyant cotton print shifts and bright skull wraps carried buckets of maize on their heads to be ground, leaving their hands free to carry items for barter: shelled peanuts, live chickens, sweet potatoes, tomatoes, and greens from their streamside *dimba* gardens. They gave the place a gaudy and exotic market-day flavor. Business was conducted with much gossip, gaiety, and laughter, with much gratuitous advice from the ever-smiling Kandulu, who sat outside collecting the money—by the grace of Allah—while his young assistant ran the mill.

All the villagers here were peasant farmers, working long-held family fields and plots, but some of the men let their wives and children do the day-to-day field work while they engaged in loftier pursuits. A village carpenter made doors and windows and simple furniture from planks of native timber that was hand-sawn by two sweat-gleaming men with a two-handled pit-saw. There was also a plate and bowl maker, who conjured marvelous things out of ebony and mahogany using a hand-turned lathe. Malawi is rich in such exotic woods and they are practical, too, not often splitting or cracking from use or age.

The lathe was a metal shaft on two roller bearings, a piece of discarded mining equipment, which was nailed to a heavy log. Welded to one end of the shaft was a short, open-ended length of two-inch piping into which the tapered end of the block of wood being worked was fixed. The shaft was turned by an assistant who spun it backward and forward by pulling on the two ends of a cord wound around it. Meanwhile the craftsman, using hand-held tools, cut only on the forward rotation. Once turned, the piece would be given to another assistant who carved fancy designs upon it, making the finished article into more of a curio artifact than a simple household utensil.

The village was completely clean. There was no rubbish of any kind lying around. Although the weather was hot and rain had fallen recently, there were no flies. The earthen yards around the houses were swept daily, this being the morning chore for the youngest girls.

Once installed in their tented camp, Brian and Jillie wandered over to chat to Kandulu and to liaise with Isa, who was staying with him. They arrived in the nick of time! A young boy was dragging a goat along on a length of rope while Kandulu tested the edge of his knife.

"Kandulu is killing a goat for you," said Isa enthusiastically.

Jillie blanched. "A whole goat! That's far too generous. Please ask him not to kill it for us."

"*Aaaii*! But it is the custom of our people," protested old and traditional Isa. "He will be offended. We always kill a goat when honored guests come to stay! It is the Yao way. You must not insult him."

"Can he not make it something smaller? Like a chicken?"

Isa, exercising all his diplomatic talents on behalf of the whites who apparently did not want to be honored, conferred at some length with Kandulu. It was well known that all whites are odd. At last they finished and turned to Jillie.

"Then," said Isa, "he insists on giving you some chickens."

It was a very generous gesture. A goat sold then for seventy-five Malawi *kwatchas*, what a small village could live on for a couple of months! Kandulu had indeed wished to honor them!

The next morning Brian, Jillie, and Isa walked over to Mwambwajila Village with one of Kandulu's young relations carrying on his head the granite plaque they had brought. Mwambwajila lay a short walk away through the veldt along a wide and well-used path. It was a small village, with only a few square, pole-and-thatch huts, all belonging to members of Aly Ndemanga's family, but it did have one small flat-roofed brick-under-iron building. This had been Aly's private mosque. The Marshes were allowed to have a look inside it. It was partitioned by a low wall of bush-timber poles, the one half for Aly and the menfolk of his family, and the other for his wife, Arina, and the female relations. Although allowed four wives by Islamic law, Aly only married once.

Having heard by bush telegraph that they were coming, the whole clan had gathered. Arina, Aly's widow, is a Sena woman from the lower Zambezi who married Aly about the time that Taylor finished writing his first two books. She had converted to Islam, and she and Aly had seven children—three sons: James, Usman, and Liemba; and four daughters: Sakina, Joanna, Bitousa, and Sinabu. Liemba had gone to Allah very young, and Usman had moved to Monkey Bay on Lake Malawi to work at the harbor. The girls were all long married with families of their own and all lived in the area, their husbands being peasant farmers. Only the still-unmarried James and a few other close relations lived at the village and worked the fields.

On Isa's advice, before departing from Zimbabwe, Brian and Jillie had emptied their closets of all their old clothes and even brought some given by old family friends. Isa now apportioned them to the extended family. Clothes, even old and tatty ones, are always greatly appreciated in the African bush and an accepted currency for barter. One of the gathered was Brian's old pal, Samson Kazembi, who had been the butcher's assistant when Aly was arrested for poaching hippo at Lake Amaramba. He spoke Chilapalapa, so Brian and Jillie could converse with him, which was a tremendous asset. Few of the other residents of the village did. Then, with greetings and introductions completed, Isa unwrapped the blanket to reveal the plaque and explained the purpose of Brian and Jillie's visit.

Isa told the gathering that Brian wanted to honor John Taylor and Aly Ndemanga by putting up a memorial commemorative to them at the place where John Taylor's ashes has been scattered. He proposed to build a cairn of stone and cement and place the plaque on it. If they agreed to this, would they please show him where they thought it should be built?

This piece of news was greeted with great enthusiasm, and each member of the family came forward and squatted down to have a good look at the tablet. From all the undertones, chatter, and gesticulations, Brian soon realized that things weren't going according to plan. Arina then rose and hurried to her hut, returning a few minutes later. To Brian's complete astonishment she carried an ivory-colored ashes urn, which she handed to him like the Holy Grail. Brian opened it. The urn was empty, but on a paper disc inside the cap, written in a neat hand in India ink, was the inscription:

Lambeth Crematorium London SW 17–John Howard Taylor–Cremation No 5560–date 9/4/69

"Where did you get this?" asked Brian incredulously.

"Aly was sent the ashes of John Taylor in this urn, but he did not know what he should do with them. It is not our custom to burn the body of a well-loved and well-respected person. This is a Christian rite. John Taylor was a Muslim, like us, but when he died his body was taken by the Christians who dealt with it in their way.

A MAN CALLED LION

"So Aly took the ashes to the Christian mission at Malembo, and asked the fathers there what he should do with them. They told him to spread the ashes on the water of the Shire River, where they would be washed down to the sea. But Aly knew that John Taylor would not want that to happen. He would want to remain here, with us at Mwambwajila. So Aly kept the ashes and told his sons that when he died they must be buried with him in his own grave."

"And this is what happened?" Brian asked.

"And this is what happened." All the assembly nodded together, the wave of skullcaps like a small flight of white butterflies.

"Well, if that's the case," said Brian, "instead of building a memorial, should we not place the plaque on the grave as a headstone?"

Again the white skullcaps nodded, in very obvious approval.

"Then that's what we will do. Tell me where I can find a builder and I will drive to Namwere to buy the cement."

"I am a builder," said Samson Kazembi, Aly's brother-in-law. "As a young man I worked in your country as a builder, building tobacco barns on the farms. I still have my tools and can do whatever you require. If you give me the cement, we have a wheelbarrow in the village, which we can use to collect sand and stones."

They walked to the graveyard, a short way from the village and set in a grove of shady trees. As soon as the party arrived, the family, with Isa in attendance, held a service over Aly's grave. Brian and Jillie, being Christians, were not invited to join in, but they did say they could watch and take photographs if they wished. The gathering removed their shoes before entering the cemetery, a fine point which Jillie and Brian had neglected to recognize. To ease the embarrassment of this faux pas, Kandulu and Samson praised their foresight in having two tusks engraved on the plaque instead of a cross, in which case it could not have been accepted.

The service over, the plaque was positioned in a manner to which the family agreed, and that was that. The Marshes would have liked to stay until the job was completed, but that would not have been possible. Aly's son, Usman, would have to be sent for and certain rites performed by him. Jillie and Brian were planning a secret rite of their own, one which they were sure John Taylor would have heartily approved.

They stayed at the village for a few more days, getting to know the family better and to ease out a bit more information about Taylor and Aly. Then all too soon, it was time to leave. Isa wanted to head out to find the remnants of his own family whom he knew had fled to Malawi to escape the Mozambican war. He had the address of a village down the border to the south where he knew they had settled, and it was agreed that they would leave at first light the following day.

But on this last evening at the camp, Brian and Jillie set themselves up for their own secret rite, every detail as carefully planned as a night commando raid. They started to assemble their specialized equipment just as the sun went down and the Yaos were involved with the last prayer of the day. In the background they could hear an emerald-spotted wood dove calling. . . .

CHAPTER FOURTEEN

Brian brought out the Igloo cold box, which had once been packed with ice and which now held a bountiful supply of clean, iced water. He tilted it so Jillie could tap some into the thermos flask. Then, he looked guiltily over his shoulder—this was, after all, Yao country and Muslim. He most certainly didn't want them to know what they had brought, and he dug out the bottle surreptitiously. There was no movement outside their camp. Lacking artificial light, the rural African settles down early.

He placed two folding camp chairs into the back of the station wagon and Jillie followed with the woven rattan picnic basket. In it were two glasses, the thermos, and one of John Taylor's favorites, a bottle of Black Bush Irish whiskey. John had once told Brian when he was visiting him at Aly Ndemanga Village that his preference was Irish, but none was available in Nyasaland at that time, so Brian always brought him a bottle of Scotch. Well, if he hadn't been able to share Irish whiskey with him then, he'd be more than glad to share it with him now!

There was no road from Nombo to Mwambwajila, only a wide, well-used footpath through the bush, just sufficiently wide to get along it in the station wagon. They drove without lights, the rising golden moon just past the full, so they did not need them. Strangers to Africa marvel at the luminescence of the African moon, which provides a glow rather like seeing in daylight with exceptionally dark glasses. Colors are visible, but somewhat muted, and the whole veldt looks like a dappled, vermiculated mass of grayish, gilded fingers.

They left the Toyota in the trees near the village, and carrying the chairs and the basket, they walked to the edge of the graveyard. They did not enter it. They did not want to violate sacred Islamic ground with forbidden alcohol. Aly's and Taylor's common grave was in one moon-washed corner.

Brian broke the lead seal on the Black Bush and squeaked out the cork. It was surprisingly loud in the stillness, only a distant nightjar's trill wafting along with the moonbeams. It was obviously an old bottle, still having a cork rather than the usual serrated metal cap of modern times. God alone knew the adventures that bottle must have had to end up at John's and Aly's grave site in Malawi. He poured two good shots and splashed in a bit of water from the thermos. He and Jillie lifted their glasses. Aly's spirit would have definitely declined, being in the arms of Allah, but John Taylor's shade would most surely have sat up and taken notice.

"May its glint blind the eye of the Prophet!" Brian solemnly intoned, remembering John's favorite toast, and he could almost hear his conspiratorial laughter.

It was a warm night, with just enough breeze to keep the mosquitoes at bay. So light was it from the moon's bronze blush that they had to try hard to see any stars at all. Only the biggest and brightest gleamed dully through the bright sky, like light pricks in a pale pie crust.

Brian thought about Alexander Maitland in London. He knew how much he would have liked to be with them, and he felt extremely grateful to him for having sent John's ashes to Aly, and he was grateful to Aly for having had them placed in his own grave when he died. Their thoughtful actions had made it possible for him, and for others in the future, to pinpoint precisely the final resting place of John Pondoro Taylor. He felt grateful, too, for the extraordinary chain of events that had eventually led him to this exact point, allowing him to sit now on a quiet, African moonlit night in this still wild and remote spot, drinking Irish whiskey to John Taylor's memory while contemplating the man himself. Aye, while contemplating the man himself. . . .

*　　*　　*　　*　　*　　*　　*

John Howard "Pondoro" Taylor: professional elephant hunter; safari guide and mentor; successful author; devout Presbyterian changed to casual Muslim; English public school boy turned white African; reverse racism bigot; son of a knighted, famous Dublin surgeon; impoverished wanderer; ferocious renegade against British colonialism, yet a combatant and supporter of Britannia whenever she took the field of battle; ballistician; arms theorist; poacher; and an improbable philanthropist. There were probably other things, too. But what made a man like John Taylor tick. Humm! What, indeed?

Brian let his mind reel back over the thirty years since he first met Taylor, trying to put him in perspective. "Quite a problem," he thought, "when my subject has so many different facets."

"The biggest problem I've had with him," Brian mused, as he sat sipping his whiskey that moonlit night, "as far as knowing him and trying to understand him, was his sexuality. I didn't believe the stories I heard about him at first, mainly because he by no means fitted the naive preconception I had about a person of these leanings. It was only when I read his novel, *Shadows of Shame*, that I became convinced of the veracity of what I thought were malicious rumours.

"In today's world it would certainly be inconceivable that a fellow the age that I was then couldn't guess what was going on, but it must be remembered that I was very much a bushman, a loner, and did not mix regularly with whites of my own age. And also, in the days when I knew him, homosexuality was very much a closed matter, and certainly not the subject for newspaper reports and main street marches that such things have become today. But I was not alone in this."

Brian's old friend Wally Johnson—whom he had first met in Mozambique in 1968 and became very friendly with when they both hunted for Safari South in Botswana—was one of the old-time Mozambican ivory hunters who knew Taylor personally. Wally told him, when asked, that he had only "heard" that Taylor was "different," and didn't believe it anyway. And another old friend, Harry Manners, whom Brian had met originally with Wally in 1968 and who had once been Wally's partner, had never even heard that Taylor was "different," despite having several mutual friends. Harry dismissed it with a snort, saying that if Taylor was a homosexual, then he certainly had never been told of it and had no reason to believe it.

And then, of course, there were the comments of the Indian doctor friend of Ricky and Rene Philip who had spoken to Brian in Blantyre about Taylor all those years ago. He emphatically stated that Taylor could not be a homosexual in that particular African tribal society. The doctor had been quite sincere and correct as far as his knowledge went, but he knew nothing about the Mozambique Asena tribe.

Then, just to complicate it further, his friend, Ken Warner, editor of *Gun Digest*, had told Marsh that he knew of an old hunter from the prewar days in Mozambique who claimed to have known Taylor. The hunter had insisted that Taylor had then been living with a harem of native wives! Marsh didn't doubt this may have been so, but thinking about it now, if Taylor had native wives then there would have been a strong likelihood of half-breed children. Birth control was not very sophisticated at that time, and along the Zambezi it probably didn't exist at all.

But of one thing Marsh was certain . . . that Taylor left no colored children. He once wondered if he might have done so; a young man disappearing into the African bush would hardly be expected to remain celibate, and we've all heard the saying that "absence makes the dark grow blonder." The celebrated Englishman, F.C. Selous, was a young man who put this saying into good practice. Everybody who had worked for Taylor with whom Brian had spoken, however, denied that he held female liaisons, and this would not have been a subject they would have hidden. They had no reason to, neither love-children nor sex being things to be ashamed of in the African context, and with Taylor's love of the African people, Brian could not imagine that he would have abandoned his own flesh and blood to adopt the son of another man if he had any children himself.

Taylor makes much in his writings of the fact that he never interfered with native women, despising white men who took economic advantage of their status to use and abuse the village belles. He attributed a great deal of his own popularity with the Africans to the fact that his abstention from such matters made him better friends of the local men. He was undoubtedly correct in both his logic and his premise, but there is also the likelihood that he had no desire or need for female companionship anyway.

* * * * * * *

Marsh's thoughts wandered onto other aspects of Taylor's life. In his attempts to place in order some of the kaleidoscopic inconsistencies that constituted Taylor's life, he had contacted Professor Argyle of the Department of African Studies of Natal University of South Africa. The professor had guessed that Taylor was a homosexual almost before Brian had completed five sentences describing him! The professor believed that Taylor's adoption of Aly Ndemanga was probably more symbolic of a "marriage" than simply a technicality to have an heir. He was equally certain that Taylor and Aly had been sexual partners and opined that the fact that Aly was married and already had a large family would in no way have hindered the relationship.

"Oh well, so much for that side of him. I still couldn't work it out." So Brian replenished Jillie's and his glass and got to wondering then just how truthful in his writing Taylor had really been. He had been accused by more than one person who claimed to have met him of being "a complete fraud."

"I knew for certain that this wasn't true," Brian asserted to himself. "I had met too many experienced hunters who had known Taylor; Dan Landrey and Ian Nyschens just for starters, who had told me the opposite; and Bush-Africans who had been in the bush with him, like Sampson Nyamhoka and Samson Kazembi, who certainly would have had no reason to lie."

Others had said point-blank that Taylor's *Maneaters and Marauders* was a fictional crib of Jim Corbett's *Man-Eaters of Kumaon*. Corbett is often mentioned in Taylor's books and it is clear that he thought of the old colonel as a sort of Asian Karamojo Bell. Marsh did believe that Corbett's best seller may well have inspired Taylor. There are certainly similarities, but there was no question in his mind that Taylor did shoot a number of maneaters himself. The two Africans who had worked for him, Sampson and Samson, both indicated that he had. He would not have to look far to come across them in the times and places in which he lived and hunted in the African bush.

Marsh knew from the tales told him in the more remote places during his own travels as a crocodile hunter that maneating lions had previously been, and in parts still were, a major problem in many of the outlying areas in Nyasaland. So surely in the much wilder areas of Mozambique at the time in which Taylor lived and hunted, they would have been a major problem, too. But, if there are similarities to be seen between *Maneater and Marauders* and *Man-Eaters of Kumaon*, there are also subtle differences. Taylor did not boast of hunting man-eaters the hard way, even the "sporting" way, by following them into the jungle as Jim Corbett regularly did. Taylor didn't hesitate to admit that he shot them the easy way, even the "unsporting" way, by using a shooting-lamp at night.

Nevertheless, Brian couldn't get away from the irritating fact that his old friend John Taylor did exaggerate, and sometimes on a grand scale. The passage in *Big Game and Big Game Rifles* concerning seven eland downed with a single bullet is the best example of this. The bullet in question was the much praised .375 H&H Magnum. He could well remember what Taylor wrote:

> As far as the 300-grain solid is concerned I have, on not a few occasions, manoeuvred into a suitable position so as to get two buffalo in line and dropped them both with a single shot: These were not body shots; I put the bullet through the nearest bull's head and then into his companion's neck, when the bullet still had sufficient power left to smash it. I have several times had three buffalo dead to one bullet—heart shot. But the biggest bag of all was seven eland to one shot! (An eland may weigh from 1500 cwt. upwards). I did not intend to do it; in fact, I did not know that there were any others besides the one bull that I saw at the edge of the bush on the opposite side of a small clearing. I happened to be loaded with solids, so let rip, shooting him through the heart, and when I got there found five more lying dead in the bush beyond and one with its back broke; after which the bullet had passed through a tree about five inches in diameter and then gone on.

"Taylor, fortunately, had second thoughts about including this piece in *African Rifles & Cartridges*, apparently deciding he had gone too far," Brian recalled.

Taylor had also been accused of exaggerating the number of different rifles he had used. This, Brian had to agree, is more than probable. But, having his first book in mind, Taylor may have at one time been in a position to trade a number of different rifles for experimental purposes. Taylor's claims that he used about sixty various heavy rifles during his hunting career is suspect and does not tally with his claim that he was often out of touch with civilization for two or three years at a time. To have had access to sixty major-caliber rifles, he would surely have needed to maintain fairly close ties with places where rifles could be exchanged.

"Yet, of all the hunting stories that he told me, none were about his own mighty or heroic deeds. He was, strangely enough, a naturally reticent and shy person."

Brian thought about what Ricky and Rene Philip had told him once. When confronted by strangers while visiting their beach cottage at Namasso Bay, he would clam up and it was often difficult to get a single word out of him.

"I remembered times when I had pressed him while seated round his campfire at Aly Ndemanga Village to tell a story about the narrow escapes he must have had. He would be more inclined to respond by evoking the shades of his first principle—'never to press trigger unless sure of killing or crippling shot'—remarking simply that he had very few close shaves because of the invocation of this tenet."

For Marsh, the best account of a lion charge that Taylor ever wrote, in fact one of the best accounts he said he ever read, appeared in the pages of *Shadows of Shame*. It was so explicit and accurate that Marsh was sure it could only have come from a real-life experience. He had met hunters who had been horned or mauled who boasted of their scars, brandishing them aloft as emblems of their superiority as hunters. But Taylor made no bones about the fact that he regarded claw and horn scars as the livid keloid red badges of inexperience, and that a good hunter should never get charged from a situation of his own making.

"And then there were people who claimed that Taylor's lifestyle didn't exactly single him out as a paragon of stability. Certainly," Brian agreed, "his norms did not fit into the everyday scene of things, even in a place as wild and woolly as early Africa. This in itself would not have made him unstable. But I had to ask myself, in view of everything, just how stable a character could he have been?"

Marsh tried to answer his own question, "Certainly Taylor's disregard for the value of money didn't help his case for being considered stable any more than did his attitude towards authority or his sexual views. I don't suppose a poor person who gave away money or valuable assets, which he obviously couldn't afford, would be considered especially normal in any society, as the case of his motorcar might show."

When Taylor returned from Australia in either late 1956 or early 1957, Harry Dawkins, a brother of John, came over with Taylor and did a grand tour of Nyasaland and the surrounding countries in a Chevrolet Coupe Imp that he had purchased on his arrival. When he left after a few months to go home again, Harry gave the car as a gift to Taylor. Taylor had no use for it, and left it parked at Mwambwajila Village, Aly's home near the Mozambique border. But he could have sold it for money that he badly needed. He didn't. It sat under a tree for over a year, and when he was deported he gave it as a gift to Aly.

Now, he would have well known that Aly had neither a license to drive it, nor the funds to run it, and Aly was only able to try it out a few times before the car developed some malady that herbalism couldn't fix and it had to be towed to a distant garage for repair. Since Aly had no money to pay the repair bill, he was unable to recover it. The car was abandoned, and finally cannibalized by the garage for spare parts.

It had to be quite clear that Taylor had no thought for his own old age, or at least this seems clear. But, maybe he did! All five of his books were immediately accepted for publication on submittal and it is Brian Marsh's genuine belief that Taylor was convinced when he finished hunting his literary talents would carry him through. It is also Marsh's genuine belief that he would have been able to maintain his chosen lifestyle quite satisfactorily by the writing of one book every couple of years. And yet, even with five books published, how successful was he really as a writer? He apparently made very little money out of them, so could he really have been a success?

If we compare him to Vincent van Gogh, the Dutch artist and painter, whose works today bring millions of dollars, it would be quite valid to consider Taylor a tremendous success. Was van Gogh really a successful artist? Not in his lifetime, he wasn't. He sold only one picture during his entire lifetime! Taylor sold five books during his lifetime, and while they hardly bring in van Gogh prices today, the surviving original copies of his works are rare and can only be bought for extremely high prices. If Taylor had been able to continue writing, he would no doubt have created a market sufficiently large for him to live on and in his own view that would have made him successful.

But there were many who saw Taylor only as one of life's dismal failures, plain and simple. His last days in London, holding down a menial job, completely broke, barely able to pay the rent for a squalid room, certainly suggested that he was a failure. Yet today, he is among the four best-known hunter/writers on African subjects. Had he been able to buy his freedom from his urban prison. . . . Who knows? And nobody knows what values he held in his gut. Perhaps for him, what had gone before had made it worth it.

There was little doubt that most colonial whites of the time looked upon Taylor's liberalism as a marked sign of instability. Liberalism wasn't very much in fashion then. In fact, it was very much out of fashion. Here was an educated white man living as a "white-wog" in a white man's Africa. And worse, he was outspoken to the point of rudeness to anybody who did not agree with his bloody views! Taylor was not in any way a hypocrite. He was not the least bothered by appearing unfashionable.

When he was in London, Taylor was denied airtime on a BBC talk show on which he wanted to appear. He wrote to Alexander Maitland concerning it in a letter dated January 26, 1960:

> I can easily imagine the derogatory terms they would have used when referring to me: "negrophile" would have been the least of them; "nigger-lover," "renegade," "agitator," probably "Red" or "Communist". . . . What you folks who have never lived in Africa do not seem to grasp is, that anyone, repeat anyone, no matter who he is who shows that he likes the natives and treats them decently and fairly inevitably gets a bad, very bad, reputation. I am not exaggerating when I tell you that a convicted murderer, released after serving so many years of a life sentence will be accepted back into his former haunts without hesitation if he is known to "uphold white prestige," and that simply means "keeping the nigger down" by any means. . . .

Paradoxically, Taylor was not really a liberal in the modern sense of the word. He did not champion reform and progress. He did not believe that the African would benefit more by being "Europeanized" and brought into the European or white way of life, which was thought by many of the liberal persuasion to be vastly superior to the African way of life. Taylor was not a "white liberal" who advocated change, which generally meant destroying a culture and inflicting an alternative that he believed had proved eminently unsuitable. Taylor was exactly the opposite. He was a conservative "white-African" who resisted change.

When Taylor became a professional hunter, he shed the last of his white cocoon and metamorphosed into a "white native," living in the African manner with his followers and not apart from them as would have been customary for a white man. He slept among them at the same campfire, ate with them out of the same pots and using the same utensils, and one and all called him by his first name, "Jack"—not "Bwana Jack"—with Taylor even insisting that the smallest children call him "Jack."

At that time, probably more than ninety-five percent of the indigenous population were what Taylor referred to as "Bush-Africans." These were people who lived as they had always lived, primitively, very simply, and bound by a solid, unyielding wrap of superstition and witchcraft. The Bush-African in his natural state, however, has always been noted for his high moral codes. Whites never dreamed of locking their houses, even on remote farms, in the Africa of Taylor's time. The thought that they might get robbed never entered their minds. Taylor wrote of leaving all his valuables not required on his hunting forays in unlocked tin trunks inside an open hut at his base at Nyungwe on the Zambezi, unattended for months at a time:

> When I arrived I found the trunks untouched. It wasn't that the local natives didn't know they were there: They'd been in and out of the hut to get an occasional empty beer or wine bottle. They didn't consider that stealing, and neither did I, because they knew they only had to ask and I would have given them—being empty they were no use to me! But there wasn't a single footprint in the sand of the floor anywhere near those boxes of mine, showing that a single solitary native had ever been sufficiently tempted to see if they were locked.

So much for his so-called negative sides, what about the positives? There could be no doubt that Taylor is best remembered among the African hunting community for his controversial ballistic theories that culminated in the formula that produced what he called a bullet's "Knockout Value." Taylor devised his KO system as a way of trying to validate the effectiveness of a bullet's terminal results based upon its diameter, weight, and speed.

Hunters of all persuasions, being a traditionally very opinionated lot, have given as many interpretations of Taylor's Knockout Values as there are hunters. If there happen to be eight of them at the long bar at Riley's in Maun, you will likely get eight different appraisals of Taylor and his theories, ranging from what streams out of the south end of a northbound male bovine to the highest praise. His ballistic theories have been misquoted and ridiculed by men who should have known better and touted to the skies by people with ideas as inaccurate as the KO theory's detractors. Nonetheless, they still talk about the theory and John Taylor, its father. The theory is a regular feature of any printed discussion of ballistics in gun books or magazines the world over.

Brian mulled over the paradox that was John Pondoro Taylor, bringing himself back to reality reluctantly. He realized the moon had risen quite considerably, transmuting itself from rich honey to a bright, clear white that almost appeared pale blue and by the same token, that the deep, amber line of the Black Bush bottle had somewhat declined:

A MAN CALLED LION

"I had begun to squirm around in my camp chair a little. I don't know how long we had been sitting there, but the chairs Jillie and I were sitting on were becoming a little bit uncomfortable. Yet, we still sat on. I was enjoying the wild but peaceful aura of this little chunk of eternity in the African bush, untroubled by any sound except the occasional and gentle sigh of the breeze. I ran through my thoughts again, admitting to myself that where I could, I was trying to rationalize, but I found this a very hard process on two aspects of Taylor's life: his callous approach to poaching, and the influence his homosexual practices might have had on unsophisticated African tribesmen."

Marsh thought about the Great Tana Raid, wondering if it could have happened as Taylor said it did. If it did, it was morally as well as legally criminal; if it did not, it still serves to exemplify that Taylor had little if any regard for game laws or regulations. Yet, the vast majority of Taylor's poached elephants were shot on tribal land rather than in national parks or reserves. They almost surely would have been eliminated anyway to make room for Africa's burgeoning population growth. This doesn't make Taylor's actions morally or actually legitimate, but it does help considerably to mitigate the circumstances of his poaching, whether he knew it at the time or not.

Portuguese East Africa did not have an effective game department in Taylor's time and from his writings it becomes obvious that Taylor considered himself to be a self-appointed game ranger. Taylor shot crop-raiding elephant and buffalo without a license, which, in his view, was a justified action. The local farmers loved him for it since they got the meat as compensation for their lost crops. Taylor kept the ivory or hides as compensation for his time and ammo. Had Mozambique had a viable game department, there can be no doubt that they would have killed off very many more elephant on problem animal control than Taylor did with his poaching. Compare his estimated figure of elephant shot to those of the game rangers of East Africa and Zimbabwe: "Samaki" Salmon killed over 4,000 elephant on control work over nineteen years; "Deaf" Banks took somewhere between 2,700 and 3,000, mostly on control; and the Ugandan Game Department culled 13,096 elephant on control in ten years using African game scouts to do the shooting. That elephant have the ability to reproduce themselves with astonishing rapidity, despite a long gestation period, becomes obvious with the fact that, despite severe cropping for many years in Zimbabwe, about 2,000 elephant still have to be culled each year to keep the reserves in ecological balance.

Taylor reckons he killed 1,500 elephant, of which four out of five were poached. By comparison, the numbers he took should not have made any permanent difference. Having seen many starving villagers in the African bush who were not helped at all by the colonial Portuguese regime, he may well have done more good than harm! Certainly, his being on the tribal lands to hunt elephant allowed him to deal with the man-eaters, too. He was an experienced, properly equipped professional hunter. He therefore must have been far more effective than the ill-armed, inexperienced African policeman usually sent along by the *chefe de posto* to deal with ravaging man-eaters.

On the other question, that of his homosexuality, Taylor defended it in *Shadows of Shame* by explaining that certain practices were something of a "tribal custom" in certain areas, such as in Sena land. Bwana Ted, who was very much the "good guy" in the tale, did not go beyond the bounds of practices that were already socially acceptable. If this was so, and Taylor also did not go beyond those bounds, then he probably made no impact at all on the local people. They may have been unsophisticated in some ways but they were certainly worldly where sexual matters were concerned.

"Or am I rationalizing again?" Brian thought.

The camp chairs now seemed to have grown harder and the night had also begun to grow chilly, the moon relatively tiny as it had risen high above, and the breeze had dropped off leaving an expectant calm. It was time to pack up and head back to bed. Brian glanced at Jillie. "One more for the road?"

He poured two nightcaps, conscious of the fact that he had still not resolved much in his mind about John Pondoro Taylor. Well, so be it! He had come here really to say his good-byes and he had said them. Yet the two sat on in some sort of expectation that perhaps Taylor's shade might understand some sign that he understood their pilgrimage, sipping the Black Bush that would have brought out the glint in Taylor's eyes and listening to the piercing silence that surrounded the Marshes and the grave of Pondoro and Aly. Only the African bush can be so quiet.

From where they were sitting they could see right into Mozambique, the border only a couple of thousand yards away. Marsh's old instincts as a professional hunter came back with a jolt! Were they safe? Sitting out there brightly lit up with gleaming moonlight? What would happen if a RENAMO raiding party found them? There was a war going on within easy rifle shot. Just over there was the MMBA, "Miles and Miles of Bloody Africa," and those neat, square miles contained quite a few creatures of the sort that bite. Taylor's hunting camp at Lake Amaramba was only twenty miles away as the vulture flies and it was there, not all that long ago, that he used to shoot buffalo and elephant. Could there be any dangerous game wandering around here?

John Taylor had told of an old lion that lived in the hills behind Aly's home in the days when game was plentiful around Mwambwajila. The lion had lived there for some time. It never even tried to hurt anybody and helped to keep the bush pigs down. Taylor said how they would often hear the singsong roar of the old boy. He and Aly had run into him one moonlit night like this on the Mandimba bridge when they were cycling from their camp at Lake Amaramba to visit the family at Mwambwajila. The lion had watched them pass but made no effort to interfere with them. Nor would Taylor have interfered with the lion as it was a hunter, not a man-eater, a fellow predator whom Taylor greatly admired.

Taylor had been given the name "Chimpondoro, the lionlike one" by the Sena tribespeople of the lower Zambezi. To have been called this, when many native-given names were far from flattering, would have been a mark of high esteem from the tribesmen. Brian wondered now what had happened to the old lion that had lived in the hills behind Mwambwajila. He must have died a long time ago. He must have been an old lion then or he would not have been content to live up there alone. He wondered if his roars were the very last to have been heard around these parts.

And then they heard it, the sign that they had been waiting for. . . . From far beneath the blanket of silence, so far that it was all but smothered by dark distance, a deep, challenging, bass voice roared out. Brian and Jillie sat taut, listening and straining to catch the last groaning grunts before they melted into the remoteness of time and blackness that is the African night.

Brian looked at Jillie and then lifted his glass in a final salute to "A Man Called Lion."

J. Vancep.

BIBLIOGRAPHY

Bell, W.D.M. *Karamojo Safari.* New York: Harcourt, Brace and Company, 1949.

Dawkins, John. *Rogues & Marauders.* London: Robert Hale Ltd., 1967.

LaGrange, Mike. *Ballistics in Perspective.* Ferndale, CA: Professional Hunter Supplies, 1990.

Taylor, John H. *African Rifles & Cartridges.* Georgetown: South Carolina, Thomas G. Samworth, 1948.

——*Big Game and Big Game Rifles.* London: Herbert Jenkins, 1948.

——*Pondoro: Last of the Ivory Hunters.* New York: Simon and Schuster, 1955.

——*Shadows of Shame.* New York: Pyramid Books, 1956.

——*Maneaters and Marauders.* London: Frederick Muller Limited, 1959.

APPENDIXES

J. Vance p.

Appendix A
CHRONOLOGY OF JOHN TAYLOR'S LIFE

January 6, 1904	John Taylor born in Dublin.
circa 1910	Attends Monkstown Park preparatory school in Eire.
circa 1917	Attends Shrewsbury School.
circa 1919	Attends agricultural college, Dublin.
1921	John and his brother, Bill, arrested by Sinn Fein, forced to leave Ireland in fear for their lives.
circa 1921	John and Bill go to Canada. John returns to Ireland.
circa 1922	John arrives at the Cape in South Africa.
circa 1922	Travels to Rhodesia and works on mission farm near Umt ali.
circa 1923	Joins British South Africa Police (B.S.A.P.).
January 5, 1924	Dishonorably discharged from B.S.A.P. for releasing a prisoner.
1924	Meets Joro, his first gunbearer, and hunts along the Zambezi River until he reaches Angola.
mid 1925	Returns to Southern Rhodesia and takes job at West Nicholson Cattle Ranch as lion killer.

APPENDIX A

circa 1926   Works as lion killer on ranch in Northern Rhodesia.

circa 1927   Shoots his first elephant in Portuguese East Africa (P.E.A.). Continues to poach elephants in P.E.A. and then returns to Victoria Falls, Southern Rhodesia and again goes to Angola with Joro.

late 1927 or early 1928   Returns to P.E.A., settling in Tete without Joro, who stays in Southern Rhodesia.

1928   Taylor becomes extremely sick with malaria and Taylor's mother travels to Tete to retrieve him. Becomes engaged to Grace Dow, a longtime friend who accompanied Taylor's mother to Tete. All return to Ireland via boat.

1929   Goes to New Zealand and then Australia to work at sheep ranches.

circa 1929   Goes to New Guinea with partner to attempt to poach birds-of-paradise for their feathers.

1930   Returns to Tete, P.E.A. Because of lack of weapons, hunts elephants with muzzleloader.

1933-1940   Obtains center-fire rifles; the heyday of his elephant-hunting career.

1936   Great Tana Poaching Raid in Kenya for rhino and elephant.

circa 1937   Meets Fletcher Jamieson, who later provides Taylor with photos for *African Rifles & Cartridges*.

1938   Taylor searches for new hunting grounds and settles in Nyungwe, near Lake Amaramda, P.E.A., not far from border with Tanganyika.

CHRONOLOGY

circa 1938	Meets Aly Ndemanga (later to become his companion and servant) and Aly's brother.
1940	Learns of start of World War II and goes to Zomba, Nyasaland, to sign up with Kings African Rifles.
1943	Wounded in Burma and returns to Zomba.
1944-1945	Stays in Zomba to work for army intelligence.
circa 1945	Aly Ndemanga comes to Zomba to seek work and finds Taylor. Becomes his servant.
1945	At war's end Aly and John Taylor move back to Nyungwe. Upon his return, Taylor finds that all his rifles and hunting equipment he had left in a safe house at the start of the war have been stolen.
circa 1946	Taylor suffers economic hardship because of a lack of rifles. Finishes his manuscript for *Big Game and Big Game Rifles*, which he had started before the war.
1946	Travels to London to meet his publisher, Herbert Jenkins, gets advance and returns to P.E.A. Buys motor launch in Beria (P.E.A.) on his way back to camp.
circa 1946	Abandons Nyungwe and settles in Baroma, P.E.A.
1946-1947	Writes *African Rifles & Cartridges* in Baroma
1948	*African Rifles & Cartridges* is published by Samworth in the United States and *Big Game and Big Game Rifles* is published by Herbert Jenkins in the United Kingdom.

APPENDIX A

September 17, 1948 Fletcher Jamieson is electrocuted in a water well in Zimbabwe. Jamieson is survived by wife and small child. Jamieson's second child is born posthumously one week later.

1948-1949 Taylor buys new rifles with his royalties and starts hunting again.

1949 Returns to Nyungwe, near Lake Amaramba.

1950 Starts to write again to make a living; writes articles for magazines, as well as a new book entitled *Pondoro*. Aly poaches hippo for himself and Taylor to supplement their income. Aly also runs the launch as a ferry to earn money.

1952 Aly caught with Taylor's double rifle poaching hippo. Taylor's arrest imminent. Flees to Nyasaland. Meets John Dawkins and they go on safari together. Afterward Taylor is invited to go to Australia by Dawkins.

1953-1956 Stays in Australia for three years and writes *Maneaters and Marauders* and *Shadows of Shame*.

1955 *Pondoro—Last of the Ivory Hunters* is published in New York by Simon and Schuster.

1956 United Kingdom edition of *Pondoro* is published in London. *Shadows of Shame* is published in the United Kingdom and USA.

late 1956 Returns to Nyasaland to Mangochi Plateau at Aly Ndemanga Village.

1957 Meets Brian Marsh.

late 1957 Taylor deported from Nyasaland and sent to London.

CHRONOLOGY

1958	Moves in with Grace Dow and her sister in Kensington. Is forced to take menial jobs to make a living. Meets Alexander Maitland, who later becomes the executor of his will.
1959	*Maneaters and Marauders* published in the United Kingdom.
1960	*Maneaters and Marauders* published in the United States.
1961	Taylor contracts his first case of bronchial pneumonia; health worsens.
March 31, 1969	Taylor dies of chronic bronchitis at age sixty-five. He is cremated and his ashes sent to Aly Ndemanga in Nyasaland.
April 1983	Aly Ndemanga dies.

Appendix B
Taylor's Theories of Ballistics

Many hunters, unfamiliar with or cowed by the seeming scientific aspect of the word "ballistics," know much more about the subject than they might think. If you have ever thrown a rock, baseball, or been tempted to put your little sister into orbit, you are already an expert. Trust me.

Ballistics probably wedged its hairy snout the first time the first man picked up a rock and threw it at something now extinct. It is the same legitimate science that now computes missile flights as a baffling series of facts and theories. There are three very closely related aspects of ballistics that every young girl should know, those being: internal, external, and terminal. There! They even sound alike.

Let's relate this to the start-to-finish of a bullet's flight from the nanosecond the primer is ignited by the blow or the rifle's hammer. It then passes through the barrel, flying free through the air, to the final aspect where it smacks home against whatever it was aimed at or otherwise terminates its flight. The same concepts of a fired bullet's flight are exactly equal to, but with less technology, the internal ballistics represented in the windup of the rock in that early man's hand. The actual departure of the rock from his mitt is where the stage turns from internal to external to fly through the air unimpeded, but for air drag and wind. The last stage is how the rock actually thumps the critter it was thrown at and what damage it does or does not do.

Think about it. Pretty simple, really.

John Taylor's lasting contribution to the art and science of ballistics—really, etymologically speaking, the tendencies of a ball in flight—was with terminal ballistics. In other words, what happens when an animal, especially an elephant, is hit near the right spot. He was interested in the relative performance of different bullets of different calibers, moving at different speeds and weighing different totals of grains, which would influence their relative performance on arrival and impact with an elephant or other big animal.

In Taylor's time, all serious hunters knew what we know now: how fast a particular bullet from a particular cartridge moves through space, and how many foot-pounds it is computed to impact with, based upon its speed and weight, and calculated into a formula. But Taylor went further and added another factor: that of bullet diameter. It sounds simple, but at the time it was revolutionary. Blasphemy! Not done! But, he did it, and came up with what is known in *Big Game and Big Game Rifles* as "Knock-Out-Blow" and in *African Rifles & Cartridges* as "Knock-Out-Value." I suppose that Taylor did for the then-hoary principles of rifle ballistics what the breast implant did for flat-chested women, but you may draw your own conclusions as to the validity of this analogy. However, John Taylor rocked a lot of traditional boats and the action from the waves he created is still felt.

Let's face it, John Taylor got to shoot a lot of animals. It was his business. He noticed that many cartridges and loads of vastly different calibers appeared the same on a mathematician's pad as far as energy computed through the formula for foot-pounds was concerned. They were, nevertheless, by no means the same in terms of performance when an elephant or Cape buffalo happened to be bearing down on his uninsured epidermis. Understandably, this got his attention.

Taylor realized in the middle 1940s what is now obvious to all but statisticians whose access to the written word is limited to braille and to those who have never fired a gun: foot-pounds are a completely misleading method of testing the efficiency of a bullet under hunting and field conditions. More is the pity that he ducked the issue when he had the chance to openly propound his beliefs:

"I do not think," he wrote, "there is any necessity to go into the methods I employed to arrive at the formula I used, suffice it to say that the final figures agree in an altogether remarkable way with the actual performance of the rifles under practical hunting conditions."

Why he did not say that the key to his formula was the insertion of bullet diameter as a factor, rather than just speed and weight is not known. Speed could make up on paper for weight and give a totally inaccurate practical result but a technically correct prediction of bullet effectiveness. An intoxicated orangutan with a missing toe could figure out that his "secret" formula was simply to take bullet weight in grains, multiply it by bullet diameter in inches (or decimals thereof), multiply this figure by the velocity in feet per second and divide the whole lot by 7,000. Why 7,000? The result fits better into a shoe box this way, that's why. It threw

TAYLOR'S THEORIES OF BALLISTICS

off amateur mathematicians before the cut-rate hand calculator, and it just happens that there are 7,000 grains to a pound.

Taylor said of his mathematical offspring, Knock-Out Values:

> They permit an immediate comparison being made between any two rifles from the point of view of the actual punch delivered by the bullet on heavy, massive-boned animals, which are almost invariably shot at close quarters, and enable the sportsman to see at a glance whether or not any particular rifle (calibre) is likely to prove a safe weapon for the job. In the case of soft-skinned nondangerous game, such as is normally shot at medium and long ranges, theoretical mathematical energy may possibly prove a more reliable guide, provided a suitable weight of bullet is chosen for the weight of the animal against which it is to be used. But here it really does not matter so much, because it is unlikely to be a matter of life or death [the hunter's].
>
> To explain what I mean when I say that my figures give a surer and more accurate indication than do the figures for mathematical energy [foot-pounds], let us take the case of the .416 and .470-bore rifles: If you take a frontal head shot at an elephant with a .416 and miss the brain by a small amount, you will probably not knock him out. His hindquarters will give way and he will squat there like a huge dog for a few moments; then, if you do not finish him off at once, he will heave to his feet again, slew round, and clear off. But if you had taken the shot with the .470, and missed the brain by the same amount, that elephant would have been knocked out entirely, unconscious—and would have remained down for anything up to five minutes—yet the theoretical energies [foot-pounds] of the rifles are the same. The point is that my figures allow the heavier bullet thrown by the .470 to come into its own—as it does in actual practice—whereas theoretical energy would seem to make it even more powerful than the .465, yet you would find the latter hitting a heavier punch if you were to use both weapons. That the punch delivered by the .416 is sufficiently heavy for all normal requirements is immaterial and irrelevant; the point is that it does *not* hit so heavy a punch as does either of the other rifles mentioned, and my figures clearly show this.

Taylor's Knock-Out Values are excellent as they utilize the concept of bullet resistance to tissue, the resistance of a larger diameter bullet being greater than that of a small diameter slug. His terminal Knock-Out Value figures are the considerations and measurements of three factors: speed, weight, and diameter formulated as explained above. As seen, Taylor doesn't completely eliminate foot-pounds as being of no value; he does suggest that they may be of use in matters of longer range nondangerous game, providing certain design and weight characteristics are met. But, we haven't looked at bullet energy expressed by foot-pounds yet, so let's do so now.

Bullet terminal energy is, in the English-speaking world, expressed in imperial measurement, in units called foot-pounds.

APPENDIX B

First, you would expect those damned fools would decide whether they want feet in length or pounds of weight. However, one foot-pound, simply expressed, is the amount of energy it takes to raise one-pound weight a distance of one foot against the action of gravity. Conversely, a one-pound weight dropped a distance of a foot acquires one foot-pound of energy.

There are two ways of figuring this out: The first is to take half the mass times the velocity squared. However, this requires more work than that normally used by backyard ballisticians like me: Take the velocity in feet per second, multiply it times itself (square it), multiply that by the bullet weight in grains, and divide the whole ferschlugginger mess by 400 and 450,250. This will give you a nice, neat little package of foot-pounds, which you can bring home to mother or use to impress your friends. It certainly did mine!

At this point, I think it might be a good idea if we were to put this book down and get a beer before we get into a discussion of power. Okay. Power! Energy is not synonymous with power. Many riflemen wish this were so, especially those who shoot fast, light bullets and get all giggly about how many theoretical foot-pounds they unleash each time they twitch the trigger. I had better warn you that there is some bad news coming: Power is energy change per unit of time. Therefore, a bullet reflecting a higher foot-pound energy factor to a larger and slower bullet is by no means necessarily the more powerful of the two. Sorry, but that's the way it is. And, you folks at Weatherby, I'll try to get this law of physics changed for you. . . .

As he certainly recognized them for the saber-fanged, shifty, unreliable little runts they are, Taylor had little use for theoretical foot-pounds. He once described energy "as surely the most misleading thing in the world—where rifles are concerned." Certainly, foot-pounds are as misleading as dyed red hair, congressmen in general, and cartridge boxes with fanciful numbers in terms of velocities imprinted thereupon.

A number of writers have criticized Taylor for his comparison between the .416 Rigby and the .470 Nitro on the basis that the two calibers chosen were too loose a concept to qualify, whatever that means. Personally, I thought it an excellent comparison, considering what he was trying to do, which was to pick two cartridges with almost identical energy and explain that, because the .416 was smaller in diameter than the actual .475-inch measurement of the second bullet, they were not the same in power as the energy figures indicated. However, Taylor made a second comparison, apparently for writers confused by the first one.

In this case, he chose two very, very different calibers, the .577 Nitro Express, one of the heaviest elephant guns, and the .280 Halgar, a now-obsolete round, one of the first hypervelocity calibers. At 250 yards from muzzle, the Halgar is still whisking its 143-grain bullet along at 3,000 feet per second and the .577 seventy-five-grain slug is waddling along at 1,330 feet per second at the same distance. Yet, at that point, despite the weight and velocity differences, the two bullets have the same calculated foot-pounds of energy!

Taylor assures us that if an elephant were hit in the head by each of these theoretical bullets, but the brain was missed by "a small amount," the .577 would knock the elephant down, whereas the .280 Halgar would have absolutely no effect on the animal at all. Remember that this experiment took place at 250 yards from the muzzle where both bullets had nearly identical energy. The experiment did not take place at the muzzle where the .577 develops over 7,000 foot-pounds (Taylor's KOV 126.7) and the Halgar has just 3,780—with the Halgar churning out a KOV of only 19.7 because of its lesser weight and diameter, although greater speed.

Taylor's ideas become a lot more than theory when a professional hunter's life is in on the line. Brian and I thought we would put this Taylor concept to a practical test by asking most fellow professional hunters we know a simple question: Would they prefer to carry a .378 Weatherby Magnum, firing a 300-grain .375 bullet at better than 3,000 foot-seconds, with a muzzle energy of 5,700 foot-pounds and a Taylor KOV of 43.4 into heavy cover following up a wounded buffalo, or would they prefer to use a .470 Nitro Express with 600 less foot-pounds and a slower velocity of almost 900 foot-seconds but a Taylor KOV of 72.9? Of thirty men experienced with dangerous game queried, all chose the .470 Nitro over the mathematically superior .378 Weatherby Magnum. The message in this is pretty obvious: Taylor wasn't full of bat guano.

While we are speaking of the .470 Nitro, possibly the most popular British double-rifle caliber, or close to it, let me correct a typo or mistake that has been haunting gun books for more than forty years. Taylor lists the .470 Nitro as having a bullet diameter of .483 inches. This is incorrect; the proper measurement is .475.

APPENDIX B

Taylor may have gotten this wrong or had a double typographical error or maybe his printer had a "devil." However, this mistake was carried over from Taylor's works to *Cartridges of the World*, the handbook on all matters of caliber, both antique and modern as well as "wildcats." The result is that most people think that the .470 Nitro uses a .483-inch diameter bullet rather than a .475. Thus, as diameter is a vital criterion in the compilation of KOV, the figure Taylor gave for the .470 in his books is incorrect. He gives the figure as 71.3 and it is actually 72.9. Not much, but it all counts.

Many of Taylor's KOVs are slightly off. He didn't have the availability of a library as he wrote on the banks of the Zambezi. Many times he used "nominal calibre diameter" rather than actual diameter. Thus, we have computed both Taylor's nominal values based upon modern figures for velocity, energy, and nominal diameter as well as computing actual KOVs based on figures that Taylor was not privy to in the bush. By "nominal," of course, we mean the number by which the cartridge is known, which may in many cases not be the actual diameter of the bullet fired. Even the .470 Capstick uses a .475 bullet rather than the .470 bullet that its designation would indicate.

So far, and this is certainly not a book on ballistics, we have been talking about theories of what "might" happen or what "would" happen to a particular bullet of a specific caliber under specific circumstances. There have been schemes as old as time to figure out what would happen if a certain animal were to be hit by a certain bullet in a certain place. Let's be realistic; every animal is different, every animal will be in a slightly different position, and every animal will have a slightly greater or lesser degree of muscular tension. We also have to factor in such important aspects as sunspots, feet above or below sea level, the pollen count, the Dow Jones Industrial Averages, and the long-term effects of Samoan internecine strife.

Theory is one thing, but practicality is quite another, especially if your theory has developed some holes, and you are stomped or eaten by something that wouldn't know a calculator from a cucumber. Taylor really worked in reverse: He first got the field experience of using different loads in different calibers and then set out to formulate something that would tie all his findings together.

Somebody who respects Taylor's ideas greatly is Mike LaGrange, a cropping officer with the Department of National

TAYLOR'S THEORIES OF BALLISTICS

Parks and Wildlife Management in Zimbabwe. This is also a man who has given the deep-six to 6,000-plus elephants on elephant control. As you might expect, Mike LaGrange has drawn some ballistic conclusions spawned from all those defunct pachyderms. It is not curious that his are pretty much the same as Taylor's, Brian's, or mine. Mike wrote in his excellent book, *Ballistics in Perspective*, "Although energy is the mathematical expression of work potential, given similar energy values, the larger caliber weapons deliver the larger blow." Well, that's nice, neat, and concise. I also think it is a dead-accurate appraisal.

But, as some experiments Mike conducted show, the foot-pound has not been idle while its empire has been razed. It has acquired the art of the ballistic spitball! Bullets do strange things, depending on their construction, what they hit, and how fast they are going. But, sometimes, they act as rogues as Mike's experiment shows. . . .

He decided to test bullet impact by placing a sand-filled metal tube on a slide. He could later measure it to see how far the bullet had pushed the metal, sand-filled tube along the slide. He chose seven different calibers, from the .577 Nitro down to the 7.62 NATO military round. The .577 moved the tube 76.6 millimeters (3.0154 inches), while the 7.62 only slid it 3.7 millimeters (0.1456 inches), with the other calibers scoring somewhere in between. LaGrange then carried out a related experiment using for resistance a steel plate and measuring the distance of each shot from each caliber it moved. The results were at least half what was expected.

"It is evident from these experiments that the larger caliber weapons moved the plate over the greatest distance."

However, at this point, the analysis of LaGrange's results pulled a long and rusty straight razor:

"It was also noted that *the faster the weapon, the less effect it had on the plate.* [!] For example, the .458 Winchester at MV [muzzle velocity] 2,040 ft\sec. moved it 11.9mm *farther* than the .460 Weatherby at a muzzle velocity of 2,700 ft\sec., although both calibers used the same 500-grain Hornady bullet."

The italics are mine, not LaGrange's, but I'm sure I don't know why he didn't evince more astonishment at the results than he did. Maybe shooting 6,000 elephant does that to one. . . .

But, why? One would think that the harder, and therefore faster, one threw a rock at a rabbit, the harder it would hit! Well, we can only assess that velocities are as big a nest of hung-over yellow scorpions as are foot-pounds. Foot-seconds are used in the derivation of foot-pounds anyway. Therefore they are blood relatives, a paternity scam meant to astonish shooters and give writers migraines. Why does a faster bullet such as the .460 not move a resisting object, such as a steel plate, as far as a slower .458? I really have no idea. But, it does seem that there is some sort of a cutoff point when the value of velocity is negated by the velocity itself. Got to be. And, with an identical pair of 500-grain Hornady bullets, that point has to be under the velocity of 2,700 feet per second, as the .460 doesn't push a plate as far as does a .458 at lesser speed. Right? It's not necessarily over the 2,040 foot-seconds of the .458. We might find that a 500-grain Hornady bullet that is even slower than 2,040 does a better job of moving that plate than does the .458.

I'm going to pause for a few minutes while they give me my bath. Anyway, they've given me a shot to calm me down and I'm tired of typing advanced scientific theories with my teeth.

Mike LaGrange agrees that rifles carrying the higher of Taylor's Knock-Out Values noticeably put elephant down faster and harder even with brain shots. Well, the bigger diameters do more damage. Mike purposely alternated between a .375 H&H Magnum and a .458 Winchester Magnum during culls and he said, "There is just no argument. More animals get back onto their feet with the .375."

Presumably, he means those that were missed with a shot near the brain. Logically, there would be less hemorrhage with a .375 than a .458 from near misses, and we must presume that LaGrange stuck with the brain shot of which he is such a master. While Mike LaGrange is almost certainly the world's most experienced elephant shooter as well as being a superb rifle shot, any misses he has on a brain shot must be by "a small amount," almost nicks in the gray matter. It was Taylor who used the term "a small amount." Just what did Taylor mean? Let's see:

> Any rifle . . . which shows a K-O value of not less than 50 can be relied upon to knock an elephant down in any circumstances, although it may not stun him. [Taylor is clearly speaking of attempted brain shots, not body shots. It is virtually impossible to knock an elephant down with a hand-held rifle from a body shot other than in the spine.] Over 60 values are necessary if he is to be stunned and not temporarily dazed—assuming the brain is missed by an appreciable amount. . . . In dense bush it is all too frequently impossible

to do anything but knock the elephant down on a head shot, which you know cannot possibly find the brain, and then tear your way through the bush in the hope that you will be there in time to finish him off before he gathers his wits together sufficiently to do anything about it. Obviously the heavier blow you hit him, the better your chances of bagging him. As I have already pointed out, over 60 Knock-Out values are necessary to stun an elephant for anything up to five minutes or so, depending upon how close to the brain you hit him; the .500s will knock him out for possibly 20 minutes; and the .600 for anything up to half an hour. From this it will be seen that if you are armed with a .577 or a .600 you will have ample time in which to bag two, three, or even more of the first elephant's companions before bothering about him, if they are in no hurry to depart.

*   *   *   *   *   *   *

Do Taylor's Theories Work?

Taylor may be correct in principle and even often in practice, but his theory does not always work. Both Brian and I have had occasion to be disappointed with the .460 Weatherby Magnum. We expected much better performance from it based on its "numbers" than a professional hunter working for Brian got. Now, let me make it clear that I am not knocking Weatherby calibers or rifles per se. It happened to be the .460 that was long touted as the world's most "powerful" commercial cartridge (before A-Square usurped it with their .500). It has a Taylor KOV of 88.3 and is more than twice as powerful as Taylor's minimum to "daze" and nearly fifty percent above the minimum to "stun." Yet, this was the very caliber that didn't outperform the .458 Winchester by much for LaGrange in certain tests. Why?

It's certainly not Weatherby because we have all seen some fine work done in the range of their .270 through .340 magnums on smallish to moderate game up to heavy stuff, such as eland. I have never seen an elephant hit in the head with a bullet from a .460, with what I would consider a perfect side brain shot. Despite John Taylor's formula that gives the .460 such impressive paper credentials, the elephant became neither "dazed" nor "stunned." The three instances when this has happened to me with clients using the .460, I have, on every occasion, had to kill the animal. One even hit the skull three times before I shot with a .470 (twice I used the .470 and in one instance I used a .375 H&H Mag.).

APPENDIX B

When Brian's company was contracted in the 1960s for the making of "Kingstreet's War," an English film about elephant poaching in East Africa, Brian's assistant, Roy Vincent, was dressed up as the white leader of the poaching gang and positioned in front of the cameras. Brian was aloft in his Tripacer and shepherded the elephant herd being filmed toward Roy. Now thoroughly irritated at being buzzed by Brian, the herd matriarch charged as soon as Roy came into sight, which was just what the director wanted. Roy let her come while the cameras rolled.

When she was close, almost too close, Roy gave her a frontal head shot with his .460 Weatherby, which went a little high. But it dropped the charging cow almost at his feet. Roy had several other things to think about while all this was going on. He had to be sure nothing else was happening that might endanger the camera crews. The cow, however, was up again in an instant and had wheeled around. She was running away from Roy before he got off his second shot. That brought her down for good, but by Taylor's reckoning she should have stayed down on the first shot, either stunned or at least dazed. This didn't happen.

A very experienced professional hunter friend of Brian's once told him that Taylor's Knock-Out Values were something he could not relate to. In his experience they did not tally. He cited a recent example. One of his safari clients, using a .460 Weatherby, the rifle with the highest energy factor of all modern big-game calibers at the time, put his 500-grain solid bullet into a bull elephant's head with "absolutely no effect whatsoever." By Taylor's standards it should have been out cold on the ground for at least fifteen minutes! Fortunately, Brian's friend was able to put in a following heart shot that brought the elephant down.

"But, my friend," said Brian, "did admit that the bull had begun walking forwards just as the client fired. The bullet placement on the outside of the head was six inches forwards of where it should have been. In my view, as the bullet was probably angling forwards, it would not have missed the brain by what Taylor would have considered 'a small amount,' not even by what he would have described as 'an appreciable amount.' I do not think this sort of shot can be counted in this context at all."

I am not so charitable as Brian, based on what Taylor said earlier. He maintained that he took shots merely to hit the elephant on the head and then tried to run through the thick bush to finish it off. After all, the .460 Weatherby Magnum, in commercial ammo sold by Weatherby, is supposed to have 2,700 foot-seconds of muzzle velocity and 8,095 foot-pounds of muzzle energy, which interpolates to 88.3 of Taylor's KOV's. He says that only 50 Values are needed to "daze" and 60 to "stun." The client of Brian's friend didn't miss the bloody thing, he merely didn't hit the brain. He hit it in the solid part of the skull, some inches away from the brain, with 88.3 Knock-Out Values of wallop. Yet, the report is that there was "absolutely no effect whatever." Hell, even if they had thrown the Weatherby Mark V rifle at the bull, there should have been some reaction!

Who's at fault? Taylor for telling us untruths? Or the manufacturer? You must make your own decision.

Lest I earn the well-deserved ire of Messrs. Weatherby, let me be quick to say that the .460 is not the only caliber that plays weird tricks on shooters. The following examples are due to bad bullet performance. I have never heard any grumping about the performance of 500-grain 458-diameter Hornady nonexpanding solid bullets such as the .460 uses. It could well be that some of these incidents that would go to disprove Taylor's theories can be put down to bullet failure.

Immediately after the last war, Knyoch began using gilding metal to jacket the .600 Nitros, proof against metallic fouling in barrels, which had been a complaint for users of steel jackets. Some years ago I read a very interesting story that, if I recall correctly, was in the NRA's *American Rifleman Magazine*, concerning a gentleman named F.P. Williamson. He was using these new gilding metal jackets in his .600 double on safari with Kris Aschans of Ker & Downey Safaris in Kenya in 1956. Nothing wrong with my memory!

Williamson put a right and a left into an elephant's shoulder. He then took a third shot as the bull ran off, which hit the spine and anchored the bull. Then he ran up and from the side, fired six more .600 bullets into its head, all assessed later as being at the correct angle for the brain, but which did nothing whatever to the standing bull!

The astonished professional then took over the rifle and fired one round also assessed as being a perfect brain shot, with the identical effect . . . exactly nothing! Aschans then fired a single shot with his .450 No. 2 into the exact center of the seven-shot group from the .600 and killed the bull instantly. A postmortem revealed that all seven .600 bullets fired into the elephant's head had disintegrated, none penetrating far enough to find the brain. Damned lucky for Aschans and Williamson that the bull had not charged!

An elephant can be temporarily dazed by a bullet in the head. Brian recalls being with the late Victor Verster, uncle of my good friend, a retired lieutenant general of the same name. Brian's pal was the holder of the record weight of ivory taken south of the Zambezi, with a 132\107-pounder collected in Rhodesia in 1967. A bull Brian and Vic were stalking changed direction and came directly toward them and the small tree they were standing behind. The bull's obvious intention was to feed on the tree. Victor gave him a badly placed .500/.465 to the forehead. Apart from a slight weaving, he continued walking toward the men, obviously dazed, and they had to back off for a killing shot.

Zimbabwean professional hunter Clive Lenox was extremely lucky to stun, and not kill, a bull elephant that charged him. Not wanting to kill it when it charged, he ran, but tripped and fell when the bull was right behind him. He wrote about it to Brian:

> I sat up instantly and turned towards the bull, which by now had the brakes full on. I brought up the .458 to my hip, and, as the bull came sliding forward, I pulled off at its head and then felt its front feet slam into my back as the elephant came to a halt. I knew I had hit him high in the head and afterwards I was thankful that I did–for obvious reasons! The bull was now standing directly over me, penis sheath above me, that musty elephant smell filling my nostrils. He did not move for what seemed like an eternity and then took a step forward. I remember thinking to myself, he has not even stepped on me. He now started to walk slowly forward, and walked straight away from me. He stopped momentarily and turned slightly as if to return, but swung again and ran off.

The "slam" that Clive received when the stunned bull's feet thumped into his back fractured his pelvis in three places and crushed his hip in another three. It was still the best of two evils. Had his shot killed the bull, the elephant would have fallen on him.

Brian and I were sitting around the fire the other night, telling, so help us, nothing but the truth. He mentioned the comments of a game warden whom he knew that had shot, with no effect, a crop-raiding elephant in each of the temples, first on one side and then on the other when it turned 180 degrees to run. We put this down to probable but rare bullet deflection in the .470 Nitro, which has a tapered bullet that sometimes gave Taylor a spot of trouble. The new stuff, particularly the A-Square Monolithic alloy solid, suffers from none of these problems that sometimes plagued the old Kynoch stuff.

Of course, that story reminded me that no less a personage than Karamojo Bell once had a strange experience with an astonishingly old bull. I found the story in his second book, *Karamojo Safari*, and pass it on. This is not so much a story that concerns Taylor, but it does show that some elephants are surprising in their reactions to bullets. Bell, of course, was considered the finest exponent of the brain shot with light calibers, as well as its finest practitioner. He was using a 275 Rigby, the British designation for the 7x57mm Mauser, with solid, 170-grain bullets:

> In this case we were lucky to view him suddenly in the open. He was quite motionless and resembled a piece of the fantastically contorted rock formation that pierced the bush in all directions. The scene formed a glimpse into the past. One felt awed by the strangeness of it all. Thus probably was the world thousands of years ago.
>
> Certainly this elephant conveyed a sense of great size, but the ivory did not look phenomenally large. That it would weigh well was evident because it held its girth so far out of the head, and one knew that the hollows would be short from the age of the beast. Age was written all over him. His massive head was horny and mossy on top, the skin hung in wrinkled folds, and there was not the slightest sign of movement except the little eyes closing wearily from time to time. I never felt so queer as when I gazed on this relic. Usually such stillness on the part of an elephant meant that he had heard some suspicious sound and I would have sprinted silently into position to kill him. But in that case the ears would have been cocked to catch the faintest vibration. Here they drooped forlornly. The whole animal expressed weariness in every attitude. Tired of the century-long struggle, he was probably deaf and almost blind. Burdened with such a load of years, he possibly no longer felt the stings of the swarms of flies that beset him. Indeed, they set up such a hum as to suggest that the living carcass was already far gone into putrefaction.
>
> Although he was ideally positioned for the brain shot and should have dropped poleaxed to the ground, nothing of the sort happened when I fired. To my amazement nothing happened at all. There was no movement whatsoever. Again I fired for the brain. Again there was no response—just a sullen wooden thud of the bullet. One might have been firing into a clay cliff. I can tell you that a very queer sensation came over me. I lowered my rifle and gazed thunderstruck. Was he dead on his feet or what? Quickly recovering, I gave him a meticulously calculated shot in the heart. Ah! here was some response at any rate. He moved slowly forward so I ran ahead of him and tried once more for the brain, this time the frontal shot. He collapsed, very much to my relief.
>
> I have never understood what happened to the first shot. At this period of my career, I had at long last learned the lesson that the first shot must be the best-delivered one. I could not believe that this one had been ill placed,

and a close examination of the head showed it to have been properly positioned as far as I could judge. Whether the 170-grain bullet had been deflected by unusually heavy bone or held up altogether remains a mystery.

Even as expert at judging ivory as Bell was, he figured these to go about 125 pounds per side. He was happily amazed when they tipped the scales at 148 and 145 pounds, a true patriarch of pachyderms.

Today, with sportsmen and safari hunting, as opposed to professional ivory hunting, the real modern test of Taylor's Knock-Out Values designed for elephant hunting is happily not empirical. Any professional hunter worth his biltong insists that any specimen of dangerous game be given a second, "insurance" shot, no matter how dead it may appear to be. Big game has a nasty habit of getting up from apparent death and killing you. Thus, many head-shot elephant that have in modern times appeared to be dead from a first shot may have, in fact, been victims of Taylor's Knock-Out Values. Remember, big-bore ammo was as rare and precious as plutonium in the 1930s in places like Mozambique and even more scarce just after the war. Taylor could not afford an "insurance" shot because of the scarcity of ammunition supplies and the cost of cartridges. Naturally, this being the case, he would have seen a great many more elephant revive after being knocked unconscious by near brain misses than we would today. Now, they would never awaken from being knocked cold by a near miss. They would be given their quietus by a safety shot.

Fletcher Jamieson "brain shot" an elephant, which dropped instantly, its legs buckling under it so it ended up on its belly. He went about setting up his Graflex camera on its tripod while he bade his team of trackers and gunbearers to climb onto the elephant's back. The camera set up and focused, Fletch instructed his camera-bearer to squeeze the bulb when he signaled, and he climbed onto the carcass to join his men for the photo. The shutter clicked, whereupon the elephant stood up, rolling its riders off its back into a thoroughly frightened heap. Fortunately the bull was still dazed, so after hastily shaking the sand out of his rifle, Fletch quickly shot it again, very much displeased that the camera had clicked a moment too soon to capture the shot of a lifetime.

Remember Fletcher Jamieson's experience of having a "dead" elephant get up while he and all his hunting crew were having their picture taken on the carcass. I'll bet he didn't think about the price of ammo quite so hard after that.

So, whatever the truth concerning unusual situations, we believe John Taylor was basically correct in his hypothesis that a greater diameter bullet kills better and causes more deadly trauma than one of lesser diameter, provided bullet construction and design are good and the aiming is as it should be for a quick, first-shot kill. And, John Taylor himself might have given you the classic advice of the old-timer to the beginning hunter, "Get as close as ye can, sonny, and then get ten yards closer!" And then, with a devilish glint in his eye and a chuckle in his voice, he would have said, "D'ye see?"

APPENDIX B

CARTRIDGES LISTED ARE IN ORDER OF ASCENDING KNOCK-OUT VALUE

Calibre	Bullet Diameter in inches	Bullet Weight in grains	Muzzle Velocity feet/ sec.	Muzzle Energy foot/ lbs.	KOV Actual	KOV Nominal
.22 Long Rifle HV.	.223	40	1255	140	1.59	1.57
.223 Remington (5.56mm)	.224	55	3185	1239	5.6	5.5
.224 Weatherby	.224	55	3600	1582	6.3	6.3
.22-250 Remington (6mm)	.244	55	3730	1699	6.5	6.4
.243 Winchester	.244	100	3070	2090	10.7	10.6
.244 H&H Magnum	.244	100	3500	2725	12.2	12.2
.257 Weatherby	.257	117	3300	2824	14.2	14.2
.275 Rigby (7x57mm)	.284	173	2430	2260	17.0	16.5
.30-30 Winchester	.308	170	2220	1860	16.6	16.3
.264 Winchester Magnum	.264	140	3200	3180	16.9	16.9
.270 Winchester	.277	50	2900	2800	17.2	16.8
.300 Savage	.308	180	2370	2240	18.7	18.7
.280 Remington	.284	165	2820	2910	18.9	18.6
7x64mm Brenneke	.284	173	2780	2965	19.5	18.9
7mm Weatherby	.284	154	3160	3416	19.7	19.1
.270 Weatherby	.277	150	3245	3501	19.3	18.7
.308 Winchester	.308	200	2450	2670	21.5	21.5
7mm Remington Magnum	.284	175	3020	3546	21.4	21.7
.30-06 Springfield	.308	220	2410	2830	23.3	22.7
.308 Norma Magnum	.308	180	3100	3842	24.5	24.5
.300 Winchester Magnum	.308	220	2720	3620	26.3	25.6

KNOCK-OUT VALUES

Calibre	Bullet Diameter in inches	Bullet Weight in grains	Muzzle Velocity feet/ sec.	Muzzle Energy foot/ lbs.	KOV Actual	KOV Nomimal
.300 Weatherby	.308	220	2905	4123	28.1	27.4
.358 Winchester	.358	250	2250	2810	28.7	28.7
.348 Winchester	.348	250	2350	3060	29.2	29.2
.338 Winchester	.338	250	2700	4046	32.6	32.6
.340 Weatherby	.338	250	2820	4414	34.0	34.2
.358 Norma Magnum	.358	250	2790	4322	35.6	35.6
.375 H&H Magnum	.375	300	2550	4330	40.1	40.1
.378 Weatherby	.375	300	2925	5700	47.0	47.3
.416 Remington	.416	400	2380	5031	56.6	56.6
.416 Rigby	.416	400	2400	5115	57.0	57.0
.416 Weatherby	.416	400	2600	6004	61.8	61.8
.450 No.2 (3 1/2") N.E	.455	480	2175	5050	67.8	67.1
.500/.465 H&H N.E	.456	480	215	4930	67.2	68.5
.458 Winchester Magnum	.458	500	2130	5040	69.7	69.7
.450 Ackley	.458	465	2400	5947	73.0	71.7
.470 N.E	.475	500	2150	5140	72.9	72.1
.460 Short A-Square	.458	500	2420	6501	79.1	79.5
.500 (3") N.E.	.510	570	2150	5850	89.3	87.5
.460 Weatherby	.458	500	2700	8095	88.3	88.7
.500 Jeffery Rimless	.510	535	2400	6800	93.5	91.7
.500 A-Square	.510	600	2470	8127	107.9	105.8
.577 (3") N.E.	.585	750	2050	7010	128.5	126.7
.600 N.E	.622	900	1950	7600	156.0	150.4

Appendix C
Taylor's Magazine Articles

Preface

Unknown to most Taylor aficionados, he wrote a number of articles for magazines in addition to his famous books. The majority of the articles were written for a now defunct English publication entitled *Game & Gun,* with the first article appearing in the 1930s and the last article appearing in 1946. In addition, Taylor wrote a few articles for the *American Rifleman* magazine in the 1940s and 1950s. Last, but not least, Taylor wrote an article on buffalo hunting that appeared in *True* magazine in 1975.

The articles reprinted here appear in chronological order, according to the date they were first published in magazine form. In editing these articles, we tried to change as little as possible. In the reprinted articles, some minor changes in punctuation and in a few cases slight revisions were made to conform to current usage. Wherever possible, however, the flavor and character of Taylor's writing have been maintained. On occasion changes were made simply to make the passage more readable to modern audiences.

"Concerning Lions"
Game & Gun
May, 1936

Whenever sportsmen from Africa and India foregather, the inevitable argument crops up as to the comparative ferocity and killing powers of lion and tiger. It is all hypothetical of course, of mere academic interest since nothing can be proved. Personally, I consider that whatever difference there may be is negligible.

Speaking generally, both beasts are of approximately the same size, though a well-maned lion may look bigger. I think that is principally due to the mane. Taking muscle for muscle, their strength must be more or less the same. As tiger are known to kill full-grown elephant (captive) out East, while lion will only on rare occasions pull down a very young elephant calf in Africa, the tiger must be both stronger and a better killer than the lion is the argument. That is easily answered. Nobody can deny that there is considerably more game per lion in Africa than per tiger in India. Consequently, the lion has never had to devise methods of killing the larger beasts, such as elephant and rhino.

His favorite method is to spring on a beast's shoulders, close his teeth on the back of the neck and bite. At the same time one mighty-muscled forearm grabs the beast by the nose and wrenches the head round. This breaks the neck and death is of course instantaneous. Anything, such as a slight eddy of wind, may warn the quarry of the lion's proximity and make him spring forward in alarm at the instant of the attack. This will cause the lion to miss his target and land abaft the shoulder. Nine times out of ten the lion will just allow himself to slide to the ground. It does not seem to occur to the lion to bite through the spine and paralyse the animal's hindquarters. He does not think of grabbing a hind leg and pulling the beast down. He is satisfied to let the quarry go and hunt on a bit further. He will almost certainly be given another opportunity before the night is out.

As proof of this, I have frequently shot animals that have been scored diagonally right down the ribs by a lion's claws. I remember once I had shot a fine big roan antelope bull on the Angoni Plateau. On examining him, I found that he had been scored right down one side only a day or two before and, on turning him over, was carrying similar wounds on the other side. They had obviously been made some years previously. The freshly made wounds showed clearly that the lion had landed well up on the roan's back but some distance behind the shoulders. He had just allowed himself to slide off. I admit I have been told by cattle owners of lion grabbing oxen by one hind leg and pulling the beast down, but I have never actually seen it myself. That, I may add, was in a district in which all game had been shot out.

I have often been asked the reason why so many lion have the long tushes at the corners of their mouths broken off. I do not think that there can be much doubt about the answer. The lion's favorite method of killing is to bite into the neck at the same time as he grabs the animal's nose and pulls the head round. As the beast crashes to the ground, the lion springs clear. It must frequently happen that one or more of his long tushes have become jammed between the joints of the vertebrae of his prey. The jolt as the animal comes down and the lion's own movements would be sufficient to snap off the jammed tooth.

The greater my experience with lion, the more emphatically do I state that he is both a sportsman and a gentleman. I am not of course referring now to man-eaters. He does not kill for the sheer love of killing, as a leopard will. He does not kill from blood lust. He kills solely for food or in self-defense, and he only kills as much as he needs.

I have been told that a troop of lion will occasionally kill far more than they need when attacking a herd of cattle. That is exceptional. Quite possibly when the cattle break out of the kraal, the lions start to kill without knowing that their pals were all similarly occupied. Time and again I have come across two or more lions hunting together. Almost invariably the actual killing is left to one. In the case of those cattle that broke out and rushed amongst the lions, the temptation to kill and make sure of a feed proved too much for some of the latter. This accounts for the unnecessary blood being spilled. When hunting game, of course things are different.

I have seen several lion resting in the shade and a large mixed herd of zebra and hartebeest feeding in the immediate vicinity. On another occasion, as I have recorded elsewhere, I saw a zebra pulled down from a troop. His companions of course stampeded at the attack, but very soon they pulled up and looked round. On seeing that the lions obviously had all that they wanted, they began grazing again as though nothing had happened. They knew that they were perfectly safe from further attack. The ordinary hunting lion will never attack man unless provoked into doing so. He does not want to fight. He does not want trouble. He will leave you alone if you leave him alone. He does not like having to get out of your way, naturally, but he will do so rather than start a row. He simply does not want to have anything to do with man.

Apart from wild dogs, man is the lion's only enemy. All wild animals have a natural, instinctive, hereditary fear of man. The lion is no exception. He knows that man is the only creature that can kill from afar without coming to actual grips, and he fears him as the average man fears a snake. Although the experience may not be a particularly pleasant one, you may quite safely meet a lion or lions face to face when you are quite unarmed. Provided that you do not do something foolish or lose your head, the chances are a hundred to one that they will not molest you.

JOHN H. TAYLOR

"Man-Eaters"
Game & Gun
June, 1936

With rare exceptions, lions only take to man-eating when very aged. Then, with their teeth worn down, their claws blunted and their great strength and agility failing them, they sometimes take to haunting the vicinity of native villages in the evenings to catch the women that go to draw water. There can be no doubt, however, that the great majority of lions do not take to man-killing when old age comes on. They starve to death on rats and rabbits and even frogs, rather than force down their natural aversion to man.

Were it not so, then Africa would be infested with man-eaters. Since there are lions born every year, so must there be lions aging every year. It is only in districts in which the balance of nature has been upset by the extermination of game by man that the younger lions take to man-eating. They are forced to do so by hunger, and if they have cubs, they will bring the youngsters up with similar propensities.

Even then it is, more often than not, sheer accident that starts a lion on a man-eating career. He is prowling round ravenous with hunger and comes across a native or two sleeping out without a fire or any other protection. The temptation is irresistible. Probably before he quite realizes what he is doing, he has sprung on one of the sleepers and carried him off. Then, finding how easy man is to kill and how easy to eat—there is no tough hide here to be torn off—he tries again. His efforts meeting with success, he gradually overcomes his instinctive fear of man and becomes that most feared and dreaded of all beasts—the man-eater.

Only a few weeks ago at my old camp at Mangwendi, I had an unfortunate man carried away from within a few feet of where I was sleeping. It had once been a notorious district for man-eaters, and only a few miles away, over the Nyasaland border, it still is. Just here we had not been troubled for some five years or so. There would be lions roaring every night, but, as there was plenty of game about, we took no notice and never bothered to keep up the fire at night. On this particular night, the beast had come right along the path from over the border, as we found by his spoor next day, and on arrival here he had first of all prospected the village by which I am camped. Then he came sneaking over to where we were sleeping.

Curiously enough, he stepped right over two lads to get a third who was sleeping actually closer to the glowing remains of the fire. It was through the lion treading on one of those two lads and waking him up that the hue and cry was raised. The boy woke up to find the lion standing on his legs and in the act of grabbing the third boy. At the first yell, I was up and out of bed for I had previous experience of man-eaters and lit the hurricane lamp. It was a pitch black night and the grass was long round the little clearing in which the camp was pitched. A rifle would have been useless to me, as I knew. There was just a chance with the lamp of saving the wretched lad's life, if only I could be quick enough. Fortunately, there was not a breath of wind to blow out the match and I doubt if a hurricane-lamp has ever been lit quicker.

I then rushed after the lion . . . naked and all as I was. I was waving the lamp and yelling at the top of my voice. Luck was with us, both me and the lad, for I caught up with them at the very edge of the clearing. The lion, having grabbed the boy by one knee only, was having trouble escaping with his prize. He had to keep his head turned sideways as he ran to drag the lad along and not trip over him. The result was that he could not see too well where he was going and, consequently, ran his own chest into the sharp stump of a small tree that had been felled two or three feet from the ground. The jar caused him to drop the boy, and before he could grab him again, I appeared on the scene. I rather fancy that the spectacle I presented must have proved too much for his nerves. He leaped round to face me but, with a vicious snarl, wheeled again and bounded into the grass. It is extremely improbable that he had ever previously faced a stark-naked white man, yelling and roaring at the top of his voice, waving a lighted lamp in one hand and wildly rushing straight at him! Now that was probably that lion's first attempt at man-eating. He had been prowling along ravenously hungry and had found us sleeping in the open right in his path. He was in the last stages of starvation as we found a couple of days afterwards when he broke into a hut in another village and killed a woman and three children. He was shot for his pains before he could get out again.

That a lion's hereditary fear of man takes a deal of overcoming is, I think, pretty conclusively proved. The fact is that when a wounded lion gets hold of a hunter, he does not seem to know quite what to do with him. He appears completely to lose his head. Of course the pain of his wound, to say nothing of the shock, if the usual dumdum bullet has been used, will tend to produce this condition. On top of that, it seems as though his old fear of man is still battling, even against his berserk rage. He will grab a hand in his mouth and chew it or an arm or a leg. It does not appear to enter his head to take the man by the throat and just shake him. One very rarely hears of a hunter being killed outright by a wounded lion. Those who lose their lives generally do so through blood poisoning setting as a result of the mauling.

PONDORO

"COINCIDENCES"
Game & Gun
September, 1936

Curious coincidences take place in the bush. I shot a big warthog one day that had been attacked simultaneously by two leopards the night before. He was very sick and had only travelled about fifty yards from the spot where he had been attacked. I back-spoored him, for it is very rare in this part of the world that leopards hunt in pairs, and found that he had been approached from both sides. It seemed pretty clear that neither leopard knew of the existence of the other. They both sprang together. In their surprise and confusion on finding that they were trying to take what must have seemed another's kill, the pig managed to make good his escape.

It is by no means unusual that an animal should be stalked simultaneously by two different enemies. A number of years ago I was stalking a fine sable bull up Barotseland way. He was feeding on the far side of a small clearing and I was able to approach to within about thirty yards or so. I was on the point of firing when I noticed a magnificent black-maned lion stalking the sable. He was almost within springing distance, so I very cautiously exchanged my rifle for a camera. With any sort of luck, I was going to obtain a unique photograph. Inch by inch, the lion crept closer. When at last I saw his hind feet wriggling for a sure foothold, I prepared to snap the picture. He sprang. I clicked the shutter of my camera and picked up my rifle. The lion had broken the bull's neck by his favorite method and was walking round his kill, licking his chops and lashing his tail. I waited until he exposed his broadside and a single shot was sufficient. It was a most successful morning: a fine sable, a magnificent lion, a black-maned one at that, and a unique photograph.

On another occasion at Mangwendi in the lower Zambezi Valley, I was looking for some fresh meat for the pot. I came on a bunch of kudu cows in the open, some fifty yards away or thereabouts. The grass was knee-high. This was in a tsetse fly belt and there were no restrictions on shooting cows. As the remainder of the troop stampeded on the heels of the shot, there came a series of angry, baffled grunts as a large tawny-maned lion bounded away. He had been stalking the cows somewhere between me and them and must have been almost within springing distance. No wonder he was peeved!

Yet another somewhat similar coincidence gave me one of the finest sights that I have ever witnessed in the African bush. It also took place in the lower Zambezi Valley in the Moravia district. I was returning to camp about midday after a successful elephant hunt, when on crossing a clearing in which the grass was up to my chin, I heard a kudu coughing in a small but very dense thicket on the far side of the clearing. The little thicket was only about a quarter of an acre in extent, so I proceeded to advance straight across the clearing. When I was within fifteen feet of the bush, I heard a shot on the far side. It was a shotgun, so my cook boy was apparently trying to get a guinea fowl in the native lands that commenced there. The shot was answered by a crash in the thicket, and in the next second a fine kudu bull came full tilt through the bush straight for me. I swung up the double rifle, which I was carrying, and waited for the bull to win clear to the open. As he bounded out, not more than five yards from where I was standing, he saw me and slewed round.

My heavy slug—I was loaded for elephant—smashed both his shoulders. He turned a complete somersault and lay facing the direction whence he had come. As I fired, out of the corner of my eye I saw a tawny shape come streaking through the bush after the bull. Naturally, I imagined that it was one of his cows, since it was only a glimpse that I got. I had all the meat that I wanted now, so I did not intend to shoot. I brought the rifle down from my shoulder with the intention of reloading that barrel when I suddenly found myself looking straight into a lioness's open mouth. It was on a level with my own.

The tawny shape that I had glimpsed was not a kudu cow. The lioness must have been stalking the bull, and pretty close too, when the shot on the far side of the thicket had stampeded him right onto the muzzle of my rifle. In baffled fury and a wild hope of being able to catch him, the lioness had come tearing after the bull. She must have been ravenously hungry to have been hunting so close to a large native village in the middle of the day. She did not see me, though she seemed to be looking straight at me. I am convinced that she never heard the crashing roar of my big Express, so great was her anxiety to find and catch the bull. She leaped high in the air to see over the grass. Then seeing her quarry lying almost at her feet, but facing her and not wishing to land on his horns, for she could not know that he was dead, she gave her body one mighty twist, turned completely over in midair, her heels over her head, and came down on the bull's shoulders.

It was all so utterly unexpected: the finding of a lioness when I was looking for a kudu cow; the utter improbability of finding lion so close to a large native village at that hour of the day; the speed with which it all happened and prevented any possibility of my getting in a shot. Although it takes some time to tell, the whole thing only lasted for a split second. Although she was eating my meat, she doubtless thought that it was hers, and in that grass where I could not have seen her until I was within a matter of two or three feet (and she would undoubtedly hear me approaching), I had not the slightest intention of arguing with a ravenously hungry lioness as to the rightful ownership of the kill! She had possession of it, wanted it badly, and would almost certainly refuse to part with it without a struggle. I retreated a short distance, made a detour round her and looked for a tree to climb that would enable me to see her in the grass.

J. H. TAYLOR

"VELOCITY AND KILLING POWER"
Correspondence to the Editor of
Game & Gun
March, 1937

Sir,—Together I suppose with everyone else who handles a rifle, I have been following with intense interest the correspondence dealing with this subject. It seems to me that most people seem to miss what, in my experience, is one of the most important points: the spot where the bullet takes the animal. Any modern rifle that fires suitable bullets will kill in his tracks any animal shot between the shoulders from in front and from above, irrespective of any question of velocity, since the spinal column will have been severed. In the same way, if a man sits up for a tiger and shoots him between the eyes from a height, of course he will drop stone dead.

I have experimented with a great many rifles during the years that I have been hunting, and for what they are worth, I am only too glad to offer my observations on this most interesting question of killing power. For years I put the "Critical Striking Velocity" at roughly the same figure as "Argus," i.e., 2,400 f.p.s. or thereabouts. Some little time ago I killed a kudu bull at what I estimated to be nearer 250 than 200 yards, but not quite the full 250, with the 270-grain bullet from my .375 magnum. This rifle I had sighted for 200 yards for this bullet. The bead of the foresight covers the spot that you wish to hit at that range. This gives me a bullet drop of roughly 4½ inches at 250 yards. (I mention this because it has an important bearing on my final determination of the exact range.) I was comfortably wedged between two convenient trees, so that I was rock steady. I could only see the bull's shoulders between two bushes, so I could not aim as I used to do just behind the shoulder. I placed my foresight on the hindermost edge of his shoulder blade and some three or four inches higher than usual, to allow for the bullet drop. I did not think that he was quite 250 yards away.

On the shot he went down as though struck by lightning. I immediately jumped to the conclusion that the bullet must have touched a twig, been deflected somewhat, and crashed into his spine abaft the withers. On examining him, however, I found that it had done nothing of the sort but had taken him exactly where my foresight had been. The range, therefore, must have been almost exactly 200 yards, which means that the striking velocity of the bullet could not have been much more than 2,200 f.p.s. or thereabouts. Yet the bull had been killed instantaneously, which would seem to indicate that the critical velocity is appreciably less than 2,400 when the bullet strikes the right spot.

I have shot, I suppose, hundreds of similar animals through the heart without touching a bone, other perhaps than a rib. Save that they have collapsed much sooner than they would have, had they been shot with a lower velocity, there was nothing very remarkable about their death. Since that occasion I have made a point of placing my bullet whenever possible through the hindermost edge of the shoulder blade and more often than not death has been literally instantaneous.

It would be interesting to know if the dark blotch on the shoulder of Colonel Alexander's buffalo in the photograph that accompanied his first letter is the bullet wound.

Captain Norton mentions dropping a buffalo in his tracks with his .375 magnum. Did he kill it, or merely knock it out? And where did the bullet take it?

Although I cannot claim to have actually "poleaxed" him, I brought a charging buffalo to his knees and his nose with a 300-grain solid from my .375 magnum that was placed just inside the point of the shoulder from in front. He just rolled over and died. The range was between eight and ten paces. He had been badly stubbed by the first shot, which had taken him just under the boss of the horns but too high for the brain. By the time I had torn my way through a matted tangle of brambles and closed in to make sure of him, he was just "coming to." He immediately scrambled to his feet and came for me, but he was obviously still badly dazed and without his full strength. Nor had he time to get up full speed.

Major Marriott states that he saw a charging tiger shot in the mouth with a soft-nosed .375 magnum at a range of about twenty yards and come on as though untouched. Did the tiger stop the bullet or did the bullet just pass through some part of the mouth or jaw and then waste its energy on the surrounding landscape? I personally have stopped several charging lions with my .375 magnum. Although I prefer, probably from force of habit, a heavier bullet for such work, nevertheless I use the rifle when necessary with every confidence. It has never let me down yet, and I see no reason to suppose that it ever will.

Incidentally, when shot with "ordinary" rifles, animals usually fall on the wounded side, presumably owing to the muscles contracting or losing power first on that side. Can anyone explain how it is that when shot with a magnum they as often as not fall on the other side, not only when "poleaxed," but even when they have been able to travel some little distance? I have frequently noticed this, both when using solid as well as expanding bullets.

JOHN H. TAYLOR
Portuguese East Africa

"Averages"
Game & Gun
June, 1937

An article, "Hits to Misses," in a recent issue proved, at all events, of absorbing interest to me out here on the Zambezi. True, it dealt with bird shooting on your side of the water, but nevertheless, it gave a very excellent idea of what constitutes a "good average." Big-game shooting is, of course, a very different proposition, so much so in fact, that the two sports cannot be compared, save only on the question of heads or tails collected per 100 rounds of ammunition fired.

Out here in the big-game shooting districts of Africa, you hear equally impossible claims being made, though almost invariably they are made by the inexperienced man. The hunter, who knows his job, also knows that extravagant claims of what he has shot with his last hundred rounds are just so many insults to the intelligence of other experienced hunters within earshot.

When considering a man's average, there is one point which is frequently overlooked. That is, is the man a professional hunter or only an amateur? I have several times had nonprofessional sportsmen tell me that I ought to have a much better average than they have, since I am at the game all the year round. They are lucky to get a couple of months a year in the bush and generally only a bare six weeks or less. The whole thing is summed up in those two words "professional" and "nonprofessional."

The amateur wants good trophies: good tusks, good heads, and good skins. He need not fire unless he likes what he sees, and there are rarely two really good heads standing together, although of course, there are exceptions. In other words, he is out essentially for quality. The professional hunter, far more often than not, must shoot for quantity if he is to do his job thoroughly, particularly in the case of an elephant control officer or cultivation protector. Let us take the two cases separately: an average day in the life of an amateur sportsman in good game country and a similar day in the life of a government hunter.

The nonprofessional man leaves camp and sooner or later encounters game of a certain species. If there is a good head amongst them, he stalks. If the animals wind him and stampede, he need not tire himself out following them unless he likes. He can branch off and wander round until he encounters something else. Even if there is more than one good head, he is under no obligation to kill more than the one. As far as that one is concerned, he should be able to kill it cleanly with a single shot, since he can take his own time and not worry about the others perhaps wandering into the bush. He only wants the one. He drops it and moves on. In good game country he will almost certainly encounter another species before long. He again kills with a single shot. Before reaching camp, he may quite possibly spot yet another type of game and again secure his trophy without trouble—three heads for three rounds fired.

Now take the case of the elephant control officer. A troop of elephant have raided the natives' food crops overnight. He gets on the spoor at daybreak and follows the troop. As any experienced elephant hunter can tell you, it is astonishing how often when following elephant you can encounter other game at absurdly close quarters. They always seem to be particularly fine specimens. They seem to know that you are not dangerous, for they do not stampede madly away, as they usually would. You cannot fire for fear the elephant will hear the shot. It is the government man's job to catch up with those elephant and teach them their lesson.

If the wind is favorable, he may do so and get back to camp by nine or ten o'clock or thereabouts. If the wind is contrary, he may close them in thick bush and approach within a matter of a few paces, only to have a wee whiff of air come from the wrong direction and stampede the herd. This may happen time and again during the day. At length, perhaps towards the middle of the afternoon, he gets his chance. The breeze has died down and he can move round and count the beasts. He can determine which to select as examples and how many he should kill to impress upon the remainder that it is dangerous to raid.

If the herd consists of ten or twelve persistent raiders, then he will probably attempt to kill three of them. Now this would be comparatively simple if the elephant were standing in the open. During the midday heat, however, they will almost certainly be in thick bush or heavy forest. Since they know that they have been followed all day from the scene of their depredations, they will be more or less on the alert. At least, they will certainly stampede on the heels of the first shot. Elephant that are not on the alert very often will not stampede because of the difficulty of placing the danger zone in thick cover. The point is that the first step will place most of them out of sight. Although the hunter might be able to drop the leader with a clean brain shot from a certain position, it might not be possible for him to fire from there. If he did, he might not get another shot. Accordingly, he must manoeuvre into such a position that he has a fair chance of bagging his three, even if it can only be done by crippling the first two or the first and third.

Judging the most likely line to be taken by the herd when it stampedes and the most probable actions of his chosen three, he takes up his position and opens fire. His first shot may be for the point of the shoulder to break the bone. His second may be a side brain shot as the second "example" exposes his broadside. The third shot will be either a side heart, lung shot or possibly an anchoring shot by the root of the tail if the animal is travelling directly away from him. Assuming these three shots have come off as he wanted them to, he has surely bagged three elephant with three rounds. An elephant with a broken shoulder must fall sooner or later, and once down with a broken shoulder, he cannot rise again. He must be given another shot to finish him off and put him out of his misery. So also must the "anchored" one. The professional man has also collected his three tails that day, but it has taken him five rounds to do it.

The hunter retained by government for elephant control purposes that can show his fifty-five to sixty tails per one hundred rounds of ammunition fired has no need to be ashamed of himself. From sixty to seventy is jolly good shooting. Anything over seventy spells phenomenally good luck in finding the elephant in easy country, more than anything else. I am, of course, assuming a keen hunter who does his work conscientiously for its own sake and not just for the few pounds a month that his salary brings him in. The ivory hunter should show a better average than the government man. The nonprofessional sportsman should show a still better record. When you hear men speaking of an average of ninety-six to ninety-seven animals killed per one hundred rounds of ammunition fired, a large, a very large, pinch of salt is more than indicated.

PONDORO

"Rhino in Thick Bush"
Game & Gun
August, 1937

Here in the Tete district of Portuguese East Africa where I live and hunt, rhino are an infernal nuisance to an elephant hunter like myself. Time and again have I been charged by rhino when following up a troop or herd of elephants. In not-too-thick scrub or open forest you can generally manage to dodge the brute since he will usually just continue at full speed in the direction in which he was facing. But in thick bush, particularly if it is of the hawk's-bill thorn variety, it is frequently a physical impossibility to dodge. You must just stand your ground and shoot the brute, which means good-bye to any chance you may have had with the elephant. It was this, really, that introduced me to the joys and excitements of rhino hunting. For a while, since the price of ivory dropped to next to nothing and it was no longer possible to make a living off the elephant, I turned my attention to the rhino, determined to get some back on them.

Now this rhino hunting in thick bush is a game that one very rarely sees played. Really it is rather extraordinary, because it is an intensely exciting sport. The excitement begins the moment you leave camp and continues uninterruptedly until you return again. (I am of course assuming a district in which rhino are numerous.) You never know when you are going to encounter one of the brutes. You may tramp for hours without seeing one. You may find yourself being attacked within a few minutes of leaving camp.

Unless you are very close, if a rhino sights you but does not wind you, he will probably clear off. If he hears you but does not get your wind, he will usually do likewise. Even if he does get your wind, he will rarely charge unless fairly close. The distance varies with individual beasts, but if he is not within a hundred yards, he will most likely make off. In the dense, matted tangles of bush beloved by rhino, however, anything over twenty-five yards is a very long shot. The usual range will be found to work at from two or three feet to ten or twelve paces. In other words, since you are so very close to the beasts, if you do happen to encounter them, the chances are at least even as to whether he comes or not.

But the point is that if he does come, he will be coming from such very close quarters and will arrive so shortly after his first snort of warning, it is absolutely imperative for you to be very much on the alert and carrying your own rifle. The pluckiest and most willing of gunbearers cannot be blamed if he jumps for his life when he sees a rhino's horn coming straight for his midriff and is only perhaps two or three feet away. It is not fair on the lad to expect him to do anything else.

Of course when playing this game, you will frequently hear the rhino before he either hears or winds you. In which case you will just stalk up as close as possible and drop him. It may not sound very exciting, but there is always the possibility of there being another in the immediate vicinity and there is no telling what that one is going to do. If it is the mate of the one that you have dropped, it may bounce about, snorting like an antiquated traction engine and then suddenly dash off at full speed, quite possibly straight for thick bush behind which you are crouching. I assure you there is no lack of excitement.

During one very successful morning when I shot and killed five rhino, I was attacked by no less than three different animals. On another occasion, when trekking through a thick patch of thorn in which I was unaware that there were any rhino, I had one of the beasts toss me over his head and crack my kneecap, an extremely unpleasant experience, even though I had the satisfaction of killing the brute.

The question of suitable rifles for this sport is of paramount importance. The first question that crops up is whether to use a double or a magazine. Now here there can be no two opinions, no two possible opinions. A double rifle is out and away the best type of weapon. In fact in my opinion, if the bush is very dense and the rhino numerous, then a double is not merely preferable, but definitely essential. There are several reasons for this:

First: In very dense bush every unnecessary inch on the length of a rifle counts heavily against it, particularly when you may, and probably will, have to swing round suddenly. A double is much shorter and more compact than a magazine.

Second: As everybody knows, balance helps one enormously to swing and mount a rifle or gun for a quick and accurate snap shot. No magazine can possibly be as well balanced as an equally good double, owing to the greater concentration of weight between the hands with the latter type. No matter how accurate your rifle may be, if it is not properly balanced, a quick and accurate snap shot is an utter impossibility other than by a fluke. You cannot afford to rely upon flukes when tackling dangerous game at close quarters.

Third: This is definitely the most important. The rapidity with which the first shot can be fired from a double is imperative.

All powerful magazine rifles are built with a Mauser pattern bolt action in which the safety has to be twisted across from one side to the other before the rifle is ready for action. This operation takes an appreciable time and cannot possibly be performed while the rifle is on its way up to the shoulder. Accordingly, an appreciable time must elapse before you can get off your first shot. On the other hand, the safety slide on a double can be snicked forward while the rifle is actually being swung to the shoulder and mounted for the shot. There is not an instant's unnecessary delay. Of course, if you are following up a wounded animal, you will carry your rifle "at the ready" with the safety in the firing position, irrespective of the type of weapon. But you cannot walk about all day in the thick bush carrying a heavy rifle in that manner when you are just hunting and waiting for something to turn up.

Now with regard to the choice of bore, where the knocking down of a heavy and dangerous animal at very close quarters is concerned, bullet weight is of primary importance. Within reasonable limits, a small, heavy bullet will inflict a heavier blow than a larger diameter bullet of lighter weight. (An excellent, example of this is to be found in the case of the standard 400-grain bullet for the .450/.400 or .404 and the 345-grain bullet for the .423 [10.75 mm] Mauser. The former deals the heavier blow of the two, although it is of smaller caliber.) Generally speaking, however, it may be taken as a rough rule that the larger the bullet, the heavier it is, and therefore it delivers a heavier blow. At the same time, it should be borne in mind that there are exceptions. I do not know what a rhino weighs, but it is probably somewhere in the vicinity of from two to three tons. Two or three tons of bad temper coming at twenty to twenty-five miles per hour takes a deal of stopping! I should certainly not recommend a bullet of less than 400 grains in weight, and personally I prefer the 480- and 500-grain bullets. (A Holland .375 Magnum loaded with 300-grain solids can be used, though even here you are running pretty close to the margin of safety. I mention it separately because there are several other rifles throwing bullets of round about 300 grains, which are definitely not powerful enough.)

Of course, the smallest rifle used in the African bush, the .256 (6.5 mm), when loaded with bluff-nosed solids, is capable of killing the largest rhino or elephant, for that matter, in all of Africa, provided the elephant or rhino is sufficiently obliging to expose a vital spot. That, nonetheless, is a very different thing to stopping a charge at a range of only a few feet, when it may be a physical impossibility to place your bullet in the brain. A knock-down blow is essential, absolutely essential, and only a heavy bullet can definitely be relied upon to inflict it. Although there is a slight difference between them all on paper, for all practical purposes of sport there is nothing whatever to choose between the various cartridges in the .450, .465 and .470-bore groups, save only on the question of chamber pressure. On this score, the .450 No. 2, .465 and .470 have the advantage. Ejectors are not necessary for rhino.

Let me assure anybody who has not tried it, that rhino hunting in thick bush is a really fine sport, always provided that you are suitably armed.

PONDORO

"RHINO IN THICK BUSH"
To the Editor of
Game & Gun

Sir,–In your issue for August, 1937, you published an article of mine on "Rhino in Thick Bush," wherein I rather condemned the use of a magazine rifle for this particular sport, owing principally to the design of the safety on all powerful magazine rifles. They cannot be swung into action as rapidly as can a double when a quick and unexpected shot is called for. Some time after I had posted that article, however, I decided to experiment with one of my magazines and see if there was any way in which it could be carried so that a really quick shot would be possible. I chose my Holland .375 Magnum for the experiments and discovered that it is possible to carry a magazine rifle ready for almost instantaneous use and with perfect safety. Doubtless magazine enthusiasts will have known of it long ago. For the benefit of those who may not, I mention it for what it is worth.

You carry the rifle with the finger piece of the safety in the vertical position instead of over to the right. In this position the rifle cannot be fired, so that there is no fear of blowing your tracker's head off. If a sudden chance is offered or a quick shot required to stop an unexpected charge, your thumb, lying alongside the right-hand side of the safety, just presses sideways and the safety flops over to the firing position on the left. The thumb follows it and gets into the normal position on the grip. With a little practice this operation can be performed quite easily and quickly and enables the shot to be made with the minimum of delay, far more quickly than if the safety is carried in the normal position on the right of the action. If carried as I suggest, the safety can be pressed down into the firing position while the rifle is actually on its way up to the shoulder. It therefore compares favorably with the double, though I should always recommend the double in preference to the magazine for this particular form of somewhat specialized hunting.

J.H. TAYLOR
Portuguese East Africa

"On Imaginative Hunting"
Game & Gun
September, 1937

It always seems a great pity to me that those who write books on big-game hunting, with but mighty few exceptions, render utterly valueless observations that would otherwise be of intense interest, because they claim to have seen things that have been proved impossible, over and over again. I am thinking in particular of that statement that practically all writers seem to imagine is expected of them: "I saw the lion's eyes glowing in the dark."

Now I have indulged in every conceivable kind of experiment in an attempt to prove or disprove this statement. I have let the fire burn down so that the lions I could hear prowling and purring round the camp might close in. Then I would fling a cup of petrol, paraffin, or a handful of gunpowder on the glowing embers. I have sat up in a tree or on a *machan* on pitch black nights and on moonlit nights and deliberately made a noise when the lions approached close to make them look up at me. In spite of all this, I have never yet succeeded in seeing a lion's eyes glow. No animal has phosphorescent eyes. Accordingly, they cannot glow unless a spotlight is turned directly on them. Even then, unless the light is an extremely powerful one, you will not see the eyes glowing unless they are very close to you.

Another remark that is also very common is that someone has seen a native with an arm or a leg, in one account it was *both* legs, that had been bitten clean off by a croc, as neatly as though by an axe. Now a croc invariably grabs its prey and pulls it under water. It drowns its victim always. I have been instrumental in rescuing two persons from crocs at different times: one an Englishman and the other a native woman. I have seen several other natives who had been grabbed and saved by their companions. Of the two that I was fortunate enough to rescue, one had been grabbed by the arm and the other by the leg. In neither case did the croc bite off the limb as a shark would have done. It just pulled. The result was that the limb was badly lacerated by its teeth. In the case of the white man, the arm was rendered practically useless because the tendons and muscles were so badly torn.

I have recently been reading a book where the author tells us how he saw the lions' eyes glowing, took a hasty shot at them, and then jumped into the tent on his wagon and fumbled in the dark for his shooting lamp. Obviously, therefore, he did not have it lit when he claims to have seen the glowing eyes. In a latter chapter he goes on to talk about hippo and describes among other things how a hippo bit a native into two halves. Now is it possible for a hippo to do this? From an examination of its mouth, personally, I fail to see how it could. It can bite a small ironwood canoe in two pieces as easily as I could bite through a cheese straw, as I know from bitter experience. One bite from a hippo sent all my worldly possessions, including a perfectly good battery of expensive rifles, to the bottom of the Zambezi when its bite splintered my canoe to match wood. Biting through a hard substance that offers resistance to the bite is a very different thing from biting through a soft, pliable substance like a human body when the formation of a hippo's mouth and teeth is borne in mind.

Be that as it may, however, the man in question claims to have seen some extraordinary things in the bush. We all know that wild animals will, occasionally, show remarkable traits utterly opposed to the usual habits and customs of their respective species. Of course, it is not impossible though perhaps improbable, for one fortunate man personally to witness several of these "freak," events. The point is that he makes it impossible for us to credit these sights by also claiming to have seen a lion's eyes glowing in the dark when he did not have his spotlight trained on them.

A most interesting letter from the pen of that well-known observer, Mr. D.D. Lyell, appeared in the correspondence columns of *East Africa*. It reminds me of a similar experience of my own. In his letter, Mr. Lyell mentions how a friend in India was sitting up for a panther one night. On the panther approaching, the sportsman fired. The two other men who were present maintained that the animal loosed a shrill scream on feeling the lead, then bounded forwards and dropped dead. The sportsman who had fired never heard a sound. He was using a .577 B.P. Express.

The first time I ever tackled a large herd of elephant—at a rough estimate there were anything from 100 to 120 of them spread out in horseshoe formation in fairly open forest—I closed in within twelve to fifteen paces of the two best at the top end of the "horseshoe." This meant that I had elephant on both sides of me as well as in front. Eyes were, obviously, going to be of greater assistance to me than ears.

I fired. I saw the muzzle of the rifle jump slightly under the shock of discharge. I distinctly heard the "clop" of the bullet (interesting, in view of what follows). I am convinced that I never heard the roar of the rifle and I know that I did not hear another sound, not even when I fired for the second big tusker, though I again saw the muzzle jump. As the herd stampeded, there was of course the usual pandemonium, but I heard nothing. Yet I am certain there wasn't a thing that I did not see: the corrugations on the elephants' hides; one big fellow with very small tusks and an abnormally long trunk; another with queerly shaped tusks, one pointing upwards and the other very straight; another with a broken tusk; two monsters with no tusks at all; the dirt and clay and small stones thrown up as trees were pushed over quite close to me; the splinters flying as another tree was snapped off several feet above the ground.

Yet, I repeat, I never heard a sound. The din must have been terrific. My boys told me that it was and of course I have frequently heard it since. But on that occasion my eyes must have completely robbed my ears to aid my sight. I had realized the necessity of it before opening fire. It was the first time that I had tackled a large herd and I suppose I was a trifle nervous. Of course, it is not a thing I should imagine you could consciously do. Though never quite so pronounced as on that first occasion, I have several times since had somewhat similar experiences.

PONDORO

"Elephant Control"
Game & Gun
November, 1937

As soon as it was light enough to see, I started off with my two gunbearers and a lad carrying food. Almost immediately we struck fresh spoor. Two big bulls had passed only a couple of hours previously. From the size of their pad marks, they were well worth following. There was little fear of losing the spoor, which was following one of the many paths stamped out by their own great feet or by those of their pals. These paths intersected the otherwise utterly impenetrable thorn that rose in a dense, matted wall about 15' high. The thorns were of the "hawk's-bill" variety.

There is nothing to tell about following fresh spoor under such conditions. Visibility is limited to a matter of feet. Save for making sure that the bulls had not turned off on one of the occasional small side tracks, hunting was done entirely by ear. Nor was it pleasant work. For although more or less free of obstacles to a height of about three and a half feet, the path was draped with the overhang from the walls. The big grey giants could merely brush through this. Neither I could do so with my khaki drill and much less my naked boys. It meant walking along all doubled up for miles on end. Fiendishly tiring it was.

I knew that the rewards for sticking to it were generously bestowed by the god of hunters when he considered that a reward had been earned. Early in the afternoon shortly after we had had a snack to eat, sure enough, we stopped like one man as a deep rumbling was heard a little way ahead. There is no mistaking that sound once you have heard it: intestinal rumbling of elephant.

We were close to them, so I took the double .577 Cordite from my head gunbearer, snicked forward the safety catch, and cautiously advanced. As I expected, there was a small clearing stamped out round a huge baobab tree. For it is here in the shade that the jumbo rest and sleep during the hot midday hours. In those deep valleys with the hills close round and with the height and density of the thorn, no cooling breezes can be felt.

Two big tuskers were there in front of me now. Snorters they were and not more than ten to twelve yards away. With my lips almost touching my head gunbearer's ear, I just breathed a word.

He, knowing, stooped and lifted a couple of dry twigs. Gently he cracked one. In the absolute stillness that followed huge ears moved slowly out till they stood at right angles to the head. The bulls were listening. . . .

One big chap was almost facing us. I was satisfied with his position, but I wanted the other to come round a bit. I nodded my head and again a twig cracked. Slowly, ponderously, and in absolute silence—save for the faintest rustling of his hide—the monster moved round. As he exposed his broadside, I slammed a heavy slug into his brain, dropping him in his tracks. The crashing roar of my big express was drowned in the trumpeting yell of the second bull as he swung round to run. As he in turn exposed a brain shot, I gave him the contents of the left barrel and brought him down with a crash beside his erstwhile companion. It was a good enough end to the day's hunt and a pleasing omen for the remainder of the expedition. I gave thanks to the god of hunters and cut off the two tails.

Then I sat down on one great foreleg for a smoke and a short rest. As I smoked and pulled through my rifle, I felt a glow of satisfaction run through me. After all this was my livelihood. Mingled with the pleasure was a tiny wee twinge of regret as I looked at the fallen giants. I always feel it after making a kill other than in self-defense. I had to remind myself of the damage these beasts do to the natives' food crops when they take it into their heads to go raiding. This they do regularly, year after year.

Now I am wholeheartedly in favour of game reserves, vast tracts of territory made over into sanctuaries for all beasts, provided that any natives living there are first given suitable districts elsewhere in which to build their villages. I have seen what the "armchair protectionist" has not seen: the ghastly spectacle of a famine caused solely by the depredations of elephant and buffalo. This was owing to the ridiculous order made by a governor living over a thousand miles away that stopped all shooting in that particular district. If you happen to run short of anything, you have only to lift the telephone receiver to have it delivered at your door immediately, irrespective of what it may be, from a whole roast bullock to a barrel of oysters of a particular breed. You can have no conception of the feelings of a wretched native as he sees a whole year's food supply for himself and his family stamped flat and utterly destroyed in a single night by marauding elephant or buffalo.

There is no more heart-rending sight than to see a group of poor, little naked children clustering on the outskirts of one's camp, too frightened to beg and yet too desperately hungry to tear themselves away. Instead of the plump, shiny little black bodies, and the round, laughing, happy little faces that one has learned to expect, there are grotesquely distended tummies—from eating grass and leaves and roots—ribs like barrel hoops and bones sticking through the skin of elbows, knees, and shoulders. Great mournful eyes, sunk far back in deep hollows, look wistfully at the white man's well-laden table.

I, who love the big grey ghosts of the forest, have found myself cursing them bitterly—savage, meaningless blasphemies pouring from my lips as I swore vengeance.

No, my masters—have your game reserves, by all means, but not at the expense of the unfortunate natives.

All this and more passed through my head as I finished my smoke and then gave the word for the return to camp. It was inspired by a letter that appeared in the correspondence columns of a contemporary journal and in which the "slaughter of elephant in Tanganyika Territory" was deplored. Reference was made to the annual report of the game warden, where he states that some 2,716 elephant were killed during 1934. Since elephant quickly learn their lesson and, therefore, are not chivvied about eternally but still continue to breed, it stands to reason that their numbers must occasionally be cut down. Otherwise, there will be so many that the country simply cannot support them and they will raid native crops.

After all, man, be he black, white, brown, or brindled, is of greater importance in the scheme of things than any elephant.

PONDORO

"VELOCITY AND KILLING POWER"
Correspondence to the Editor of
Game & Gun
January, 1938

Sir,—There are two points, brought up by correspondents under the above heading that in fairness to the rifles concerned, I should like to answer.

The first concerns a statement that Colonel Henderson of Kenya says was made to him by three ex-elephant hunters. They claim that the bullet from a .423 (10.75 mm) rifle was incapable of penetrating an African elephant's brain from the front. One is compelled to wonder just what experience those three men had both with elephant and with 10.75mm rifles used for frontal brain shots on elephant. I know for a fact that one assistant game warden in Kenya has shot over 300 elephant with a 10.75mm Mauser. It seems inconceivable that he could have shot so many without ever taking and bringing off successfully a frontal brain shot.

I cannot remember ever taking a frontal head shot at an elephant when armed with a 10.75mm, but I drove a bullet from one of these rifles clean through an elephant's head from back to front. I had shot him through the lungs, and after running some distance, he collapsed in a small depression. When I reached him, he was lying down with his back towards me in the attitude adopted by cattle when resting and chewing the cud. I endeavored to place my bullet on the spine where it joins the skull but owing to excitement—I was fairly new to the game in those days—my bullet took the elephant some three inches to the right of where I intended. He took not the slightest notice and presently got to his feet. Standing broadside on, he offered an easy target. On examining him later, I found the bullet that had taken him in the back of the head was held by the skin between his eyes. On making an incision, it popped out into my hand and I was able to trace its course clean through his head. Accordingly, I find it difficult to see why it should have not been able to find the brain had it been fired from the front.

The second point concerns a question asked by "Jungli Bains." Colonel Alexander had told us how he poleaxed a buffalo in Assam with the bluff-nosed solid 300-grain bullet from his .375 magnum at under fifty yards range. (In reply to a question of mine, he stated that the bullet had taken it through the shoulder blade.) He then went on to describe how he shot another buffalo at a 150-yard range, hitting it behind the shoulder with a similar bullet fired from the same rifle. It was not even knocked down, much less poleaxed. "Jungli Bains" then wrote to describe how he had shot a buffalo at a 180-yard range with a 10.75mm (.423) Mauser and the buffalo was knocked down for a count of five, then got up and staggered off. On the strength of this, he claims that his rifle hits a heavier blow than does Colonel Alexander's, at any rate at ranges upwards of 150 yards.

Unfortunately, "Jungli Bains" omits to tell us where he hit his buffalo. Assuming that it was neither in the head nor in the neck, then I contend that it must have been either in the shoulder blade or spine. From my own experience I have not the least hesitation in declaring that no rifle on the market, particularly when loaded with solids, is capable of knocking down an animal weighing upwards of a ton at ranges in excess of 150 yards, if the bullet fails to strike any bone larger than a rib. Accordingly, it is obviously unfair to compare the result of his shot with Colonel Alexander's, since the latter definitely stated that his took the buffalo behind the shoulder.

Now, quite apart from the theoretical aspect of the question (from the point of view of the ballistics of the two rifles), I can assure both Colonel Alexander and "Jungli Bains" that had Colonel Alexander hit his second buffalo on the shoulder blade, he would have killed it instantly. I speak from my own experience. I have shot a number of buffalo in the same way, but the most recent, only yesterday morning, was quite the most outstanding.

I shot a very fine bull out of a large herd at a range of 177 very long strides, well stretched out strides that could not have been less than thirty-six inches in length. I used the bluff-nosed solid 300-grain bullet from my Holland .375 Magnum. The bullet took the bull on the shoulder blade and he dropped instantly. All he was capable of doing was to lift his head just a few inches from the ground and then let it fall again. He was totally paralysed and was certainly dead within not more than two minutes. Had there been even a tiny tuft of grass between me and him I should never have noticed that slight movement of his head and would have written that I had "poleaxed" him stone dead at a range of 177 yards and written it in all honesty and truthfulness. At the same time, I shot three other members of the herd at various ranges between 150 and 170 yards. All three were hit behind the shoulder (two of them with the same bullet). All three ran some distance before falling. All three loosed the same mournful bellow as they died, but the big bull never made a sound or a movement beyond that slight lifting of his horns. For all practical purposes of sport, he could be said to have been killed outright.

This, I think, effectively answers "Jungli Bains'" question concerning the relative power of the .375 magnum and .423 (10.75mm) bore rifles.

JOHN H. TAYLOR
Portuguese East Africa